THE LI'L DEPRESSED BOY™

VOLUME ONE:

"SHE IS STAGGERING"

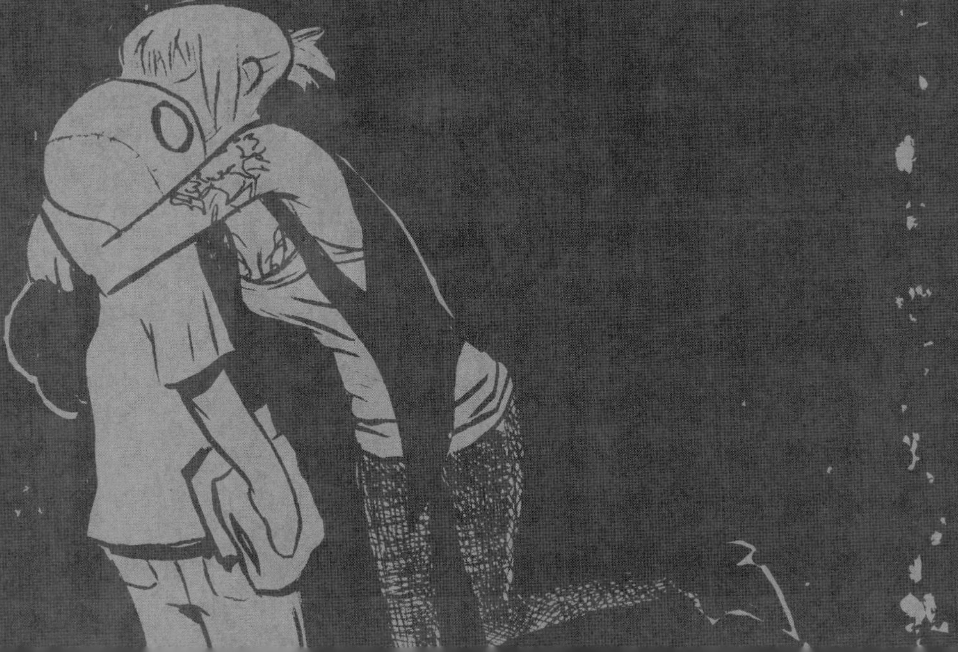

S. STEVEN STRUBLE
WRITING, COLORING, LETTERING

SINA GRACE
PENCILING, INKING

NICHOLAS BRANDT
EDITING, MOTIVATING

ZACHARY TROVER
DESIGNING

FLATS BY THIAGO RIBEIRO AND CHRIS FENOGLIO

SPECIAL THANKS TO
KEPI GHOULIE, DREW BLOOD, TENNESSEE, LAENA, ANNIE AND Z FROM THE LIKE.

THANKS FOR BEING IN OUR BOOK, GUYS!

IMAGE COMICS, INC.
Robert Kirkman - chief operating officer
Erik Larsen - chief financial officer
Todd McFarlane - president
Marc Silvestri - chief executive officer
Jim Valentino - vice-president

Eric Stephenson - publisher
Todd Martinez - sales & licensing coordinator
Sarah deLaine - pr & marketing coordinator
Branwyn Bigglestone - accounts manager
Emily Miller - administrative assistant
Jamie Parreno - administrative assistant
Kevin Yuen - digital rights coordinator
Tyler Shainline - production manager
Drew Gill - art director
Jonathan Chan - senior production artist
Monica Garcia - production artist
Vincent Kukua - production artist
Jana Cook - production artist
www.imagecomics.com

ISBN #: 978-1-60706-390-2

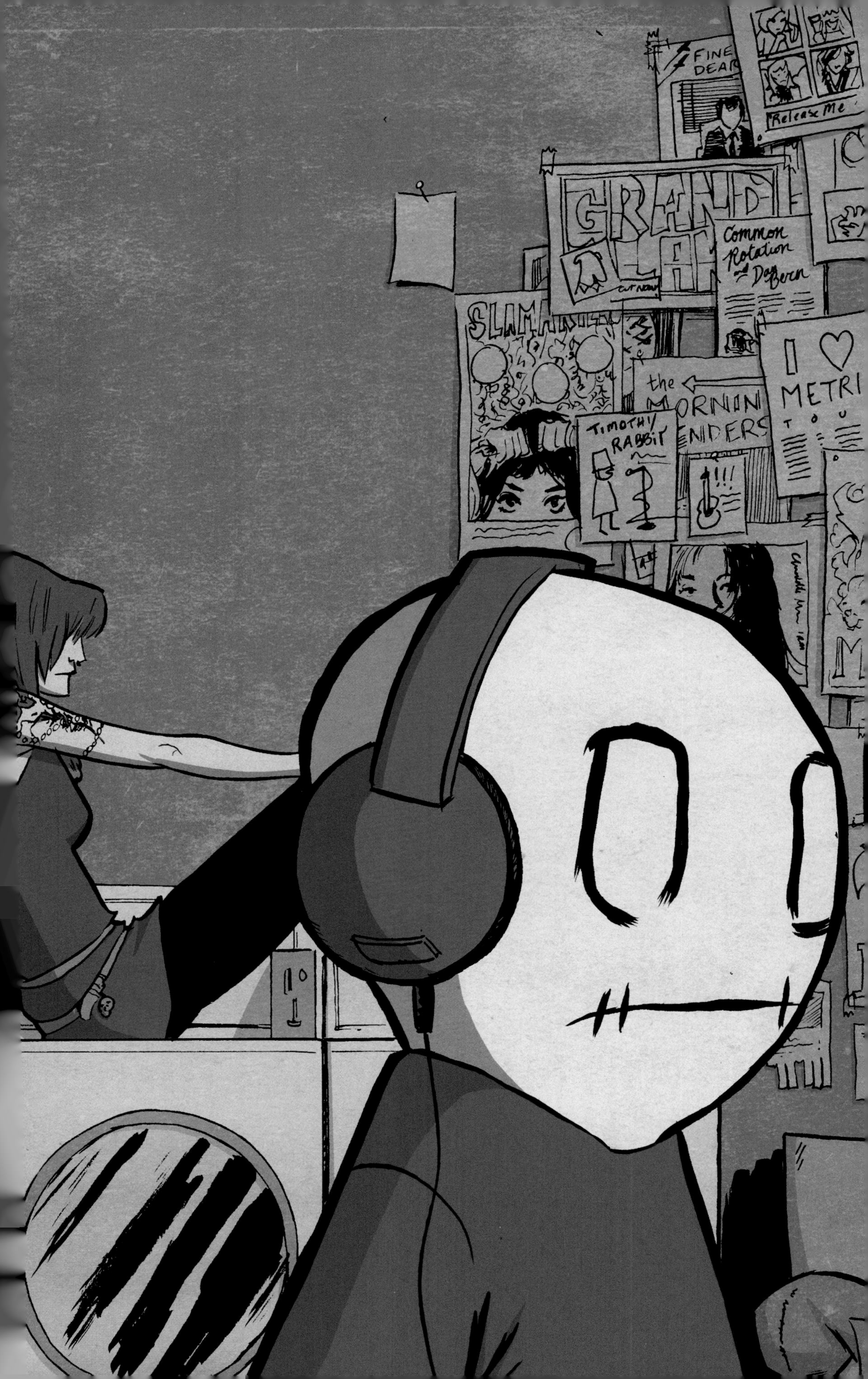
FINE
DEAR
Release Me
GRAND
Common Rotation and Dan Bern
the
TIMOTHY RABBIT
I ♥
METRI

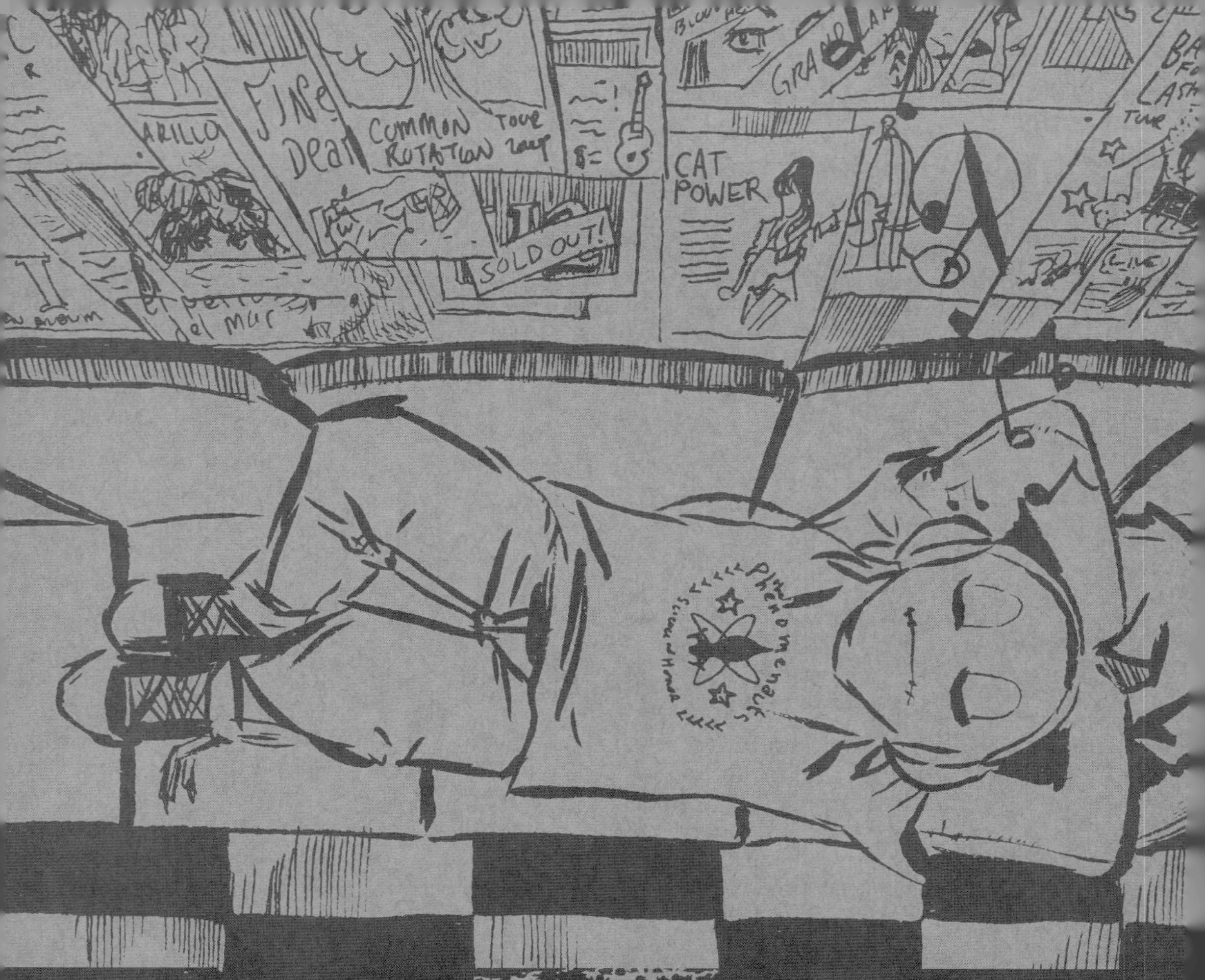
COMMON ROTATION TOUR
CAT POWER
SOLD OUT!

CHAPTER
ONE:

"(SHE'S GOT A) BRAIN SCRAMBLING DEVICE"

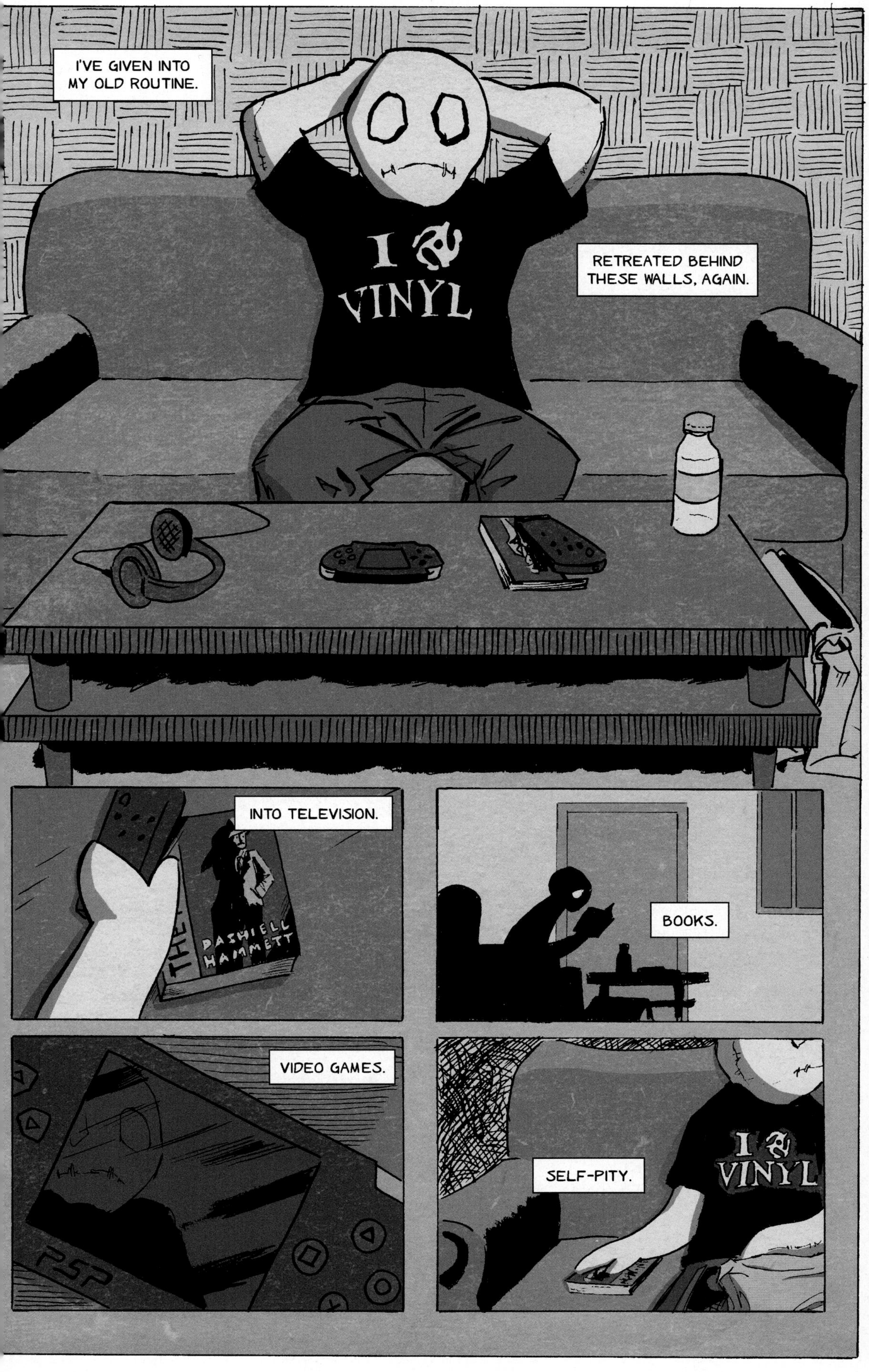
I'VE GIVEN INTO MY OLD ROUTINE.
I VINYL
RETREATED BEHIND THESE WALLS, AGAIN.
INTO TELEVISION.
THE
DASHIELL HAMMETT
BOOKS.
VIDEO GAMES.
PSP
SELF-PITY.
I VINYL

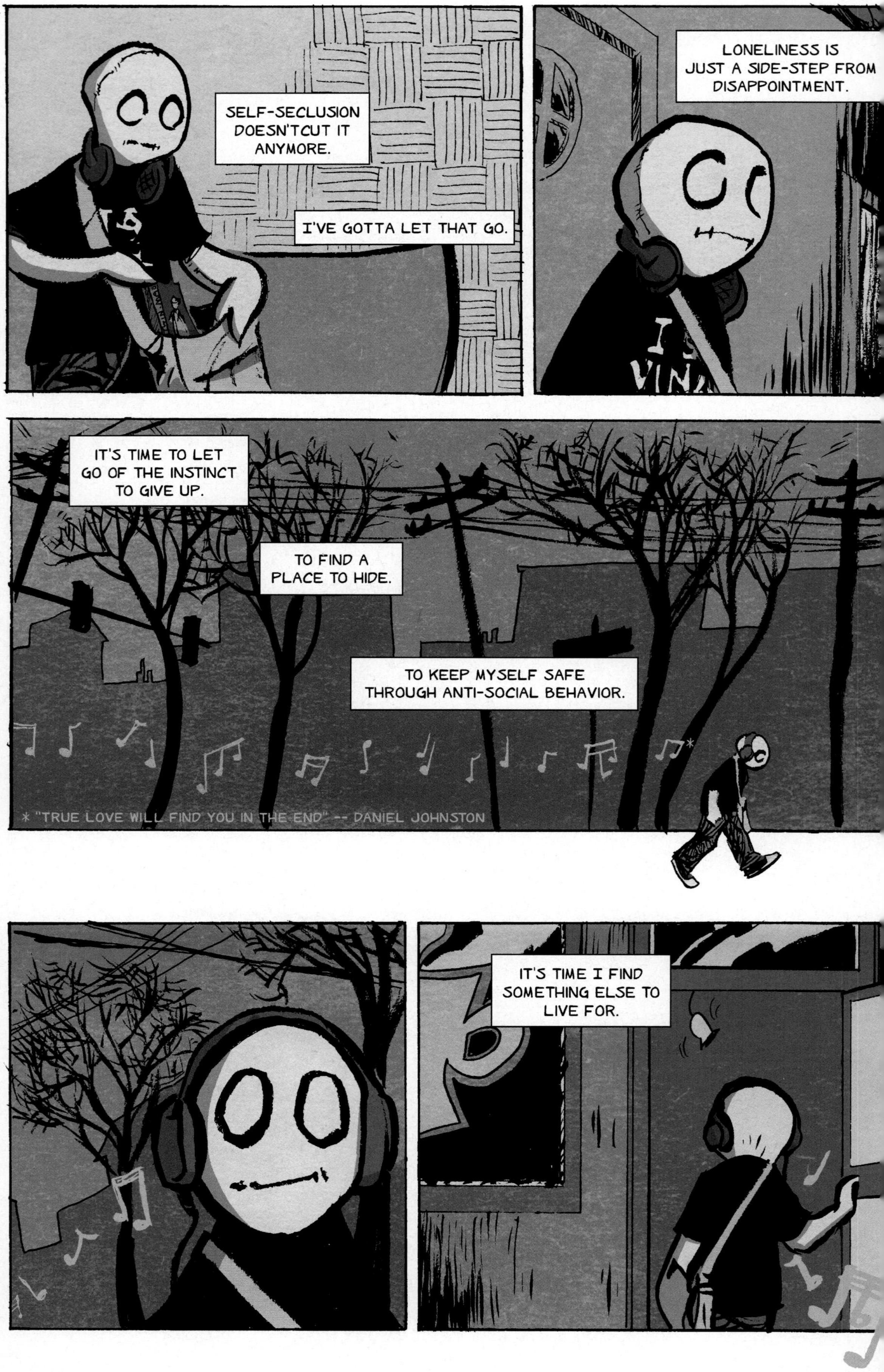
SELF-SECLUSION DOESN'TCUT IT ANYMORE.
I'VE GOTTA LET THAT GO.
LONELINESS IS JUST A SIDE-STEP FROM DISAPPOINTMENT.
IT'S TIME TO LET GO OF THE INSTINCT TO GIVE UP.
TO FIND A PLACE TO HIDE.
TO KEEP MYSELF SAFE THROUGH ANTI-SOCIAL BEHAVIOR.
* "TRUE LOVE WILL FIND YOU IN THE END" -- DANIEL JOHNSTON
IT'S TIME I FIND SOMETHING ELSE TO LIVE FOR.

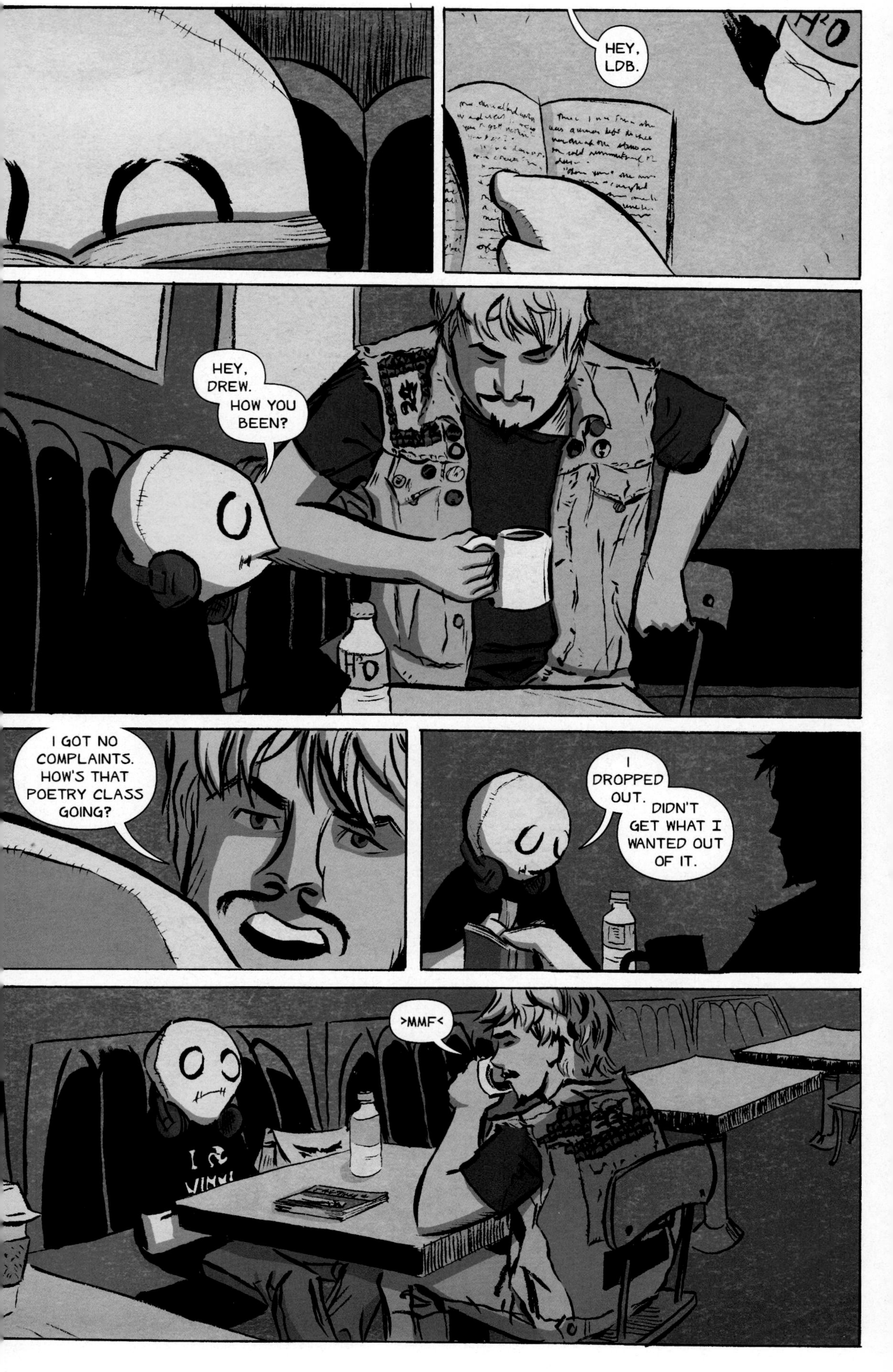
HEY, LDB.
HEY, DREW.
HOW YOU BEEN?
I GOT NO COMPLAINTS. HOW'S THAT POETRY CLASS GOING?
I DROPPED OUT.
DIDN'T GET WHAT I WANTED OUT OF IT.
>MMF<

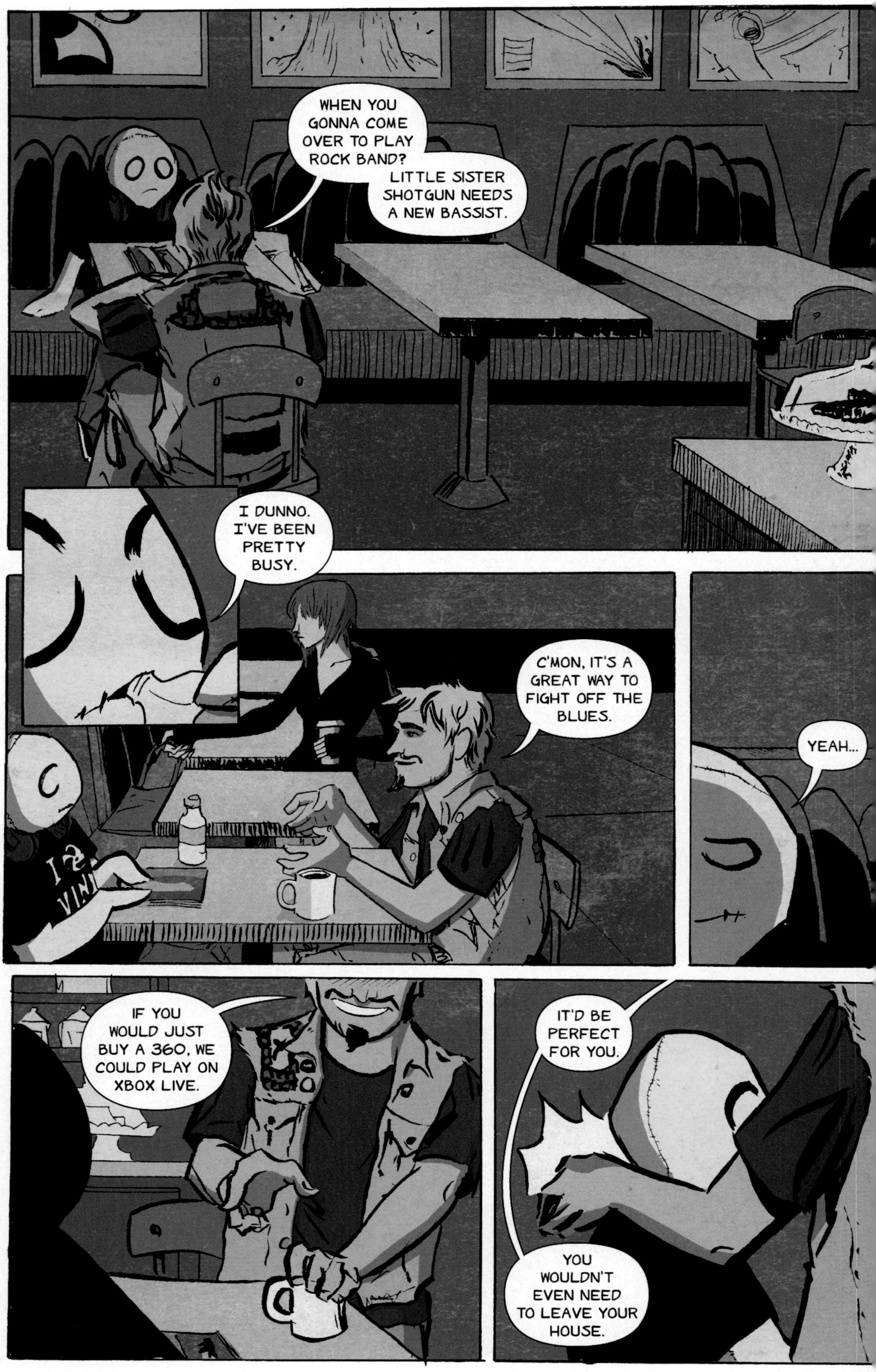
WHEN YOU GONNA COME OVER TO PLAY ROCK BAND?
LITTLE SISTER SHOTGUN NEEDS A NEW BASSIST.
I DUNNO. I'VE BEEN PRETTY BUSY.
C'MON, IT'S A GREAT WAY TO FIGHT OFF THE BLUES.
YEAH...
IF YOU WOULD JUST BUY A 360, WE COULD PLAY ON XBOX LIVE.
IT'D BE PERFECT FOR YOU.
YOU WOULDN'T EVEN NEED TO LEAVE YOUR HOUSE.

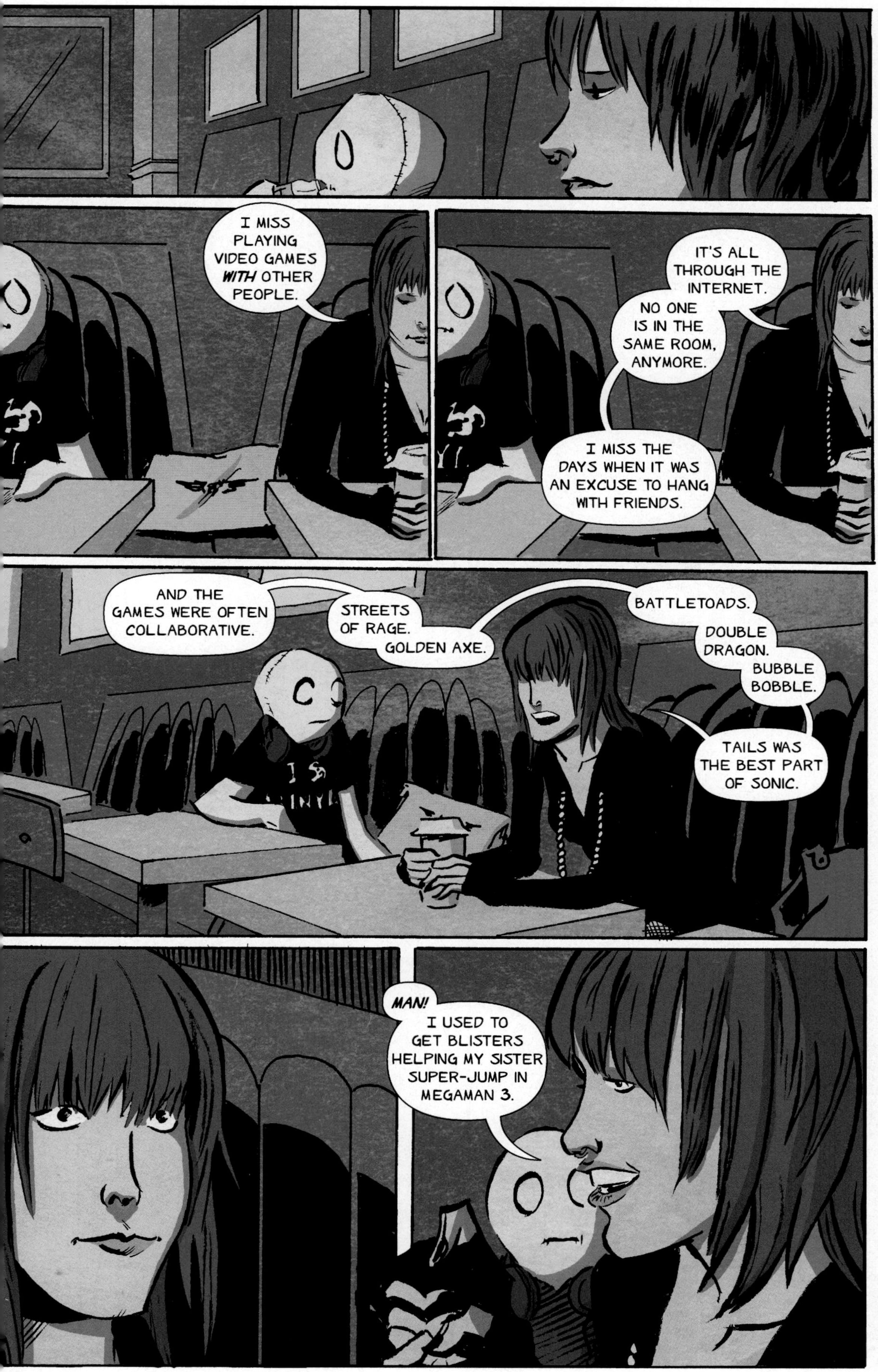
I MISS PLAYING VIDEO GAMES *WITH* OTHER PEOPLE.
IT'S ALL THROUGH THE INTERNET.
NO ONE IS IN THE SAME ROOM, ANYMORE.
I MISS THE DAYS WHEN IT WAS AN EXCUSE TO HANG WITH FRIENDS.
AND THE GAMES WERE OFTEN COLLABORATIVE.
STREETS OF RAGE.
GOLDEN AXE.
BATTLETOADS.
DOUBLE DRAGON.
BUBBLE BOBBLE.
TAILS WAS THE BEST PART OF SONIC.
MAN!
I USED TO GET BLISTERS HELPING MY SISTER SUPER-JUMP IN MEGAMAN 3.

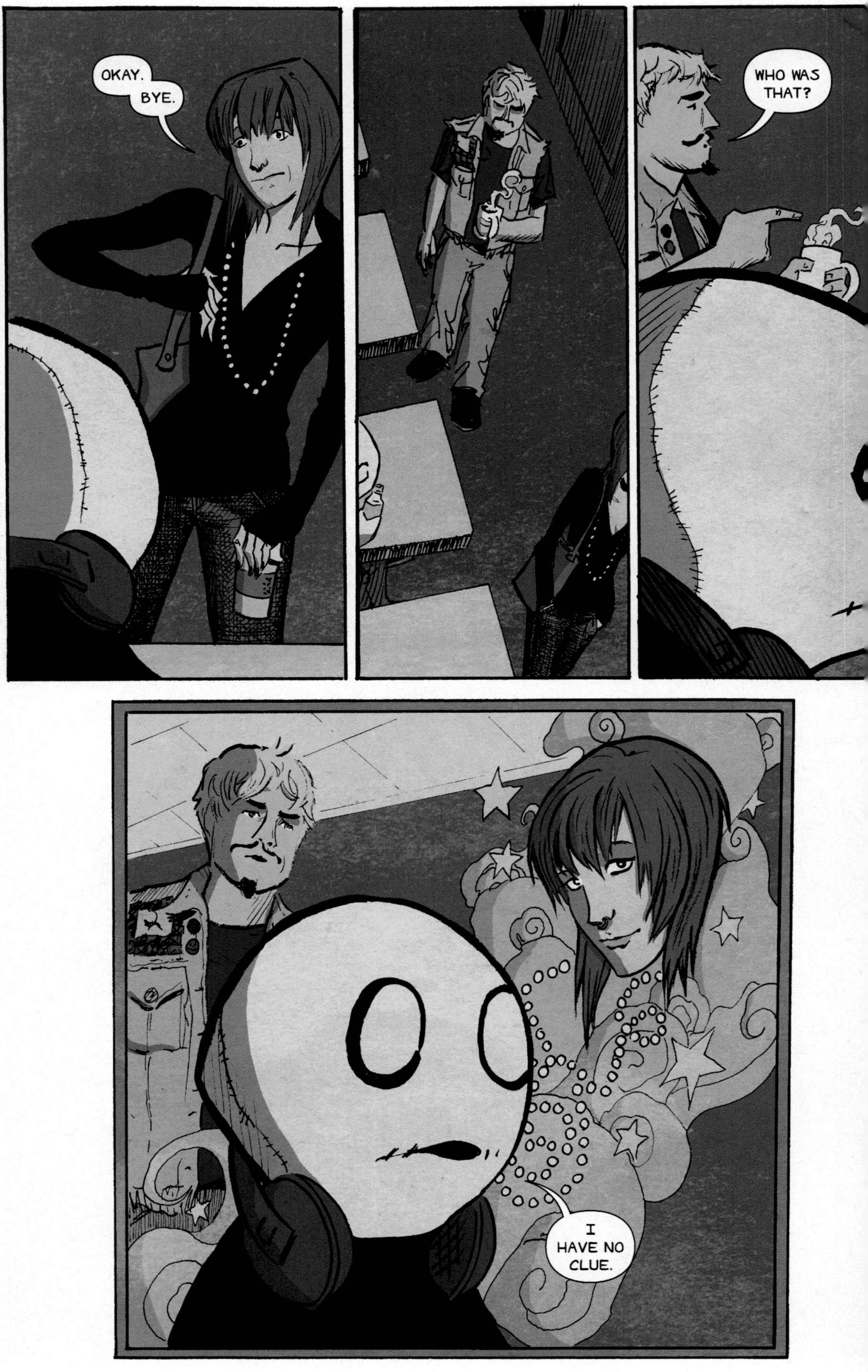
OKAY.
BYE.
WHO WAS THAT?
I HAVE NO CLUE.

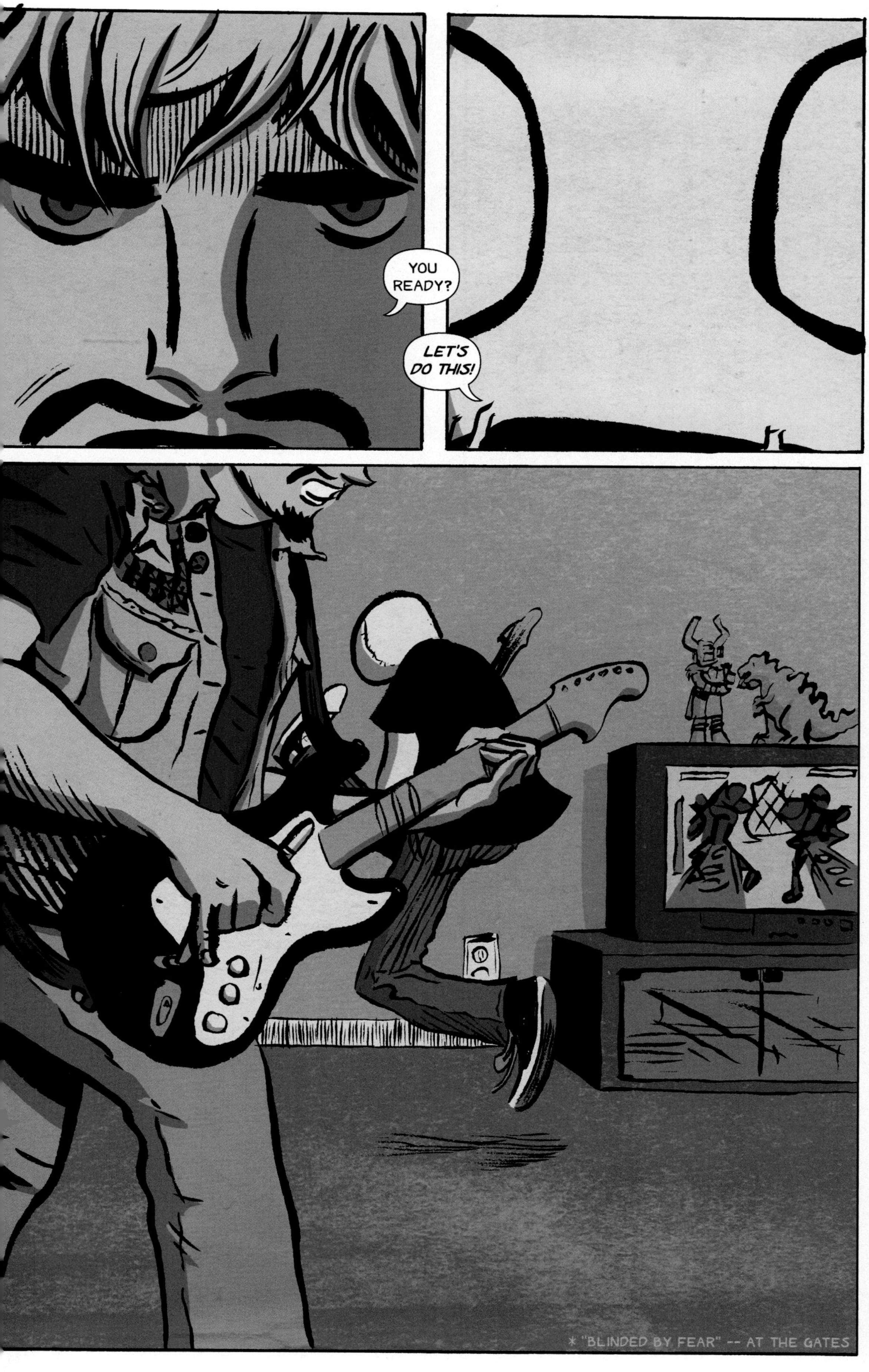
YOU READY?
LET'S DO THIS!
* "BLINDED BY FEAR" -- AT THE GATES

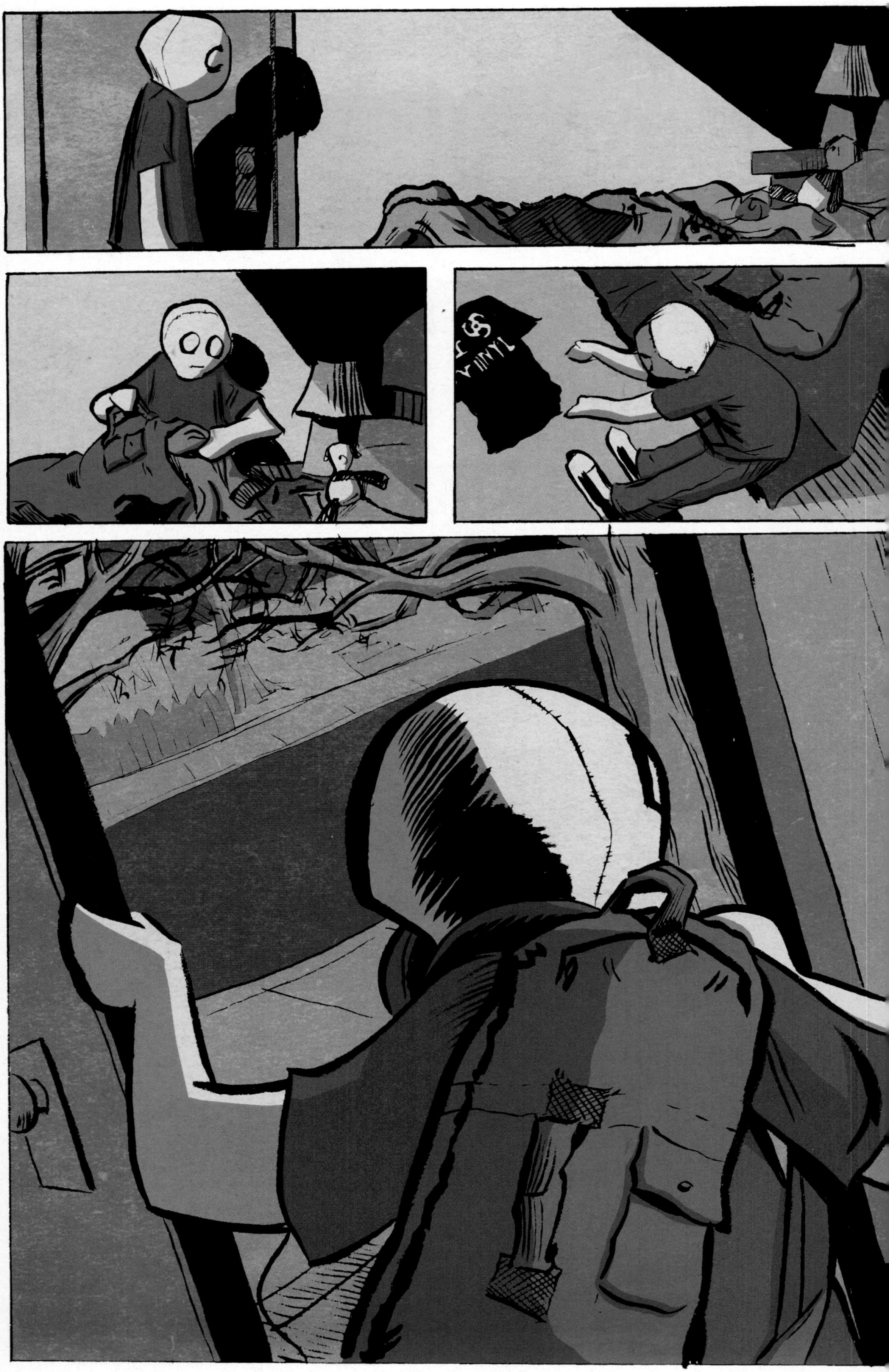

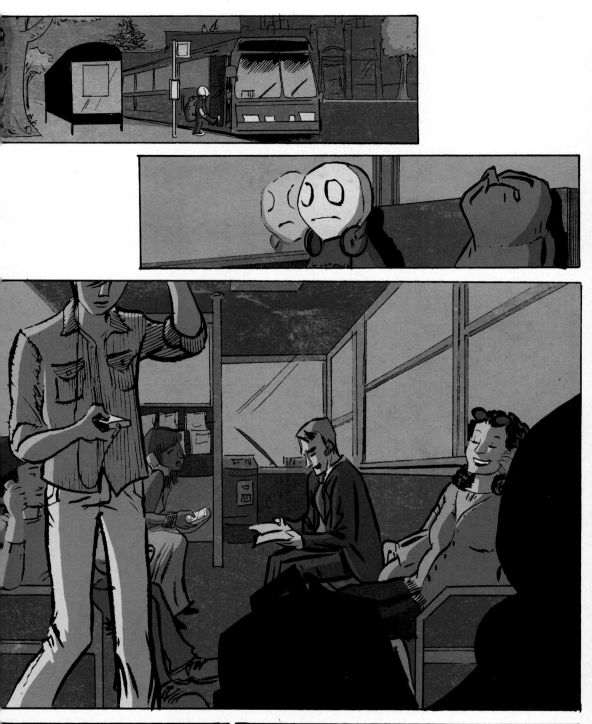

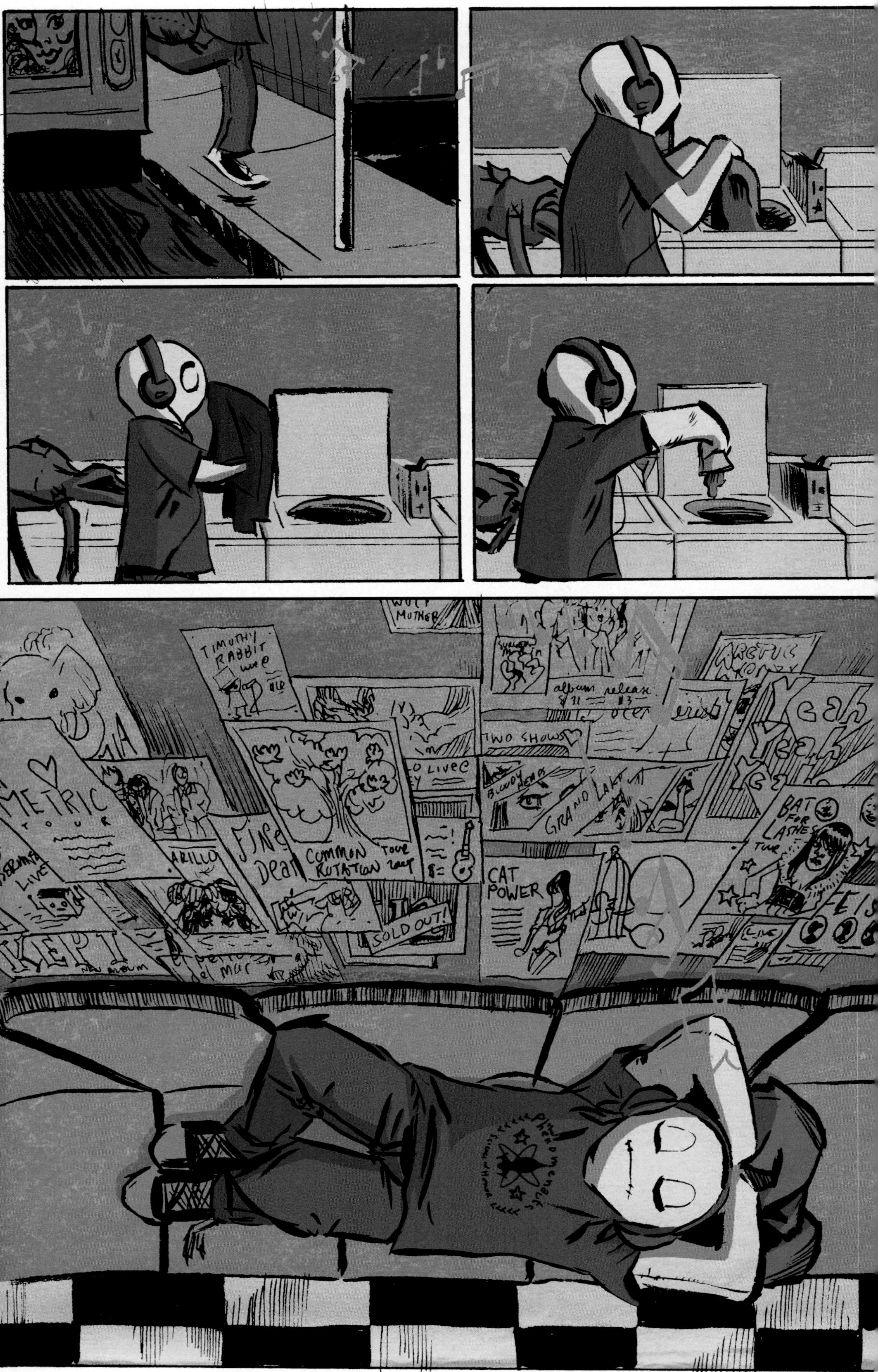
MOTHER
TIMOTHY RABBIT
album release
TWO SHOWS
I ♥ METRIC TOUR
CAT POWER
BAT FOR LASHES
COMMON ROTATION
SOLD OUT!
GRAND LAKE
NEW ALBUM
Yeah Yeah

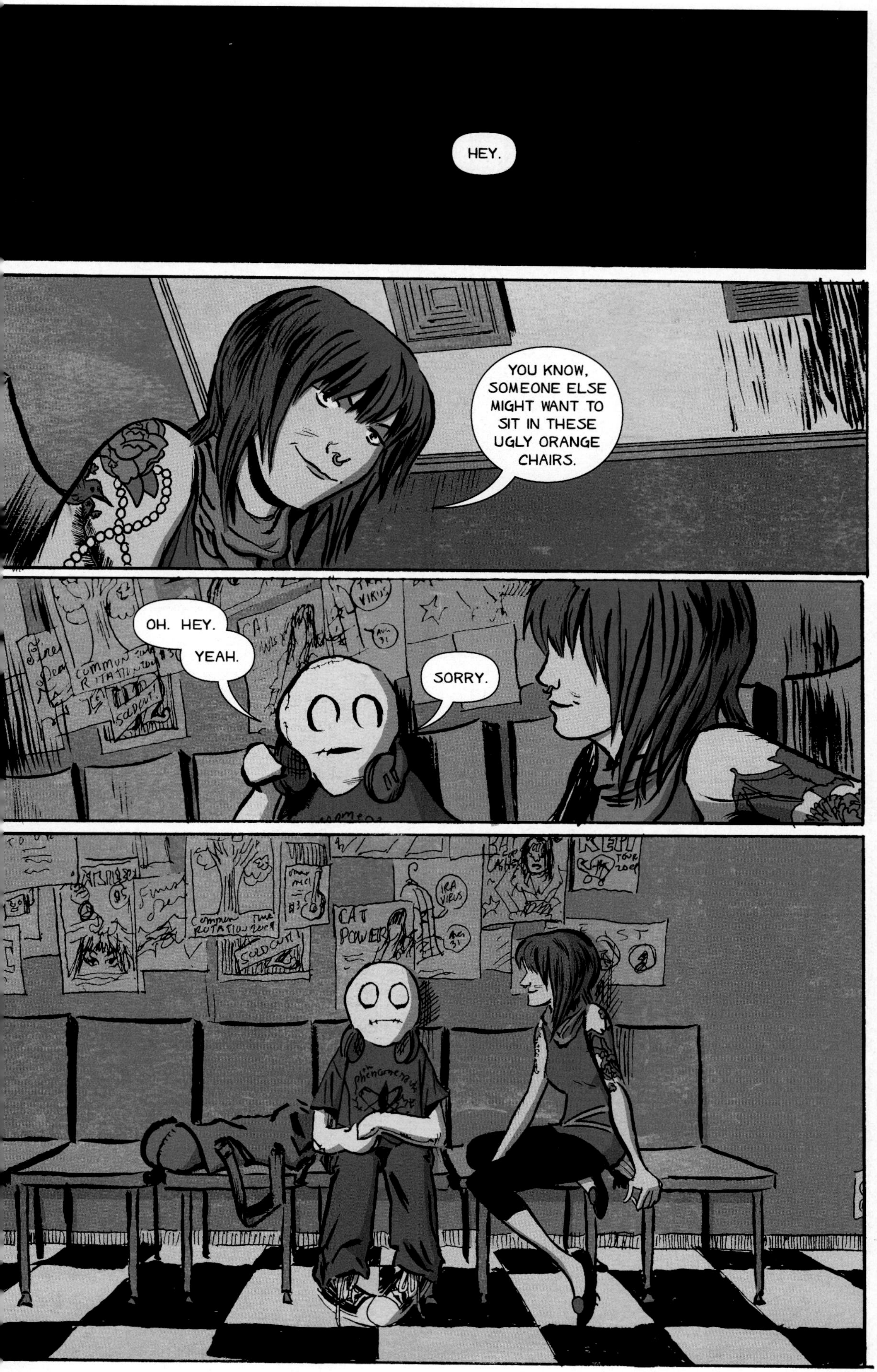
HEY.
YOU KNOW, SOMEONE ELSE MIGHT WANT TO SIT IN THESE UGLY ORANGE CHAIRS.
OH. HEY.
YEAH.
SORRY.

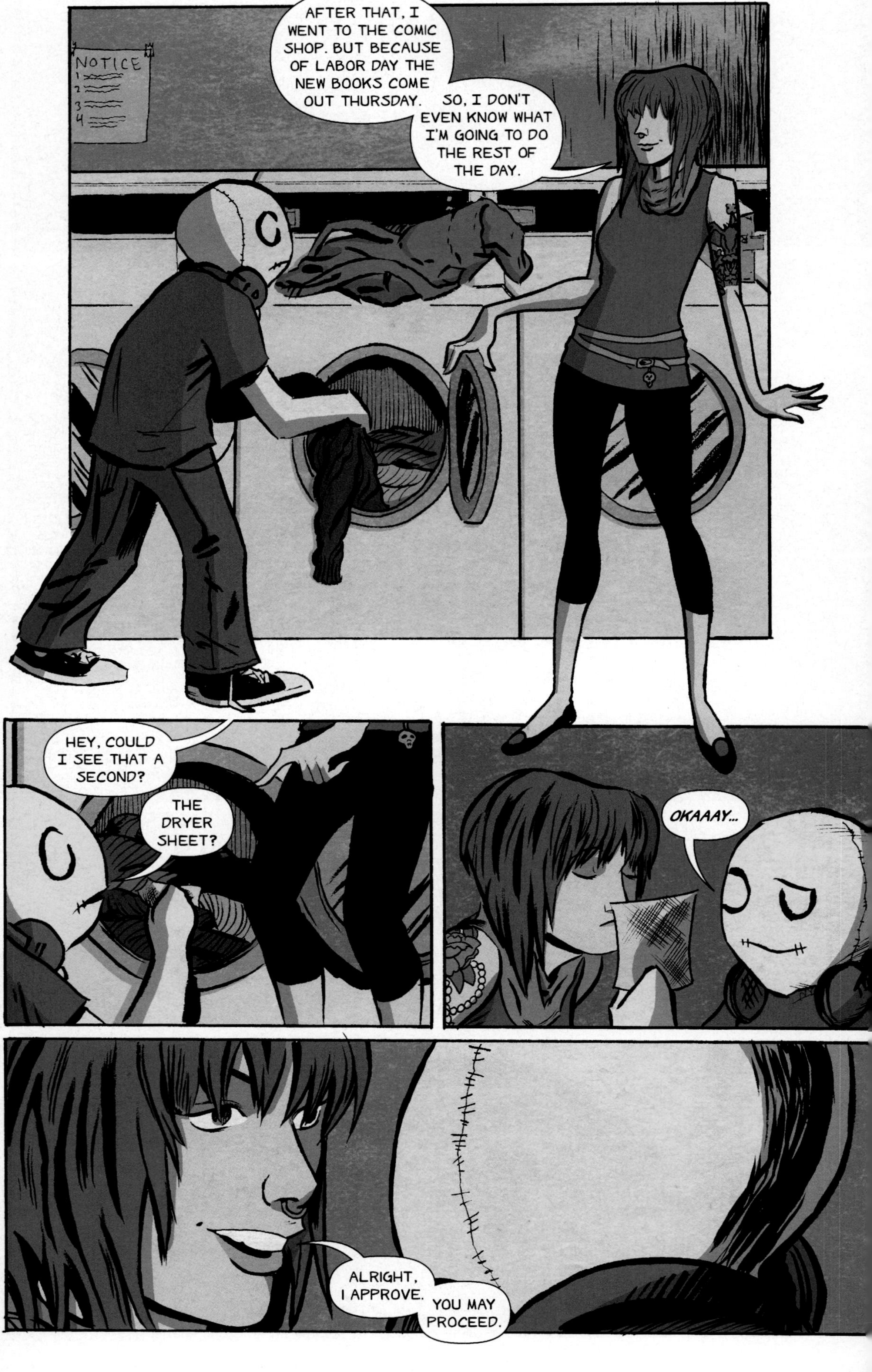
NOTICE
AFTER THAT, I WENT TO THE COMIC SHOP. BUT BECAUSE OF LABOR DAY THE NEW BOOKS COME OUT THURSDAY.
SO, I DON'T EVEN KNOW WHAT I'M GOING TO DO THE REST OF THE DAY.
HEY, COULD I SEE THAT A SECOND?
THE DRYER SHEET?
OKAAAY...
ALRIGHT, I APPROVE.
YOU MAY PROCEED.

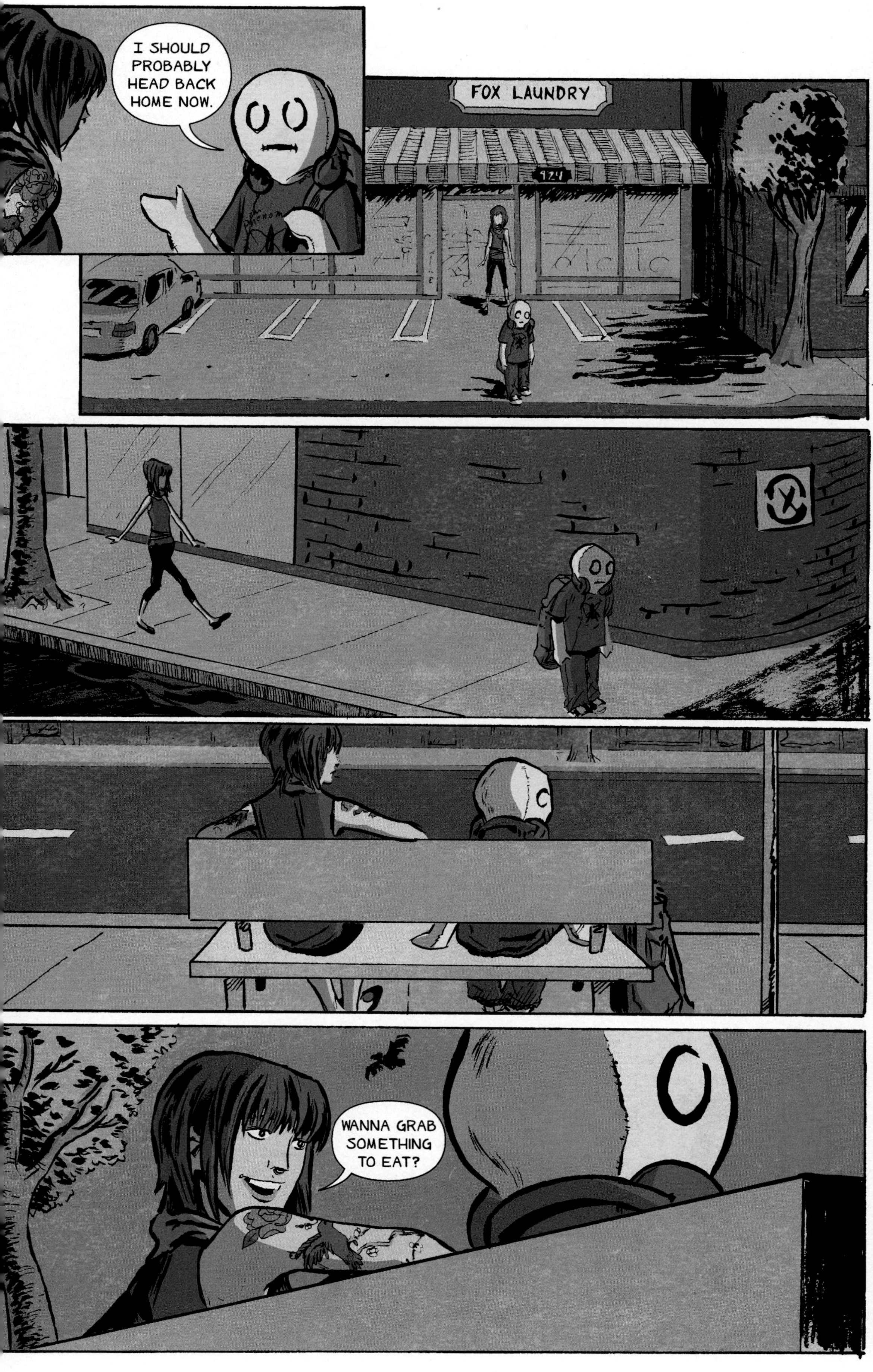
I SHOULD PROBABLY HEAD BACK HOME NOW.
FOX LAUNDRY
WANNA GRAB SOMETHING TO EAT?

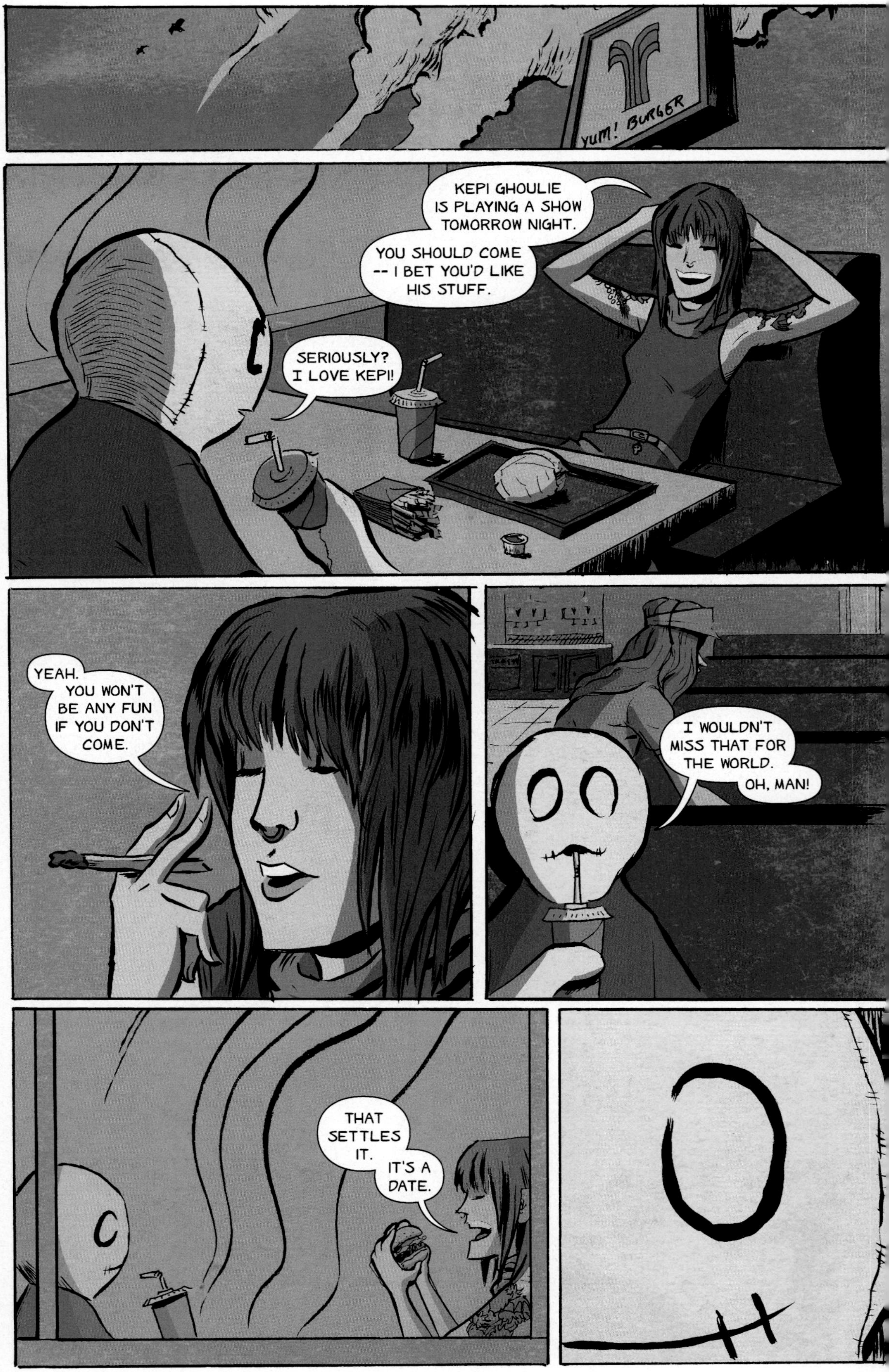
YUM! BURGER
KEPI GHOULIE IS PLAYING A SHOW TOMORROW NIGHT.
YOU SHOULD COME -- I BET YOU'D LIKE HIS STUFF.
SERIOUSLY? I LOVE KEPI!
YEAH. YOU WON'T BE ANY FUN IF YOU DON'T COME.
I WOULDN'T MISS THAT FOR THE WORLD.
OH, MAN!
THAT SETTLES IT.
IT'S A DATE.

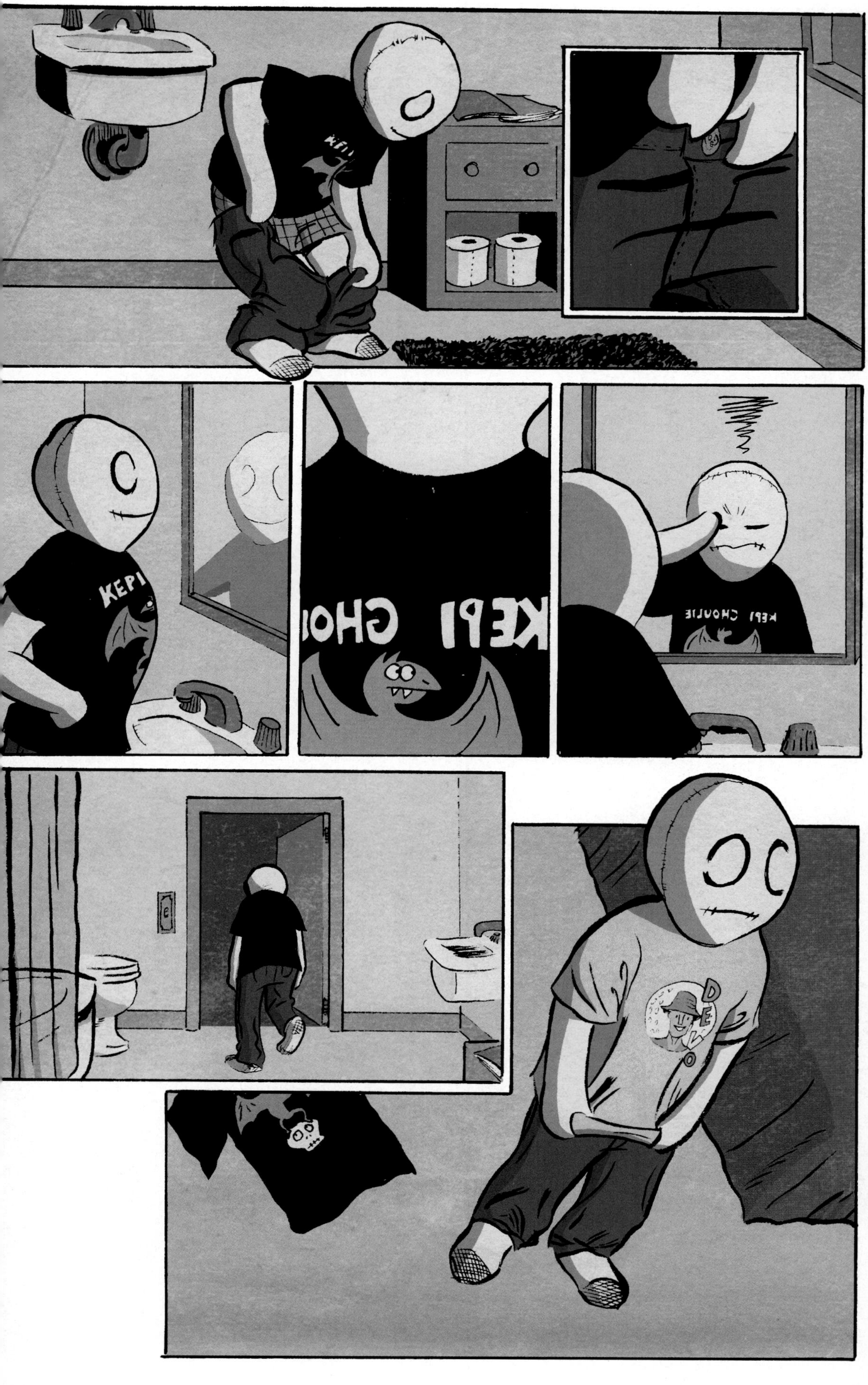
KEPI

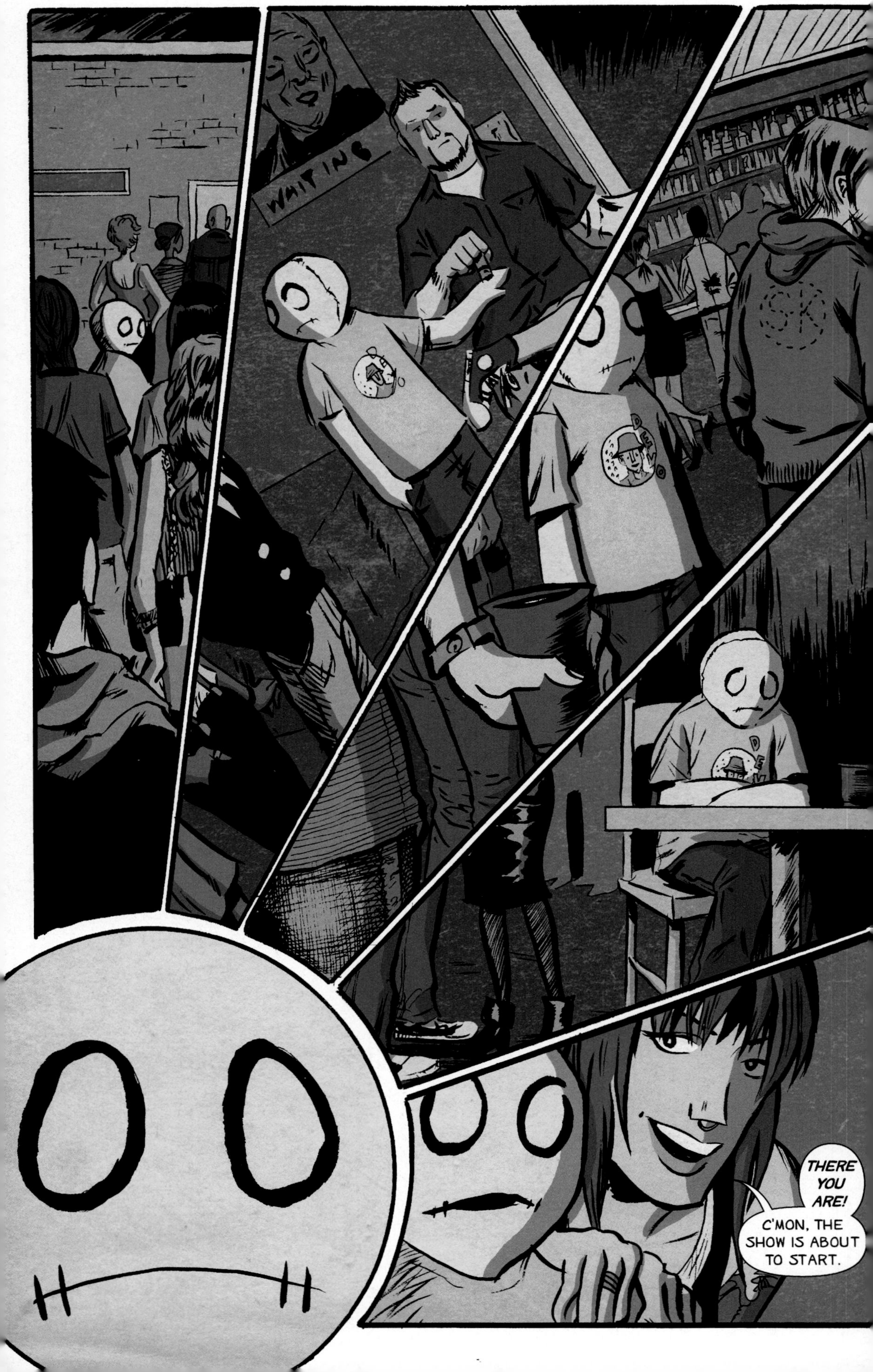
WHITING
SK
THERE YOU ARE!
C'MON, THE SHOW IS ABOUT TO START.

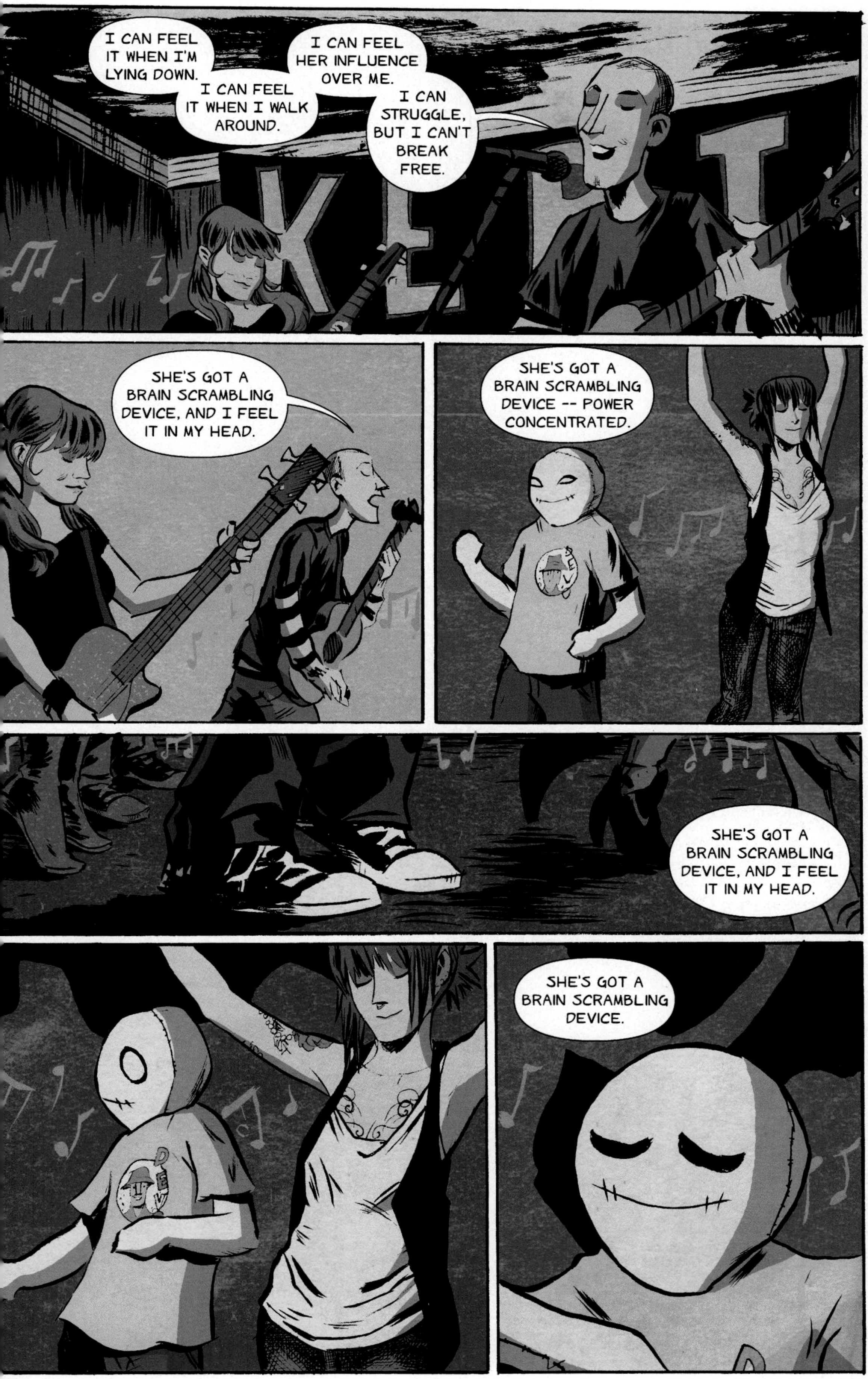
I CAN FEEL IT WHEN I'M LYING DOWN.
I CAN FEEL IT WHEN I WALK AROUND.
I CAN FEEL HER INFLUENCE OVER ME.
I CAN STRUGGLE, BUT I CAN'T BREAK FREE.
SHE'S GOT A BRAIN SCRAMBLING DEVICE, AND I FEEL IT IN MY HEAD.
SHE'S GOT A BRAIN SCRAMBLING DEVICE -- POWER CONCENTRATED.
SHE'S GOT A BRAIN SCRAMBLING DEVICE, AND I FEEL IT IN MY HEAD.
SHE'S GOT A BRAIN SCRAMBLING DEVICE.

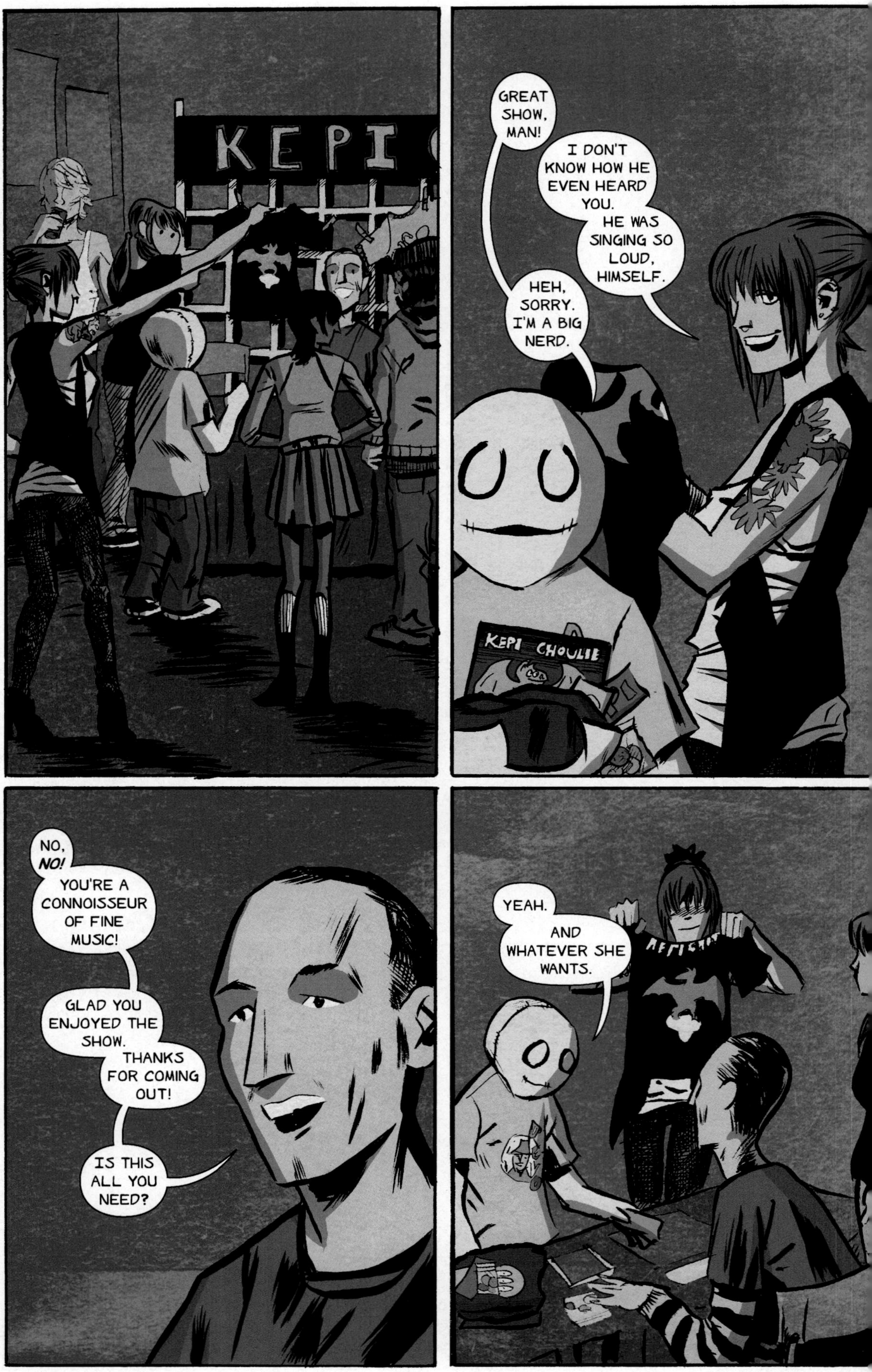
KEPI
GREAT SHOW, MAN!
I DON'T KNOW HOW HE EVEN HEARD YOU.
HE WAS SINGING SO LOUD, HIMSELF.
HEH, SORRY. I'M A BIG NERD.
KEPI CHOULIE
NO, *NO!*
YOU'RE A CONNOISSEUR OF FINE MUSIC!
GLAD YOU ENJOYED THE SHOW.
THANKS FOR COMING OUT!
IS THIS ALL YOU NEED?
YEAH.
AND WHATEVER SHE WANTS.

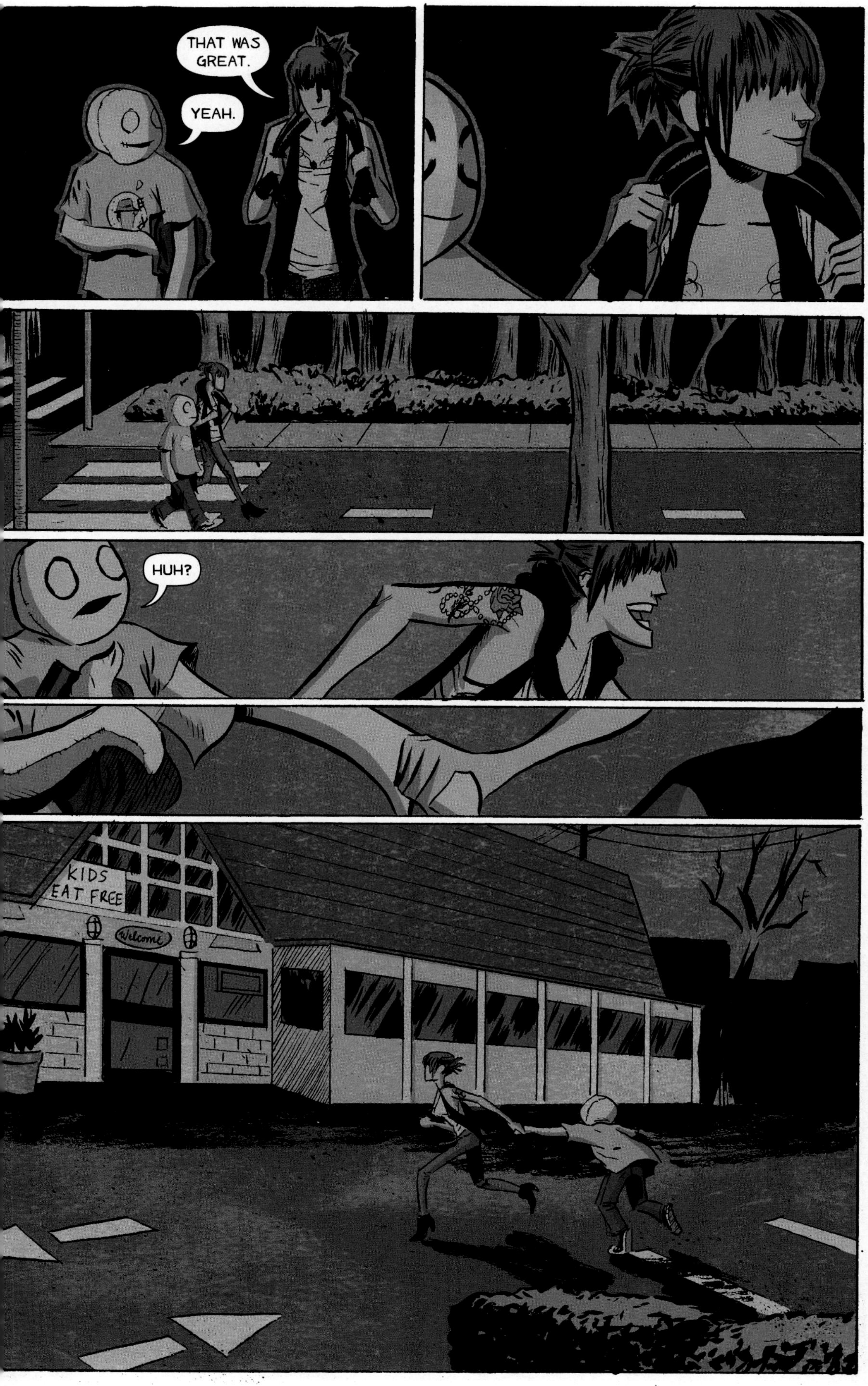
THAT WAS GREAT.
YEAH.
HUH?
KIDS EAT FREE
Welcome

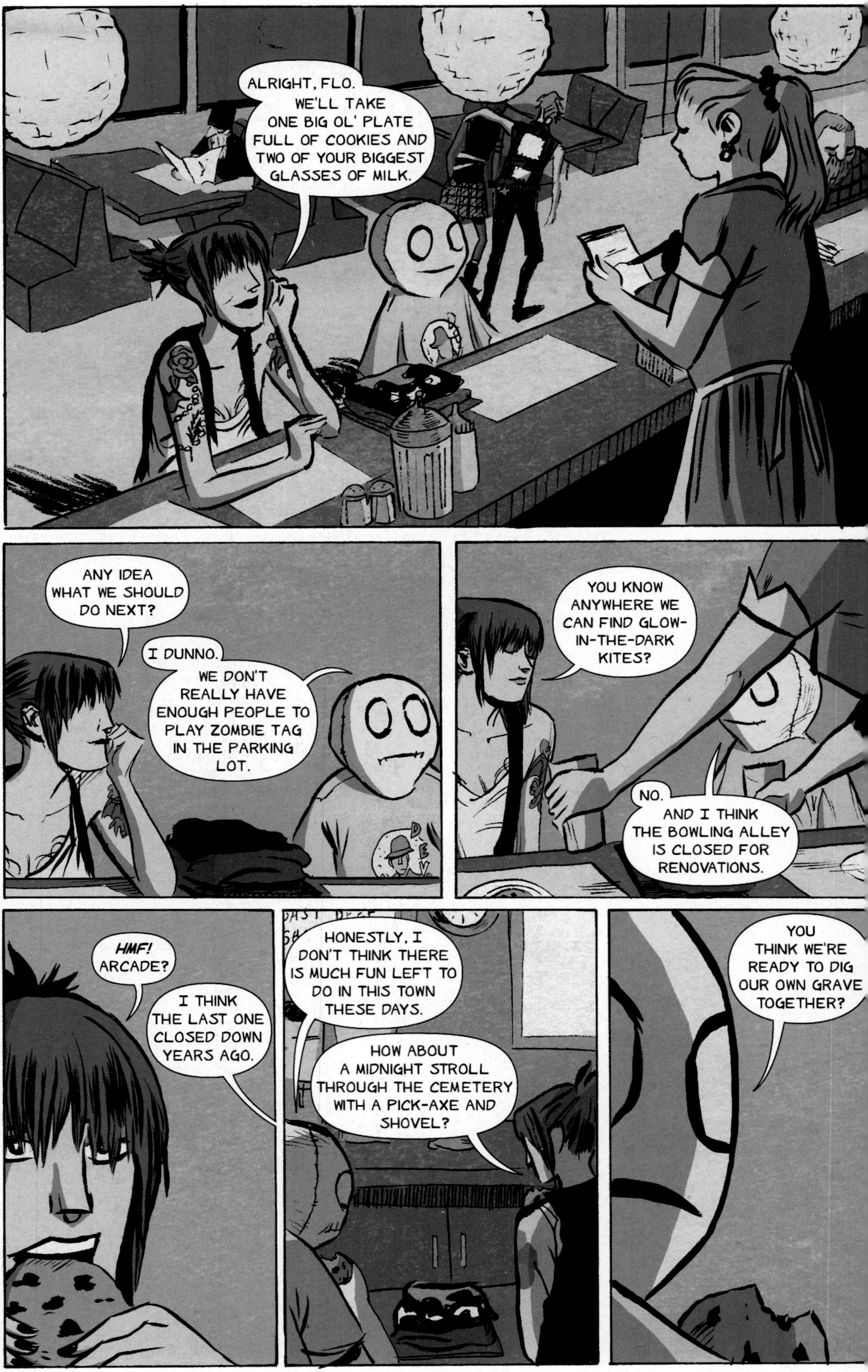
ALRIGHT, FLO.
WE'LL TAKE ONE BIG OL' PLATE FULL OF COOKIES AND TWO OF YOUR BIGGEST GLASSES OF MILK.
ANY IDEA WHAT WE SHOULD DO NEXT?
I DUNNO.
WE DON'T REALLY HAVE ENOUGH PEOPLE TO PLAY ZOMBIE TAG IN THE PARKING LOT.
YOU KNOW ANYWHERE WE CAN FIND GLOW-IN-THE-DARK KITES?
NO.
AND I THINK THE BOWLING ALLEY IS CLOSED FOR RENOVATIONS.
HMF! ARCADE?
I THINK THE LAST ONE CLOSED DOWN YEARS AGO.
HONESTLY, I DON'T THINK THERE IS MUCH FUN LEFT TO DO IN THIS TOWN THESE DAYS.
HOW ABOUT A MIDNIGHT STROLL THROUGH THE CEMETERY WITH A PICK-AXE AND SHOVEL?
YOU THINK WE'RE READY TO DIG OUR OWN GRAVE TOGETHER?

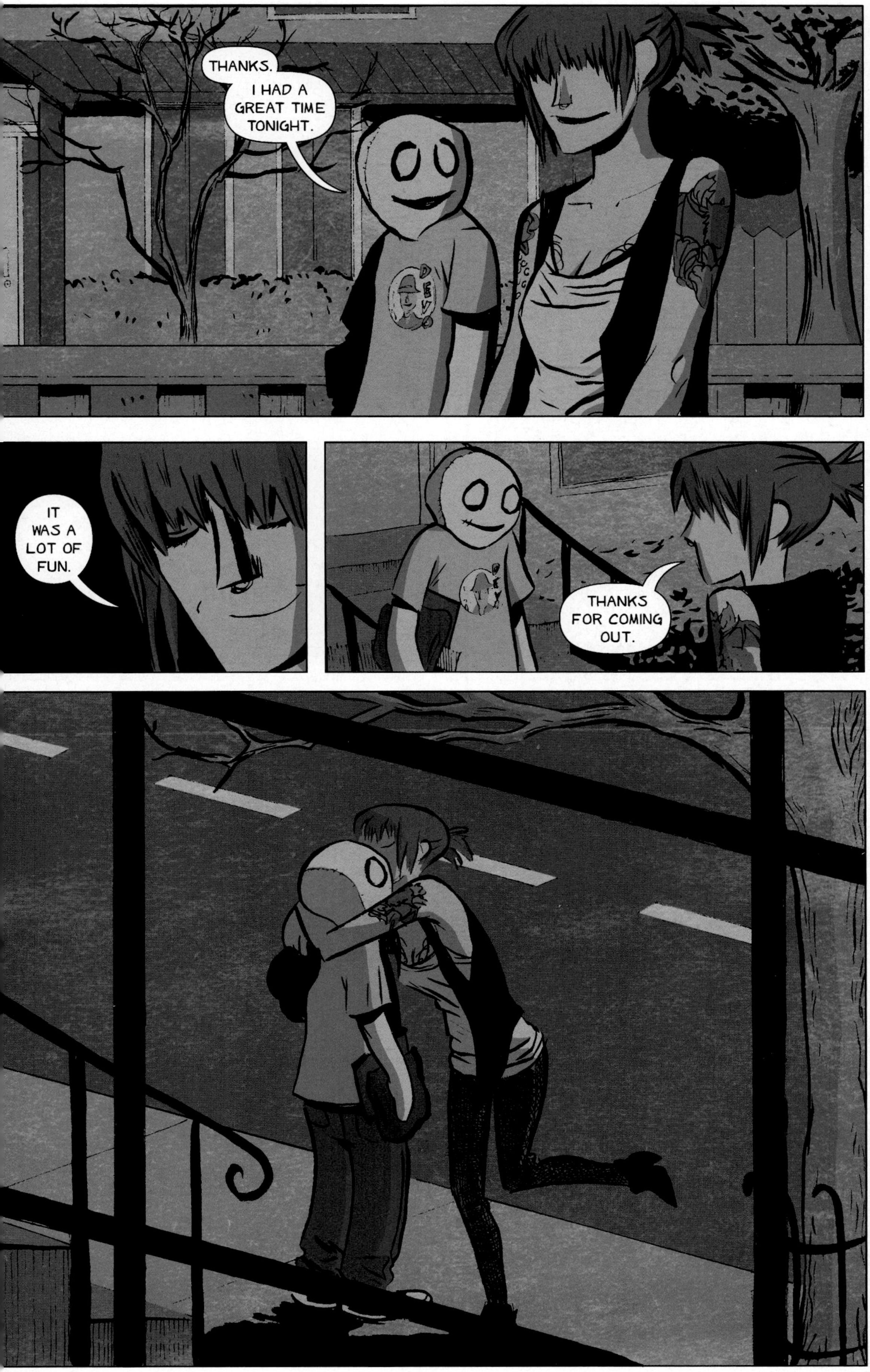
THANKS.
I HAD A GREAT TIME TONIGHT.
IT WAS A LOT OF FUN.
THANKS FOR COMING OUT.

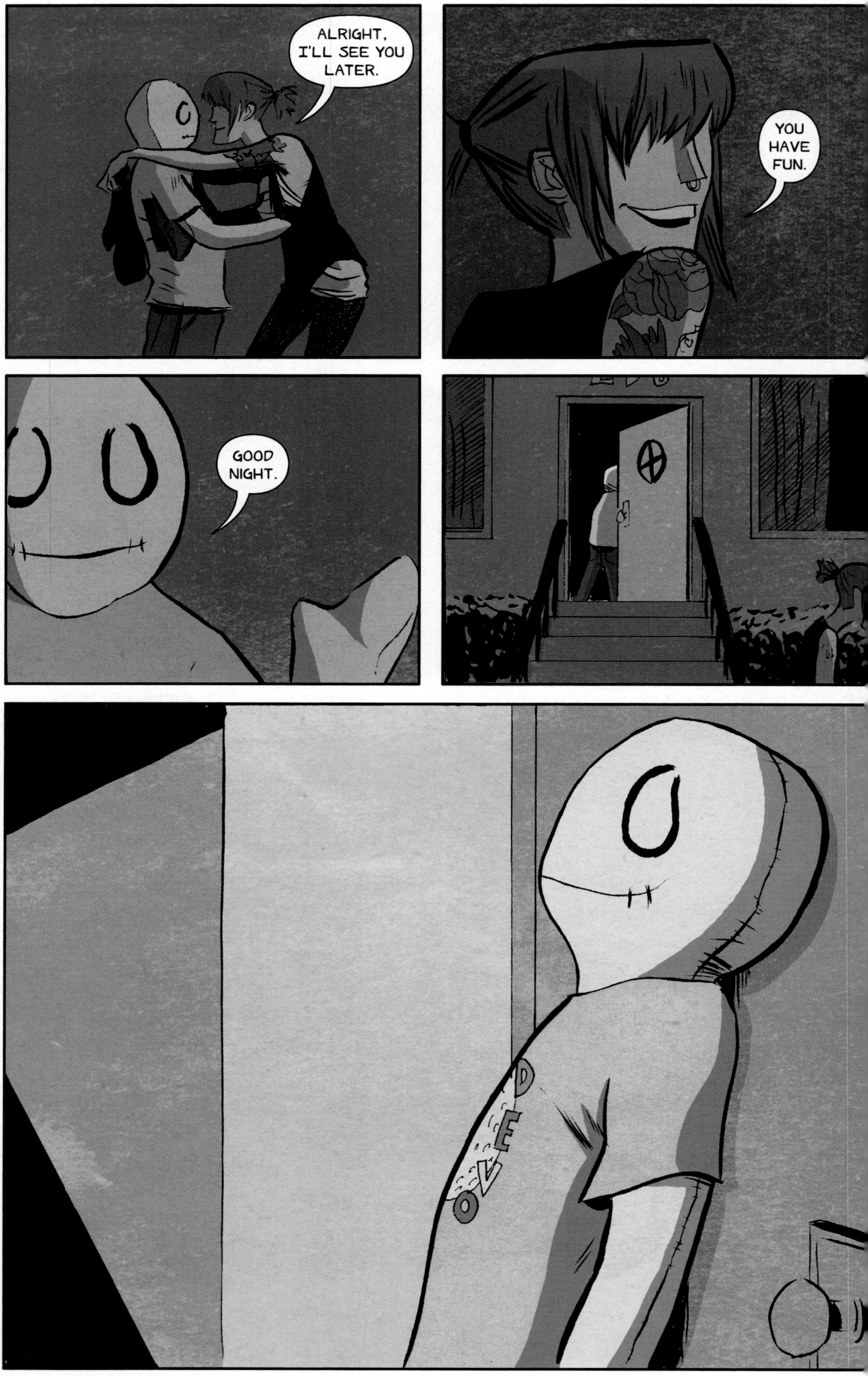
ALRIGHT, I'LL SEE YOU LATER.
YOU HAVE FUN.
GOOD NIGHT.
DEVO

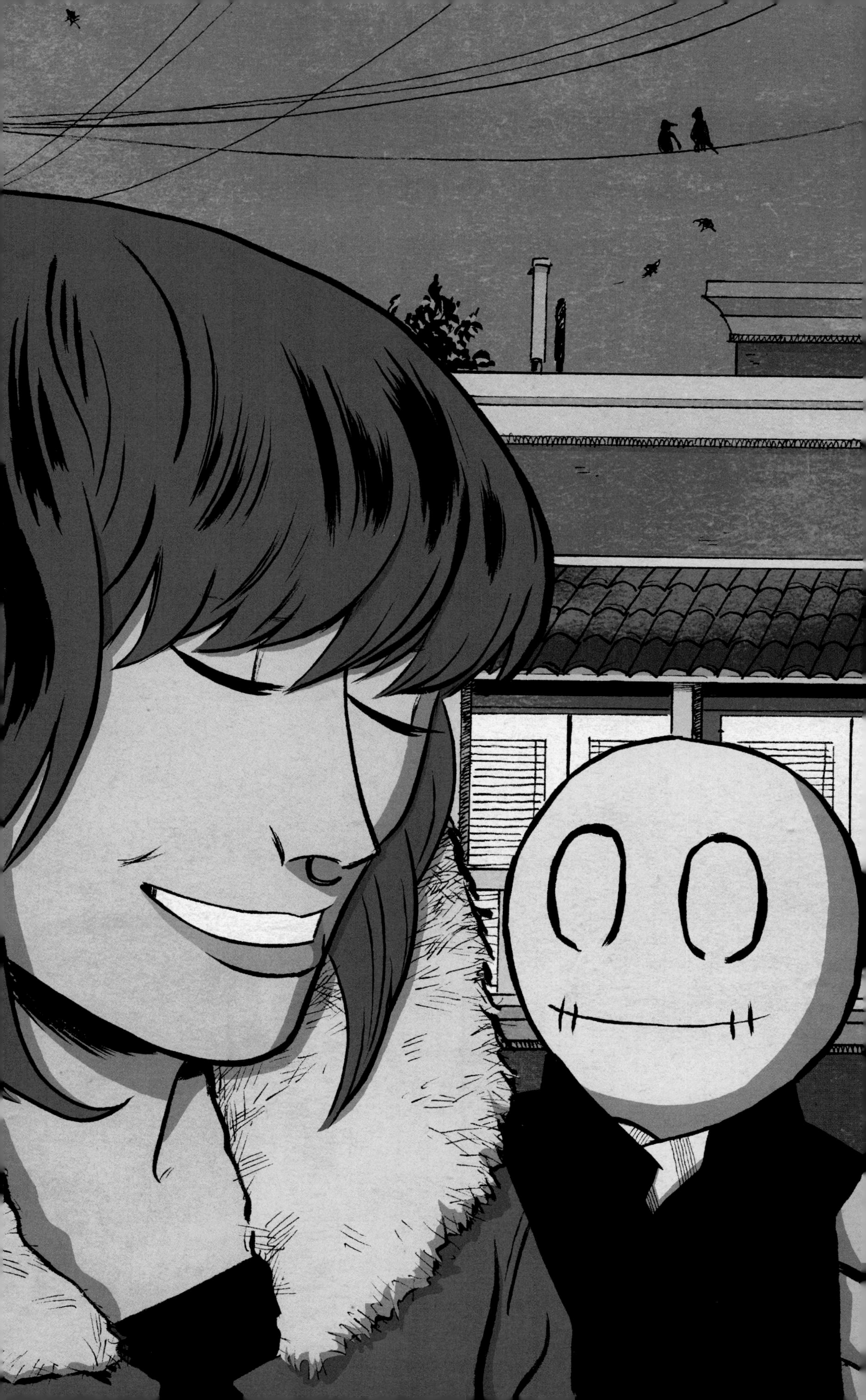

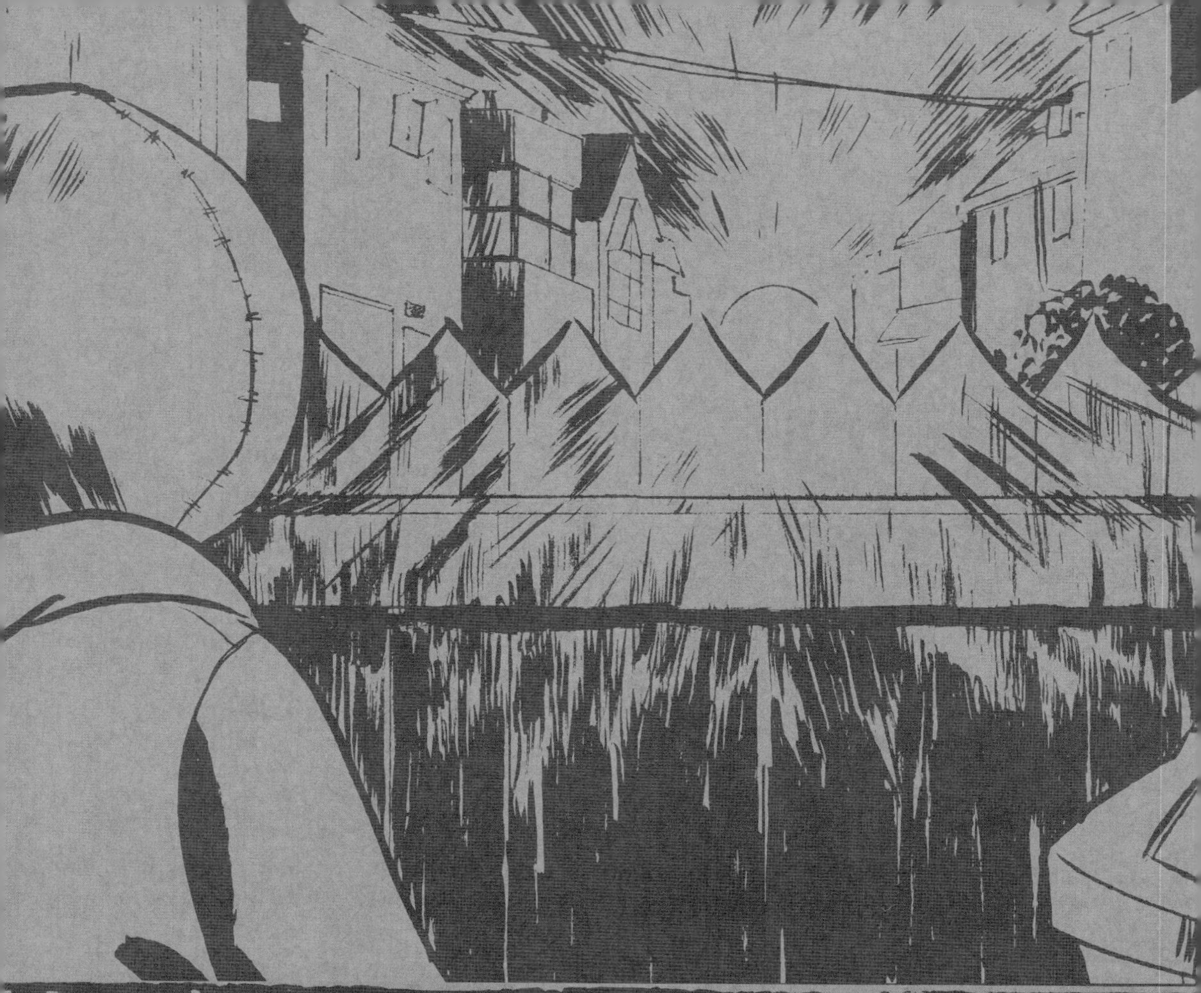

CHAPTER TWO:

"THAT'S NOT MY NAME"

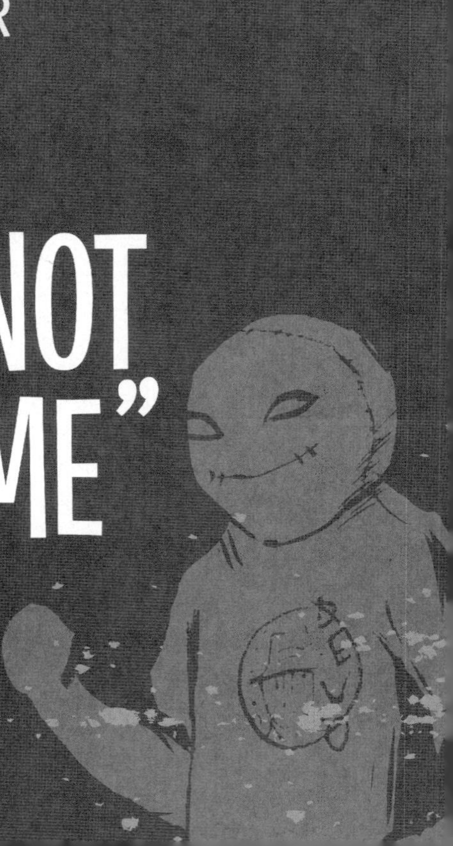

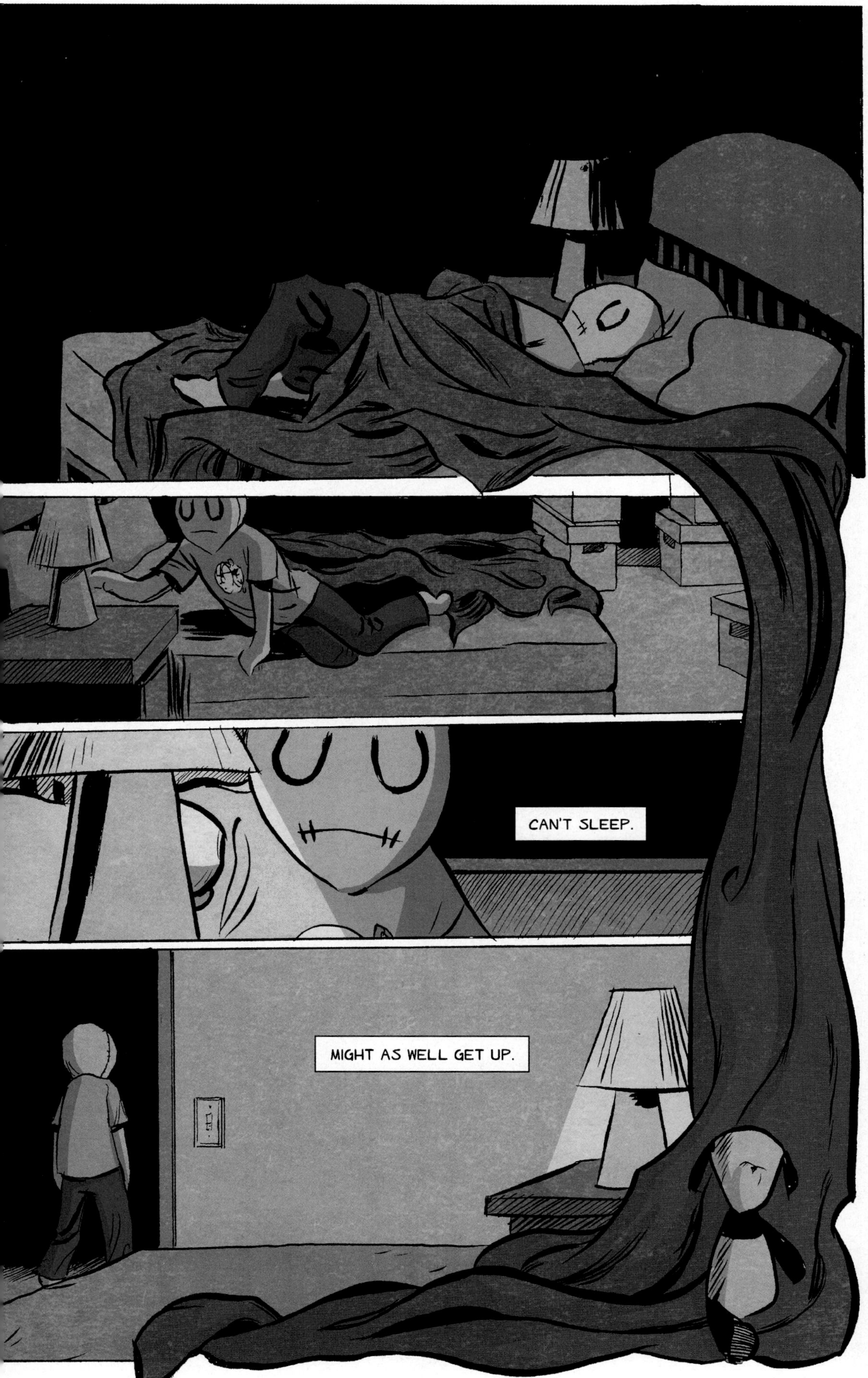
CAN'T SLEEP.
MIGHT AS WELL GET UP.

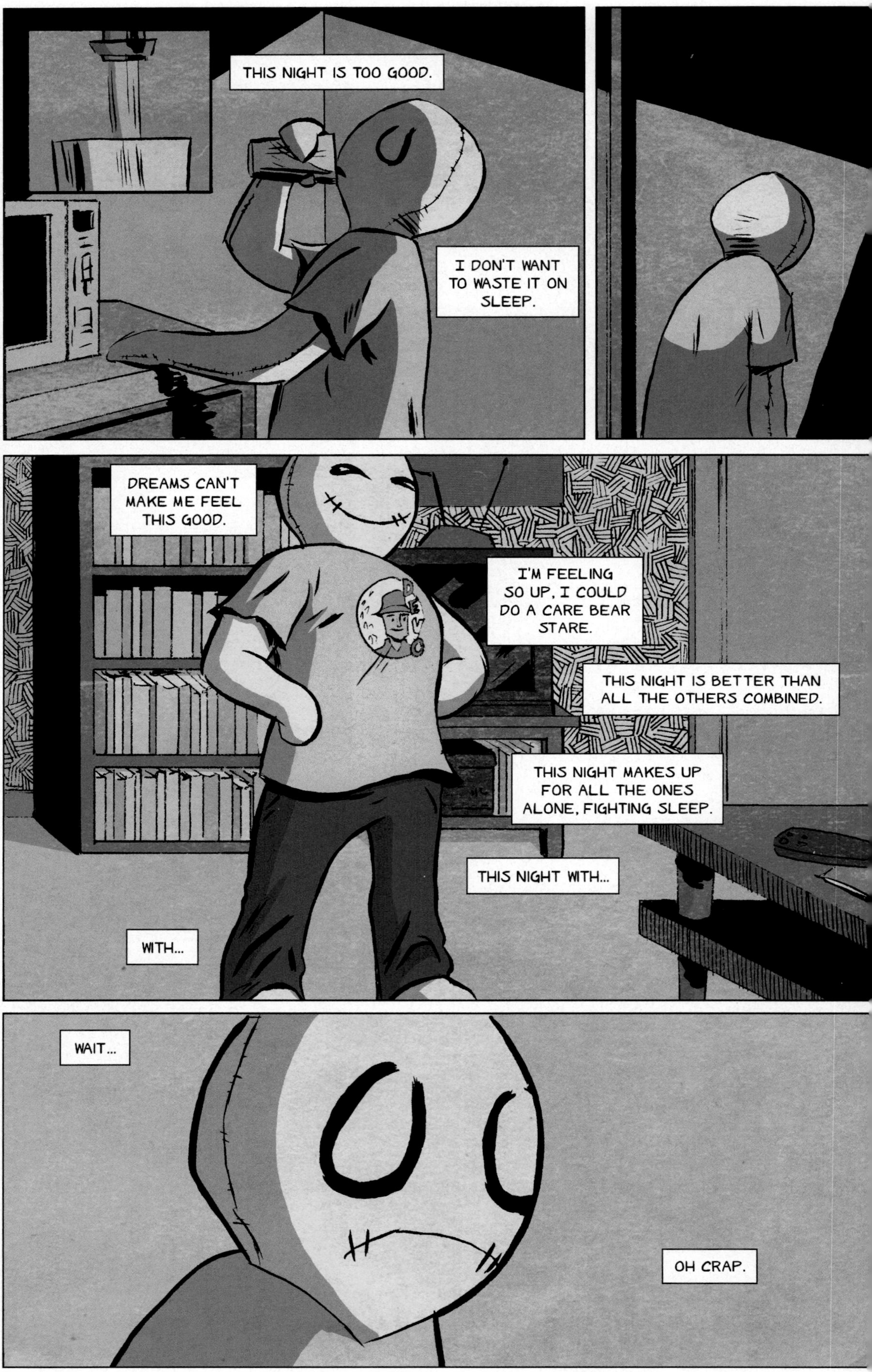
THIS NIGHT IS TOO GOOD.
I DON'T WANT TO WASTE IT ON SLEEP.
DREAMS CAN'T MAKE ME FEEL THIS GOOD.
I'M FEELING SO UP, I COULD DO A CARE BEAR STARE.
THIS NIGHT IS BETTER THAN ALL THE OTHERS COMBINED.
THIS NIGHT MAKES UP FOR ALL THE ONES ALONE, FIGHTING SLEEP.
THIS NIGHT WITH...
WITH...
WAIT...
OH CRAP.

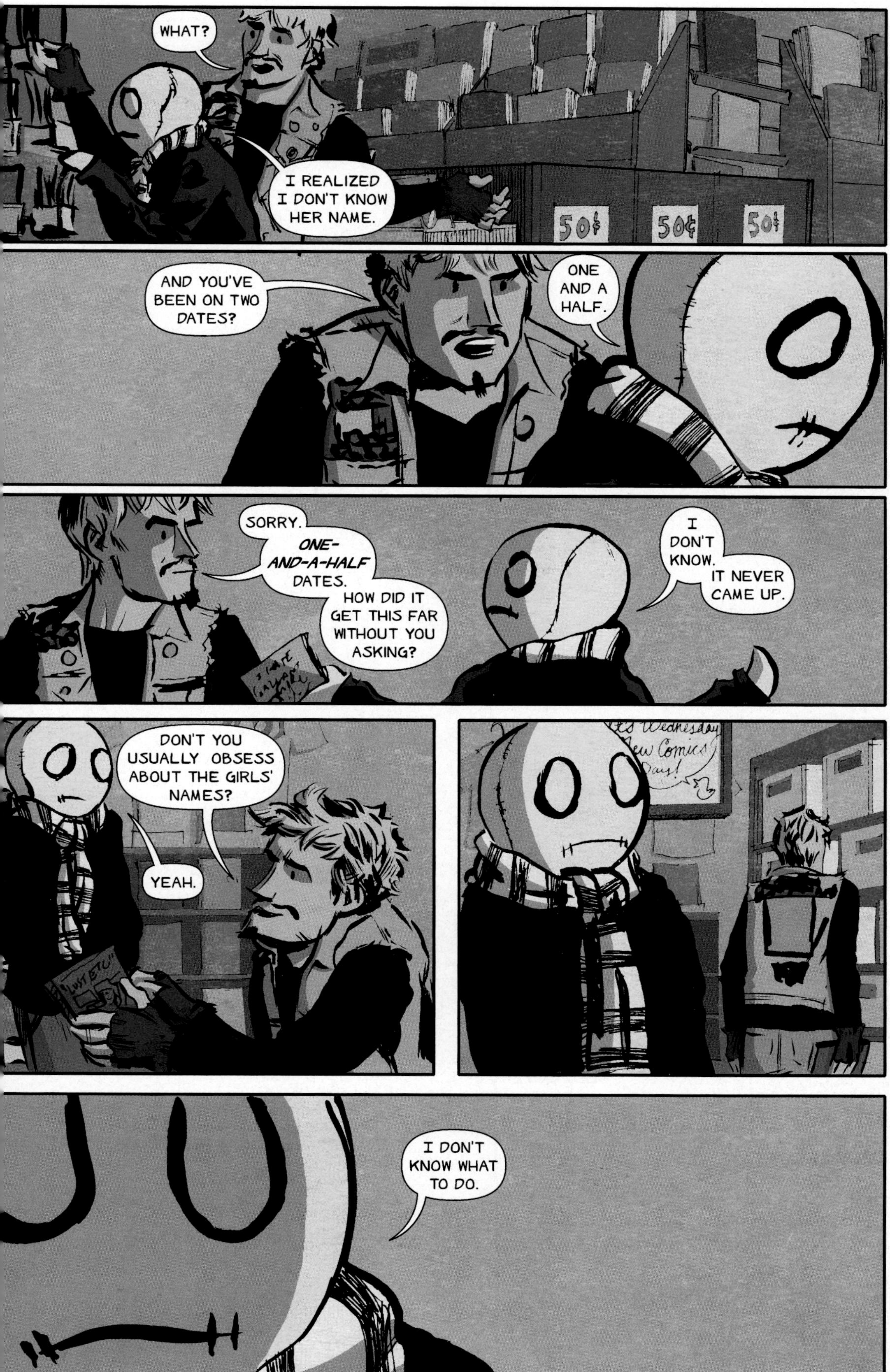
WHAT?
I REALIZED I DON'T KNOW HER NAME.
50¢
50¢
50¢
AND YOU'VE BEEN ON TWO DATES?
ONE AND A HALF.
SORRY. *ONE-AND-A-HALF* DATES.
HOW DID IT GET THIS FAR WITHOUT YOU ASKING?
I DON'T KNOW.
IT NEVER CAME UP.
DON'T YOU USUALLY OBSESS ABOUT THE GIRLS' NAMES?
YEAH.
I DON'T KNOW WHAT TO DO.

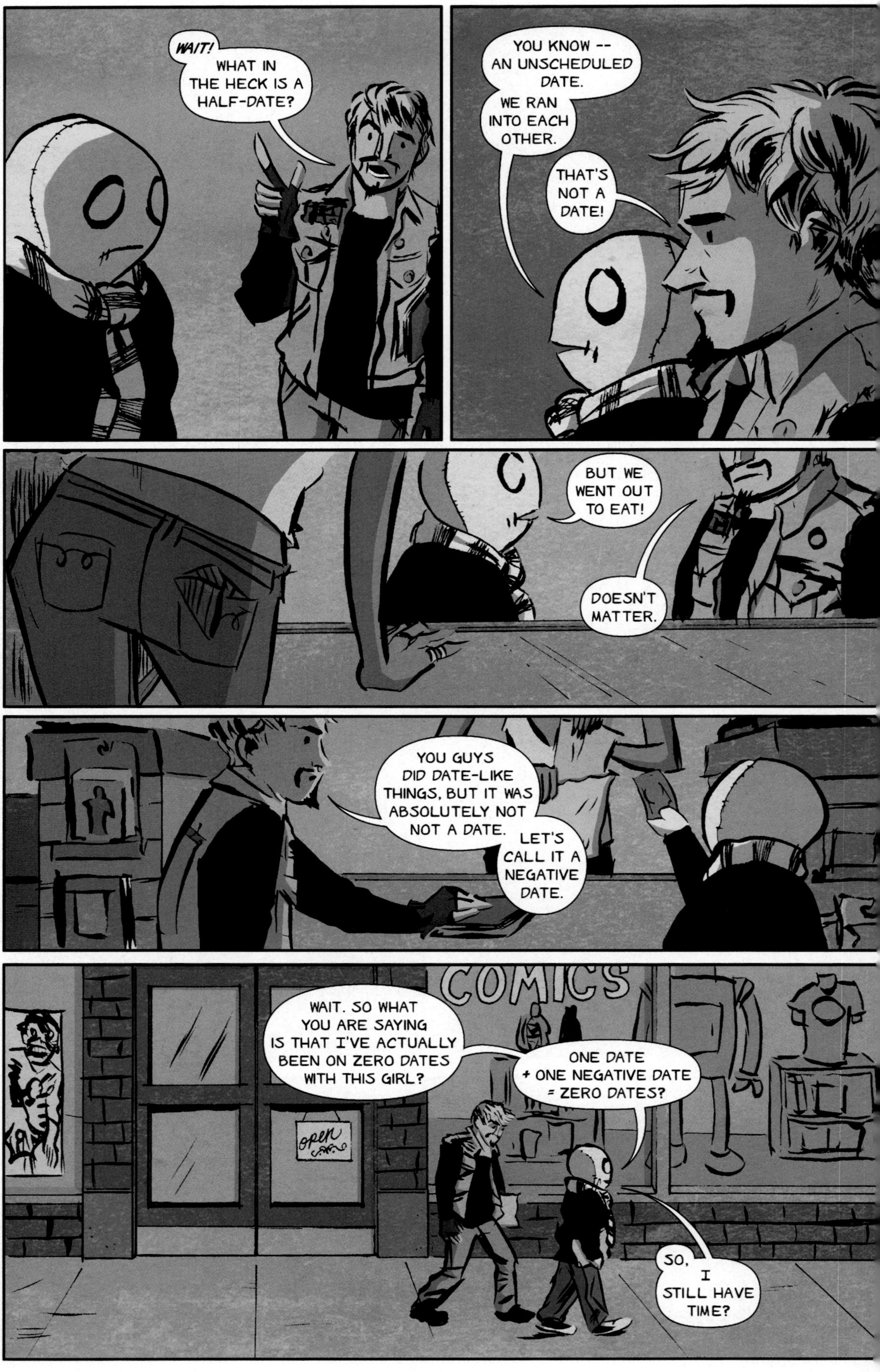
WAIT! WHAT IN THE HECK IS A HALF-DATE?
YOU KNOW -- AN UNSCHEDULED DATE.
WE RAN INTO EACH OTHER.
THAT'S NOT A DATE!
BUT WE WENT OUT TO EAT!
DOESN'T MATTER.
YOU GUYS DID DATE-LIKE THINGS, BUT IT WAS ABSOLUTELY NOT NOT A DATE.
LET'S CALL IT A NEGATIVE DATE.
COMICS
WAIT. SO WHAT YOU ARE SAYING IS THAT I'VE ACTUALLY BEEN ON ZERO DATES WITH THIS GIRL?
ONE DATE + ONE NEGATIVE DATE = ZERO DATES?
open
SO, I STILL HAVE TIME?

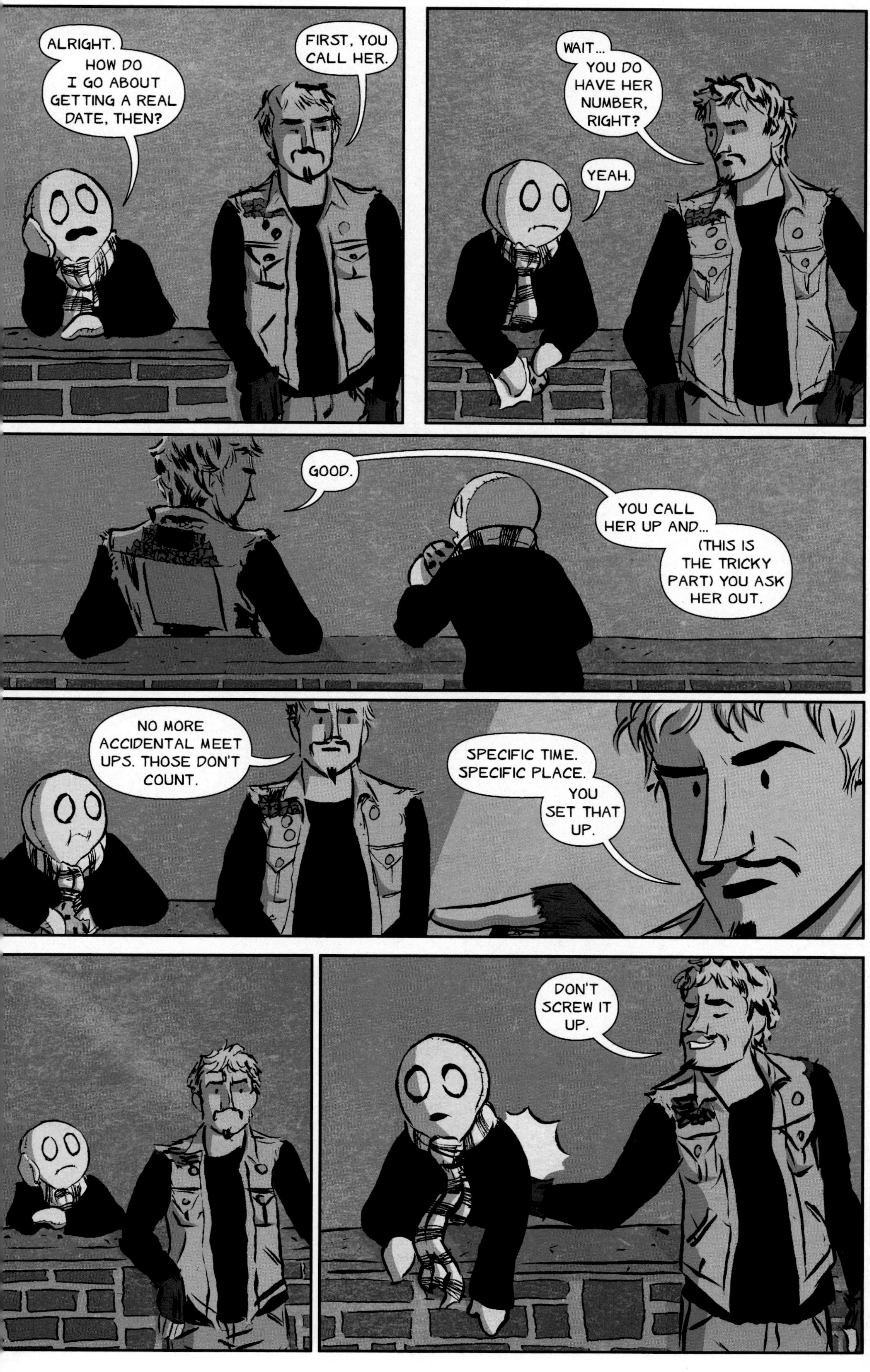
ALRIGHT.
HOW DO I GO ABOUT GETTING A REAL DATE, THEN?
FIRST, YOU CALL HER.
WAIT...
YOU DO HAVE HER NUMBER, RIGHT?
YEAH.
GOOD.
YOU CALL HER UP AND...
(THIS IS THE TRICKY PART) YOU ASK HER OUT.
NO MORE ACCIDENTAL MEET UPS. THOSE DON'T COUNT.
SPECIFIC TIME. SPECIFIC PLACE.
YOU SET THAT UP.
DON'T SCREW IT UP.

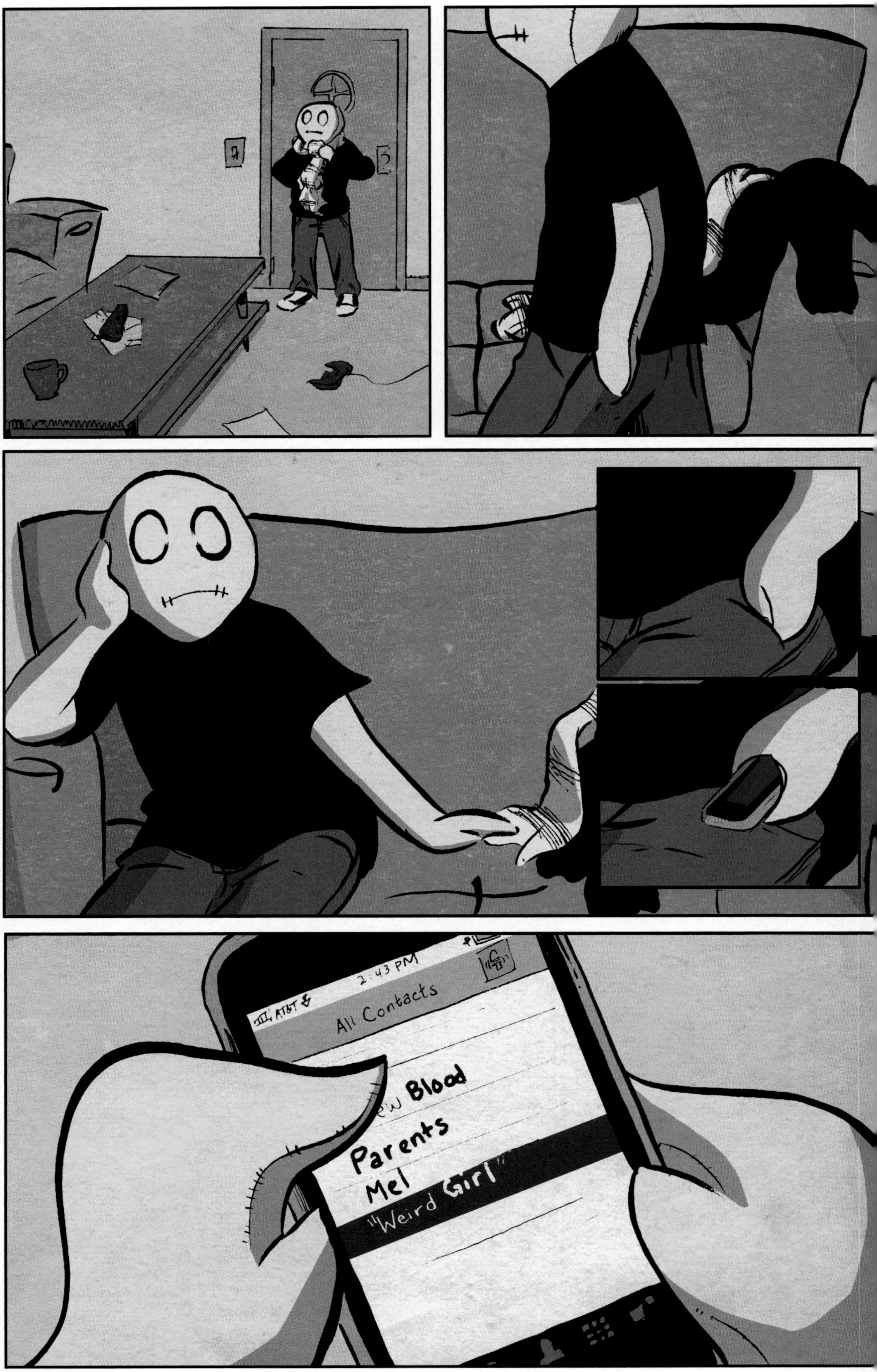

2:43 PM
AT&T
All Contacts
ew Blood
Parents
Mel
"Weird Girl"

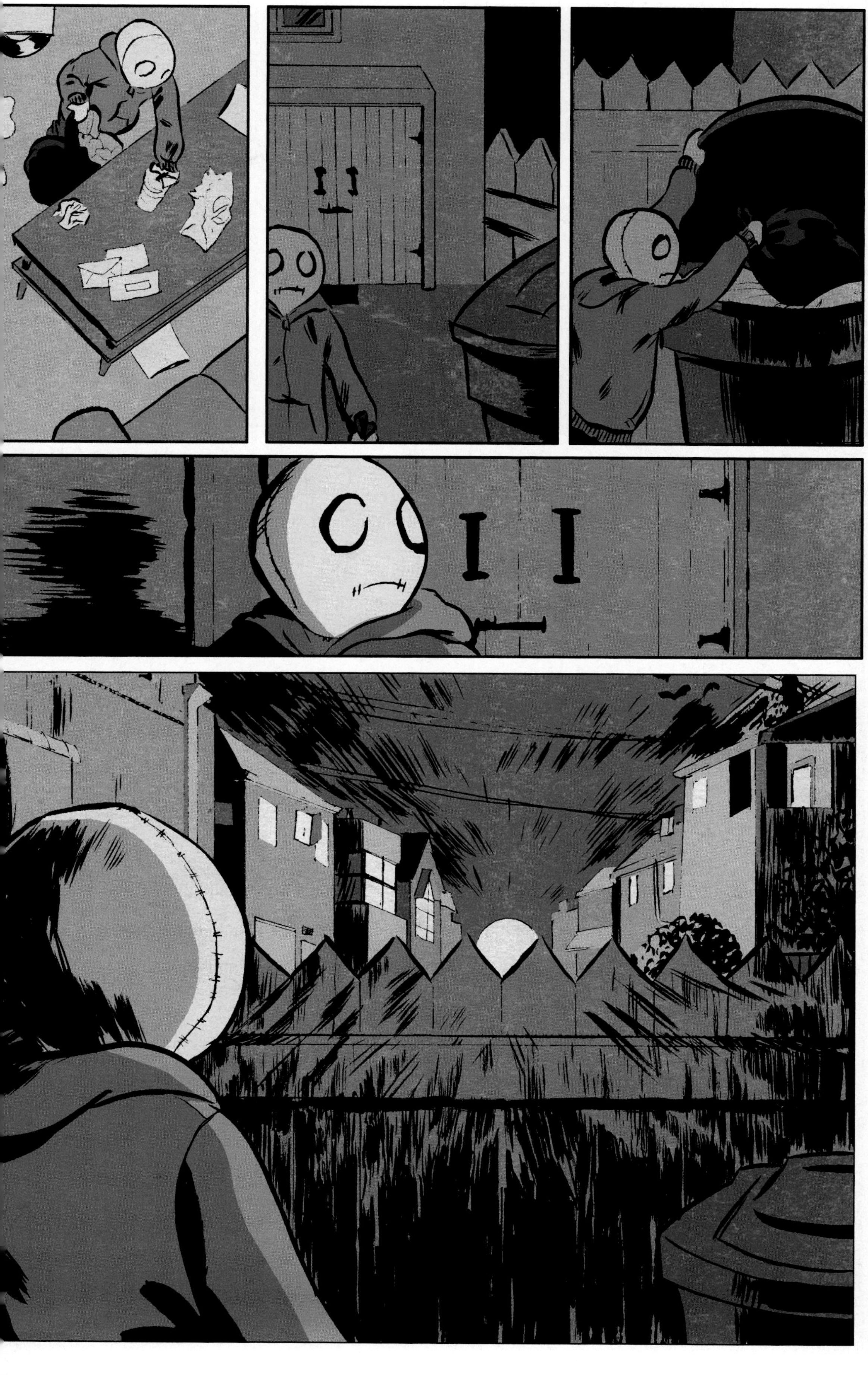

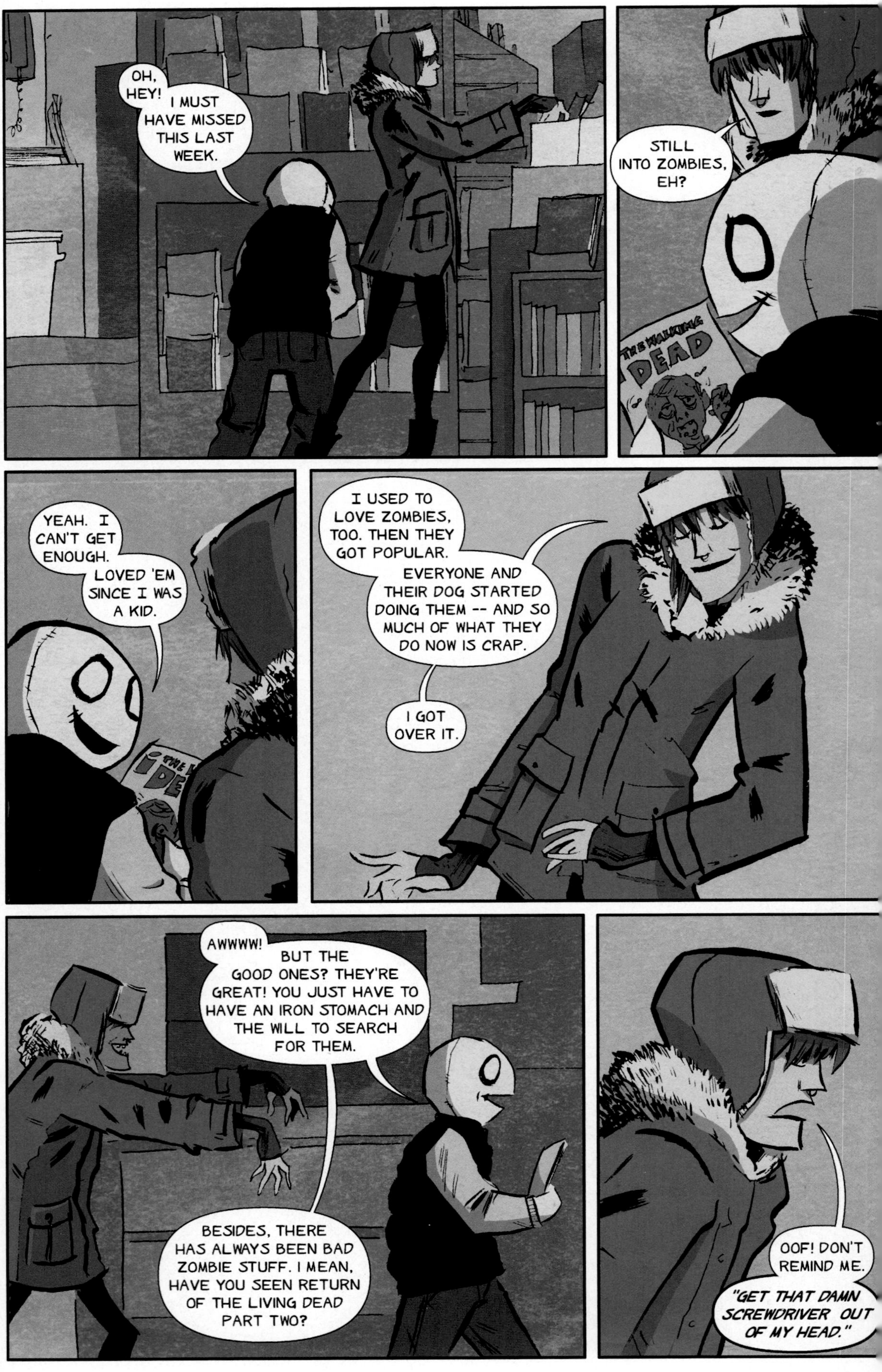
OH, HEY!
I MUST HAVE MISSED THIS LAST WEEK.
STILL INTO ZOMBIES, EH?
THE WALKING DEAD
YEAH. I CAN'T GET ENOUGH.
LOVED 'EM SINCE I WAS A KID.
I USED TO LOVE ZOMBIES, TOO. THEN THEY GOT POPULAR.
EVERYONE AND THEIR DOG STARTED DOING THEM -- AND SO MUCH OF WHAT THEY DO NOW IS CRAP.
I GOT OVER IT.
AWWWW!
BUT THE GOOD ONES? THEY'RE GREAT! YOU JUST HAVE TO HAVE AN IRON STOMACH AND THE WILL TO SEARCH FOR THEM.
BESIDES, THERE HAS ALWAYS BEEN BAD ZOMBIE STUFF. I MEAN, HAVE YOU SEEN RETURN OF THE LIVING DEAD PART TWO?
OOF! DON'T REMIND ME.
"GET THAT DAMN SCREWDRIVER OUT OF MY HEAD."

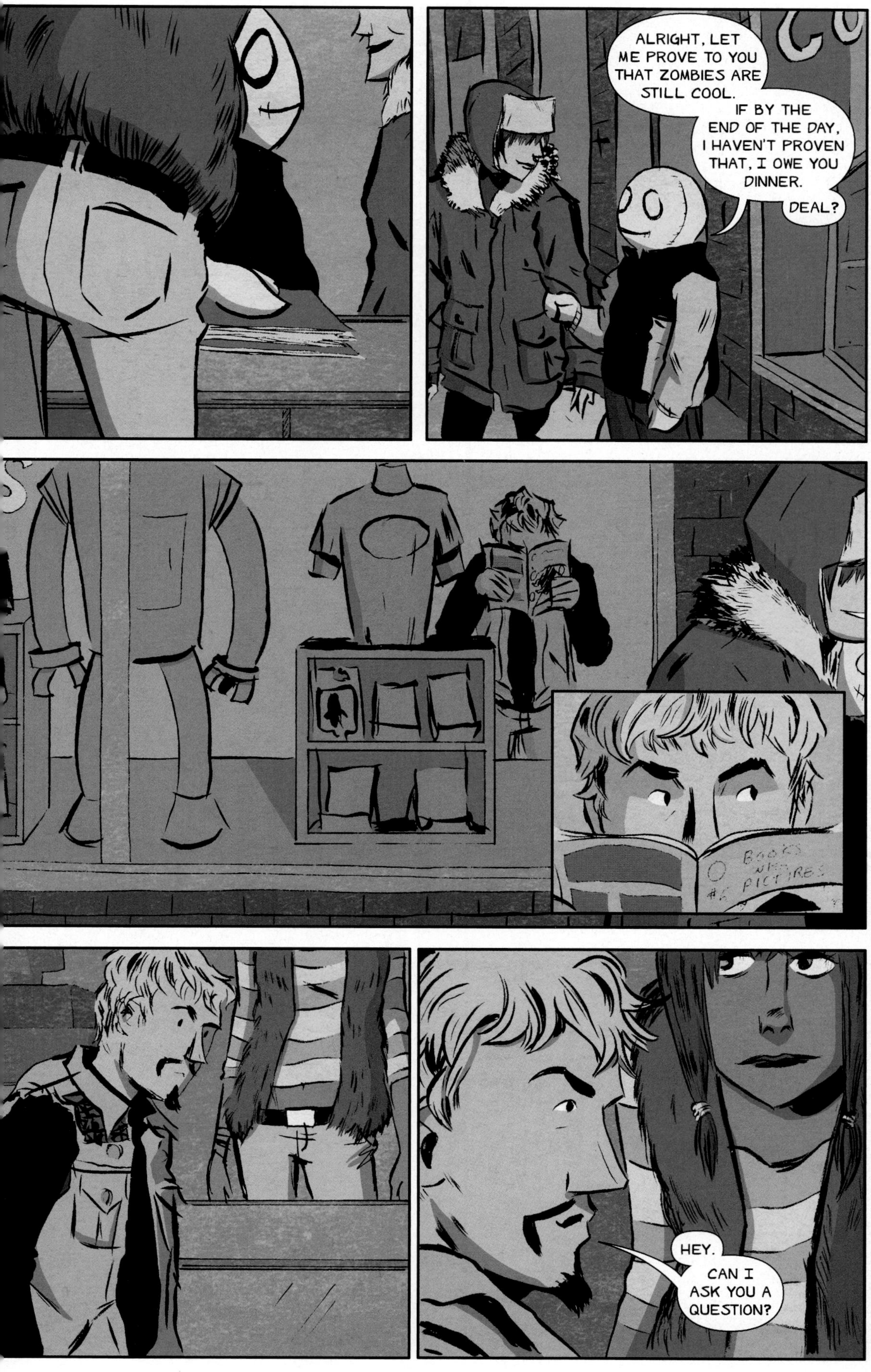
ALRIGHT, LET ME PROVE TO YOU THAT ZOMBIES ARE STILL COOL.
IF BY THE END OF THE DAY, I HAVEN'T PROVEN THAT, I OWE YOU DINNER.
DEAL?
BOOKS WITH PICTURES #6
HEY.
CAN I ASK YOU A QUESTION?

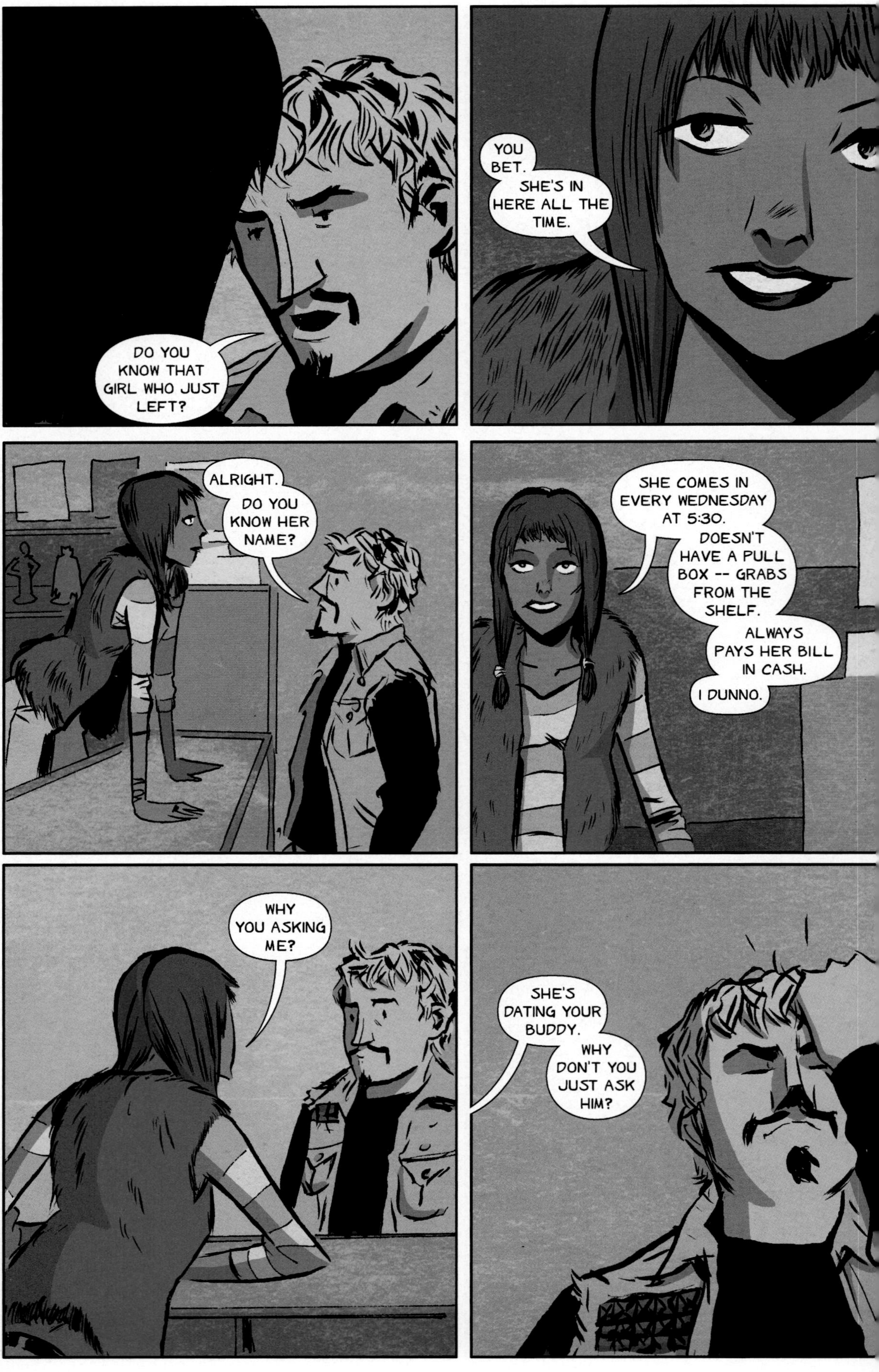
DO YOU KNOW THAT GIRL WHO JUST LEFT?
YOU BET.
SHE'S IN HERE ALL THE TIME.
ALRIGHT.
DO YOU KNOW HER NAME?
SHE COMES IN EVERY WEDNESDAY AT 5:30.
DOESN'T HAVE A PULL BOX -- GRABS FROM THE SHELF.
ALWAYS PAYS HER BILL IN CASH.
I DUNNO.
WHY YOU ASKING ME?
SHE'S DATING YOUR BUDDY.
WHY DON'T YOU JUST ASK HIM?

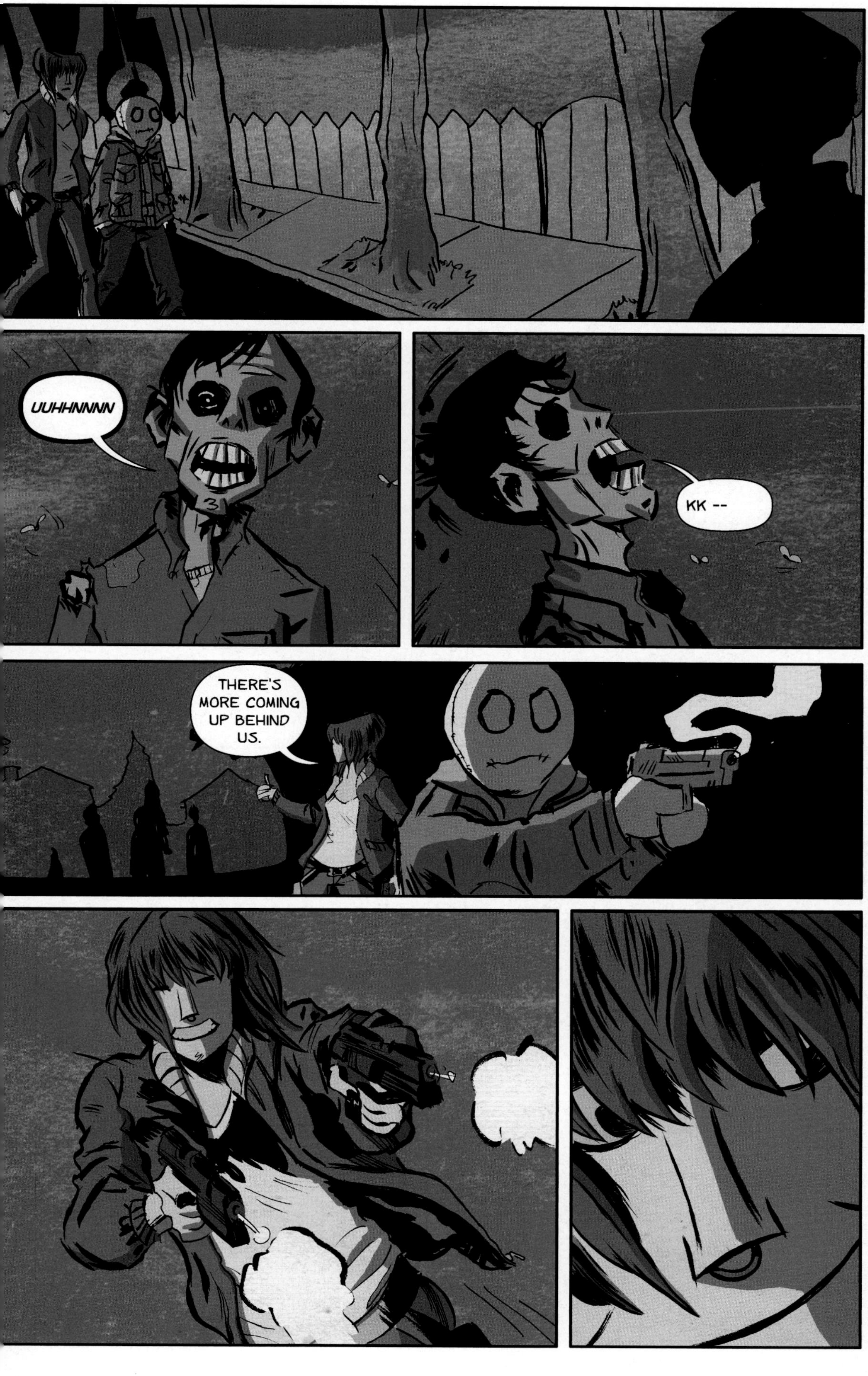
UUHHNNNN
KK --
THERE'S MORE COMING UP BEHIND US.

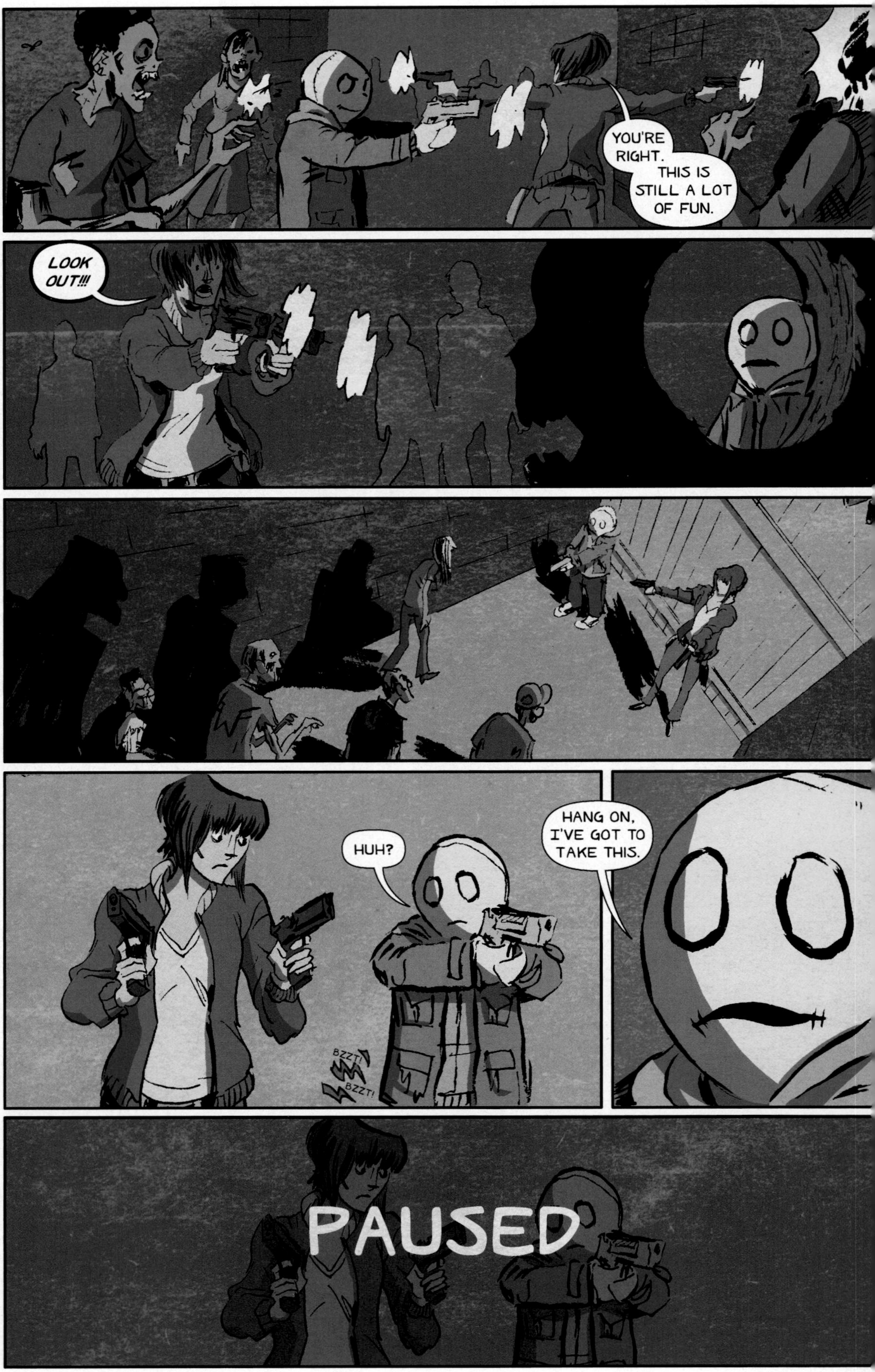
YOU'RE RIGHT. THIS IS STILL A LOT OF FUN.
LOOK OUT!!!
HUH?
HANG ON, I'VE GOT TO TAKE THIS.
BZZT!
BZZT!
PAUSED

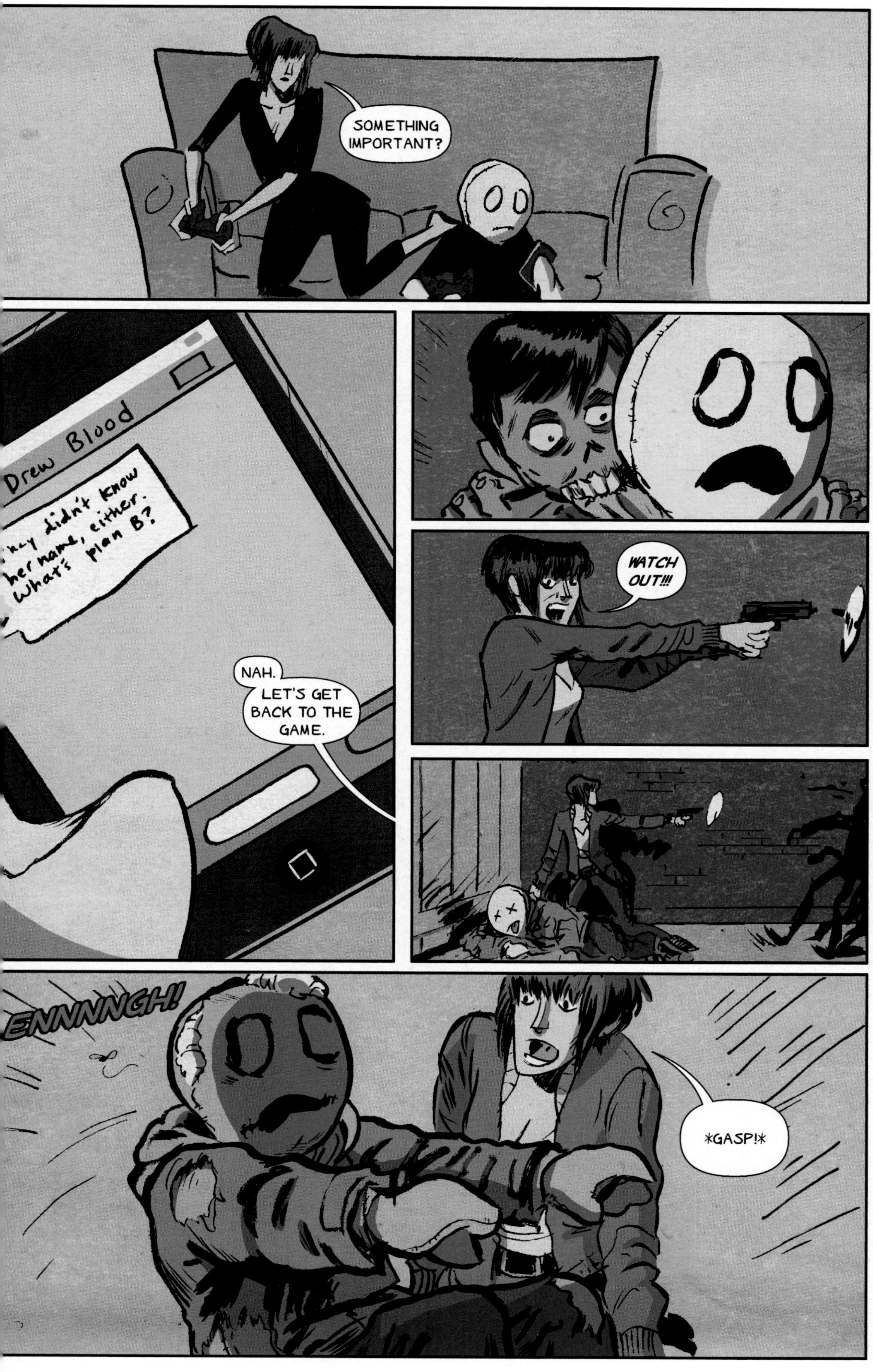
SOMETHING IMPORTANT?
Drew Blood
...hey didn't know her name, either. What's plan B?
NAH.
LET'S GET BACK TO THE GAME.
WATCH OUT!!!
ENNNNGH!
GASP!

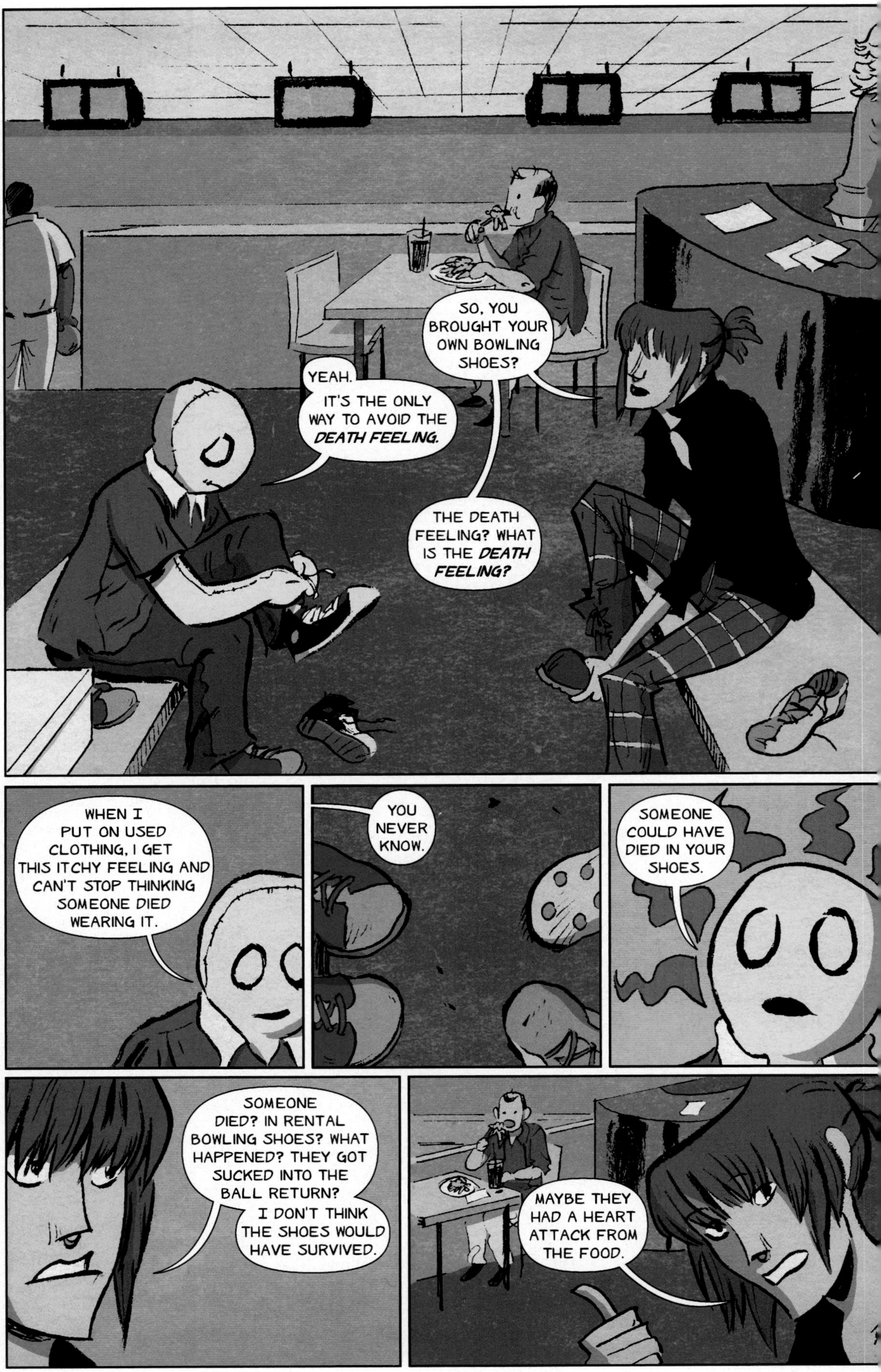
SO, YOU BROUGHT YOUR OWN BOWLING SHOES?
YEAH.
IT'S THE ONLY WAY TO AVOID THE *DEATH FEELING.*
THE DEATH FEELING? WHAT IS THE *DEATH FEELING?*
WHEN I PUT ON USED CLOTHING, I GET THIS ITCHY FEELING AND CAN'T STOP THINKING SOMEONE DIED WEARING IT.
YOU NEVER KNOW.
SOMEONE COULD HAVE DIED IN YOUR SHOES.
SOMEONE DIED? IN RENTAL BOWLING SHOES? WHAT HAPPENED? THEY GOT SUCKED INTO THE BALL RETURN?
I DON'T THINK THE SHOES WOULD HAVE SURVIVED.
MAYBE THEY HAD A HEART ATTACK FROM THE FOOD.

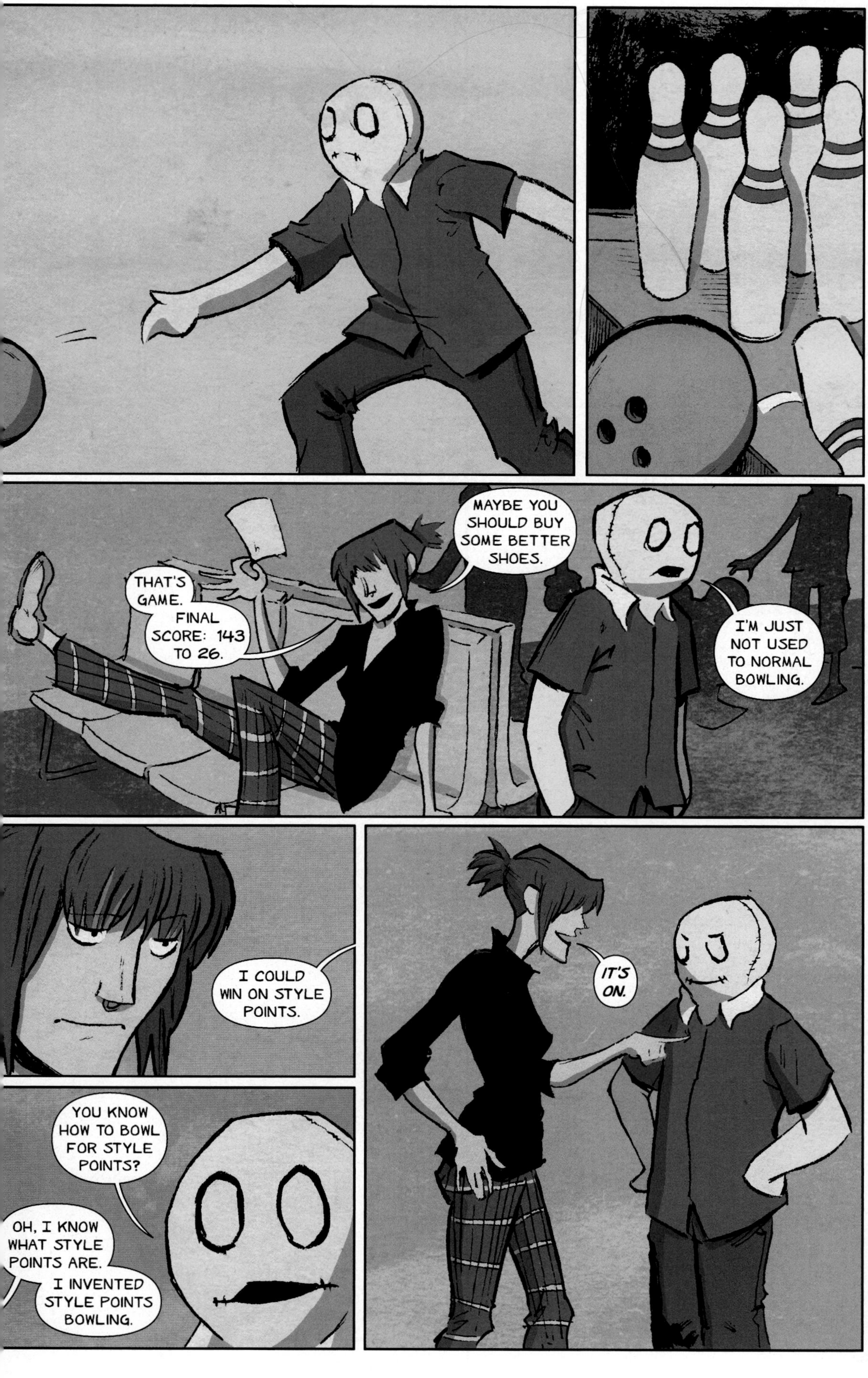
THAT'S GAME. FINAL SCORE: 143 TO 26.
MAYBE YOU SHOULD BUY SOME BETTER SHOES.
I'M JUST NOT USED TO NORMAL BOWLING.
I COULD WIN ON STYLE POINTS.
YOU KNOW HOW TO BOWL FOR STYLE POINTS?
OH, I KNOW WHAT STYLE POINTS ARE.
I INVENTED STYLE POINTS BOWLING.
IT'S ON.

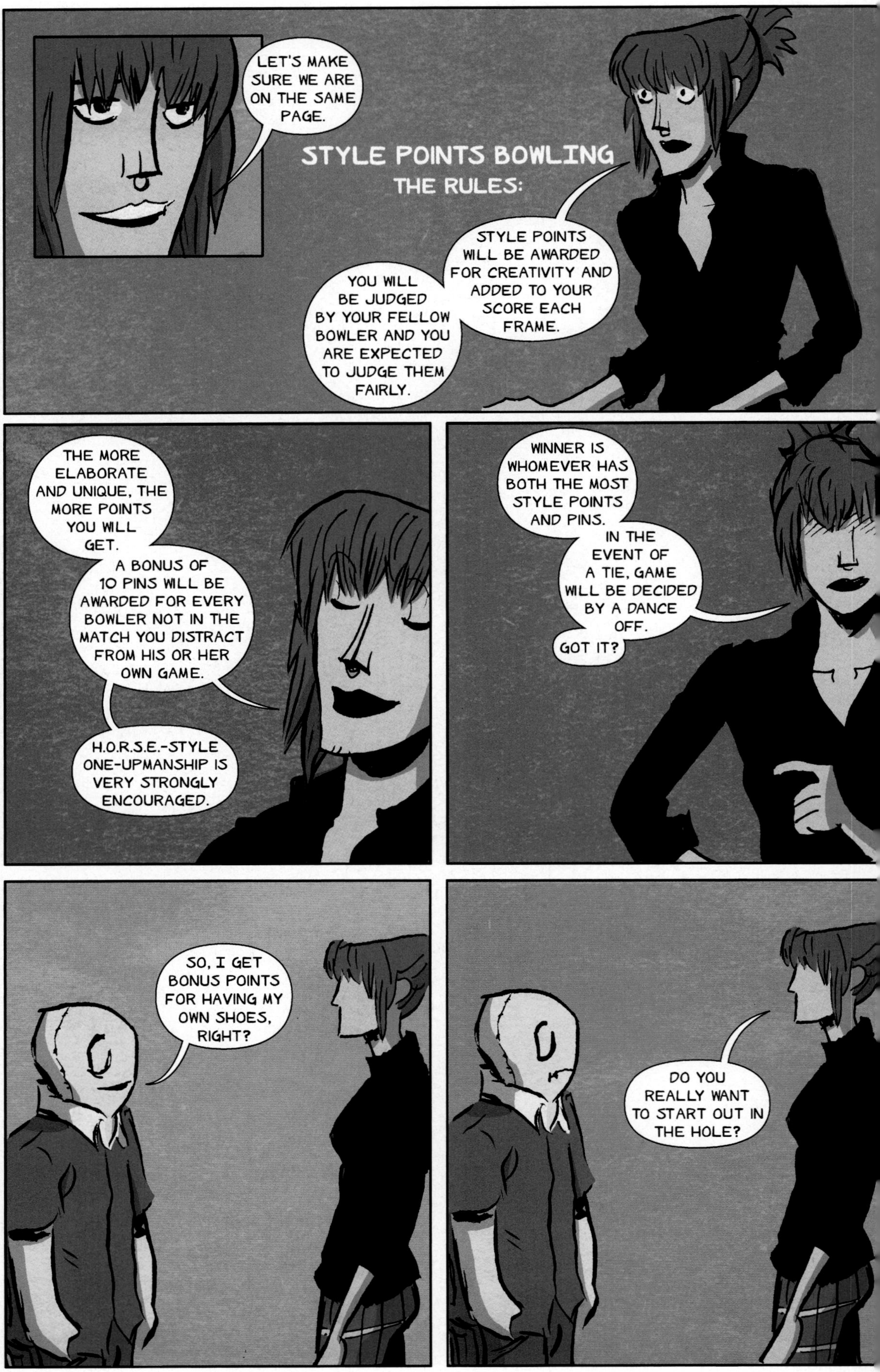
LET'S MAKE SURE WE ARE ON THE SAME PAGE.
STYLE POINTS BOWLING
THE RULES:
STYLE POINTS WILL BE AWARDED FOR CREATIVITY AND ADDED TO YOUR SCORE EACH FRAME.
YOU WILL BE JUDGED BY YOUR FELLOW BOWLER AND YOU ARE EXPECTED TO JUDGE THEM FAIRLY.
THE MORE ELABORATE AND UNIQUE, THE MORE POINTS YOU WILL GET.
A BONUS OF 10 PINS WILL BE AWARDED FOR EVERY BOWLER NOT IN THE MATCH YOU DISTRACT FROM HIS OR HER OWN GAME.
H.O.R.S.E.-STYLE ONE-UPMANSHIP IS VERY STRONGLY ENCOURAGED.
WINNER IS WHOMEVER HAS BOTH THE MOST STYLE POINTS AND PINS.
IN THE EVENT OF A TIE, GAME WILL BE DECIDED BY A DANCE OFF.
GOT IT?
SO, I GET BONUS POINTS FOR HAVING MY OWN SHOES, RIGHT?
DO YOU REALLY WANT TO START OUT IN THE HOLE?

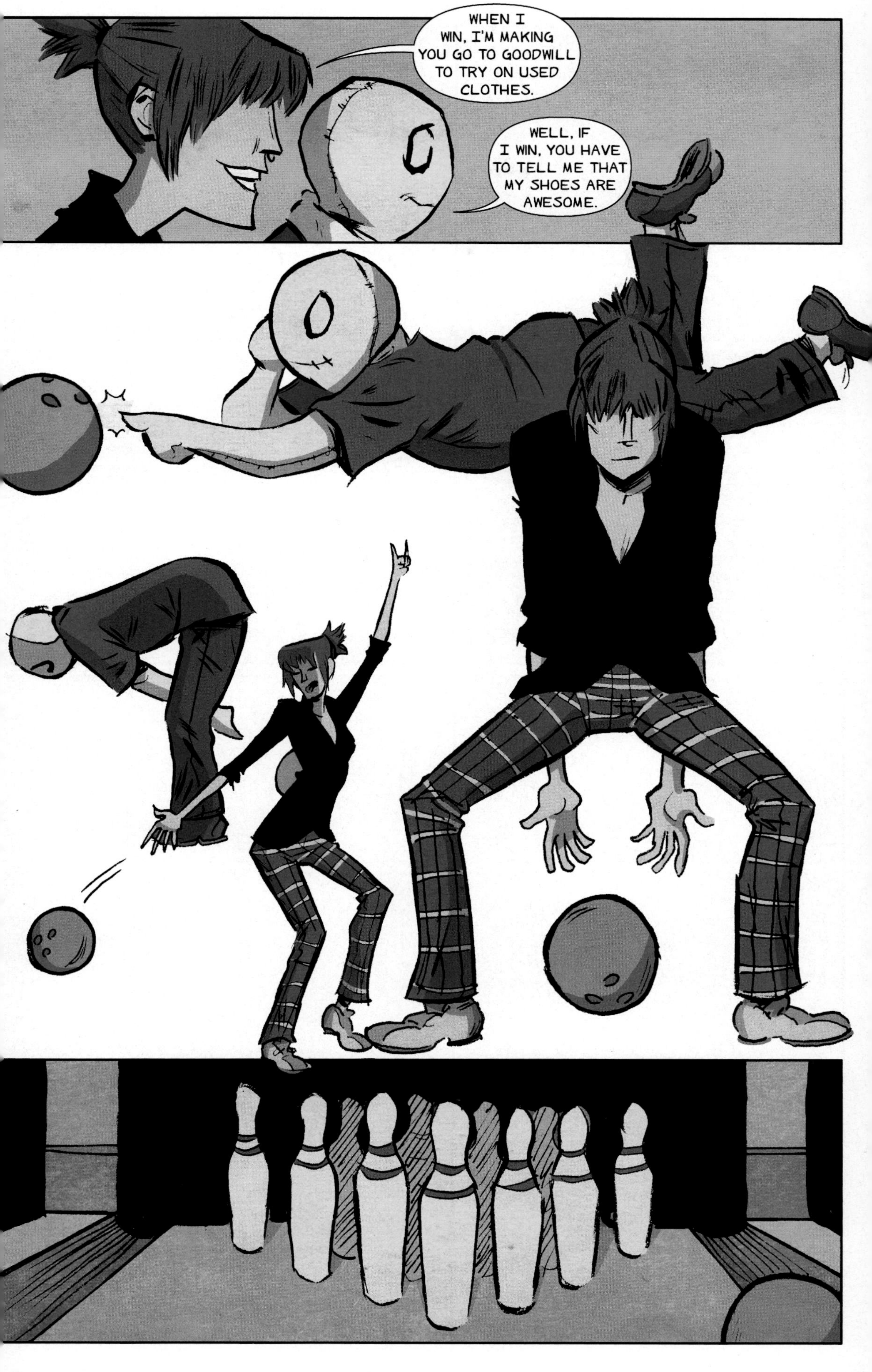
WHEN I WIN, I'M MAKING YOU GO TO GOODWILL TO TRY ON USED CLOTHES.
WELL, IF I WIN, YOU HAVE TO TELL ME THAT MY SHOES ARE AWESOME.

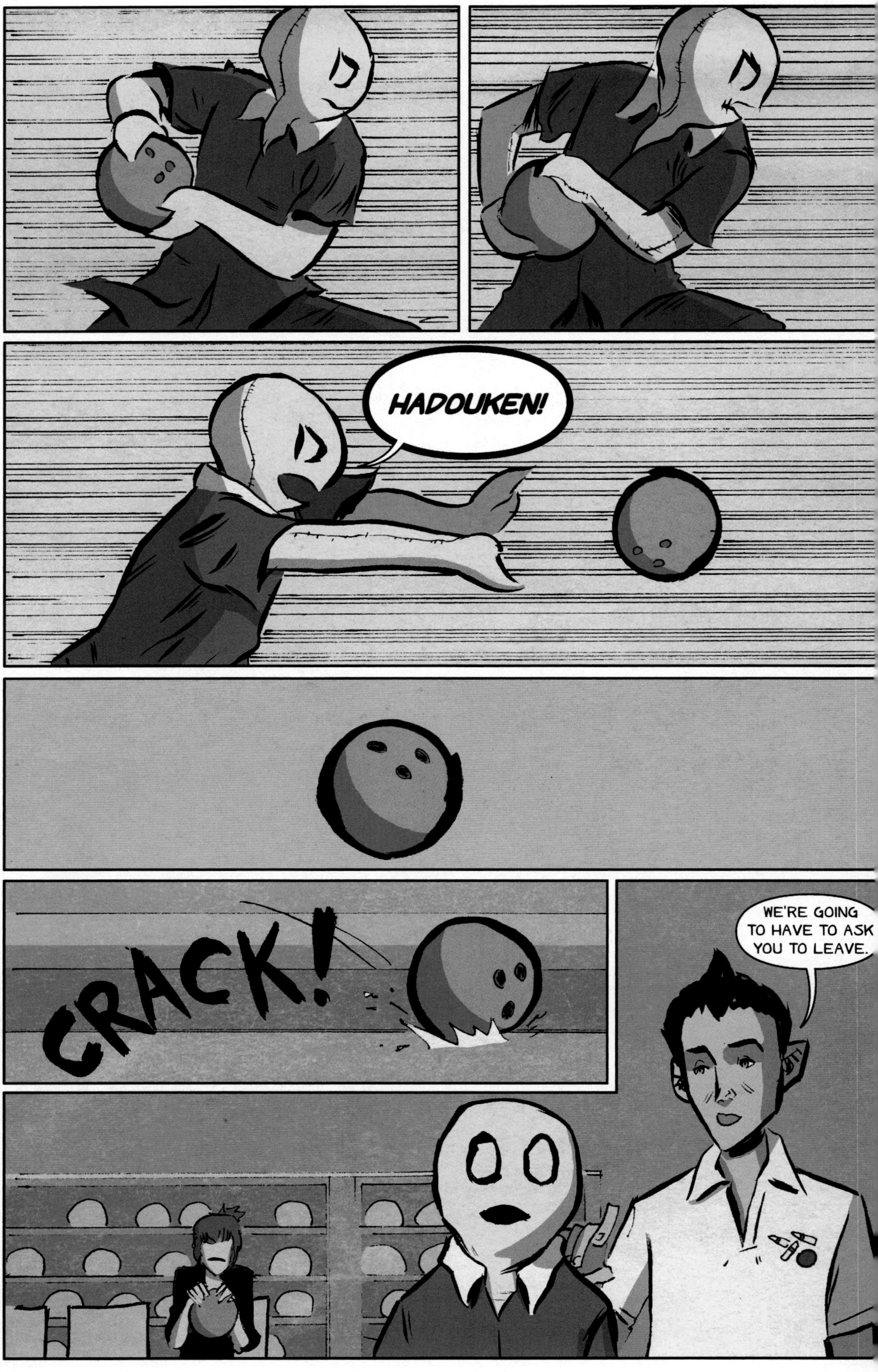
HADOUKEN!
CRACK!
WE'RE GOING TO HAVE TO ASK YOU TO LEAVE.

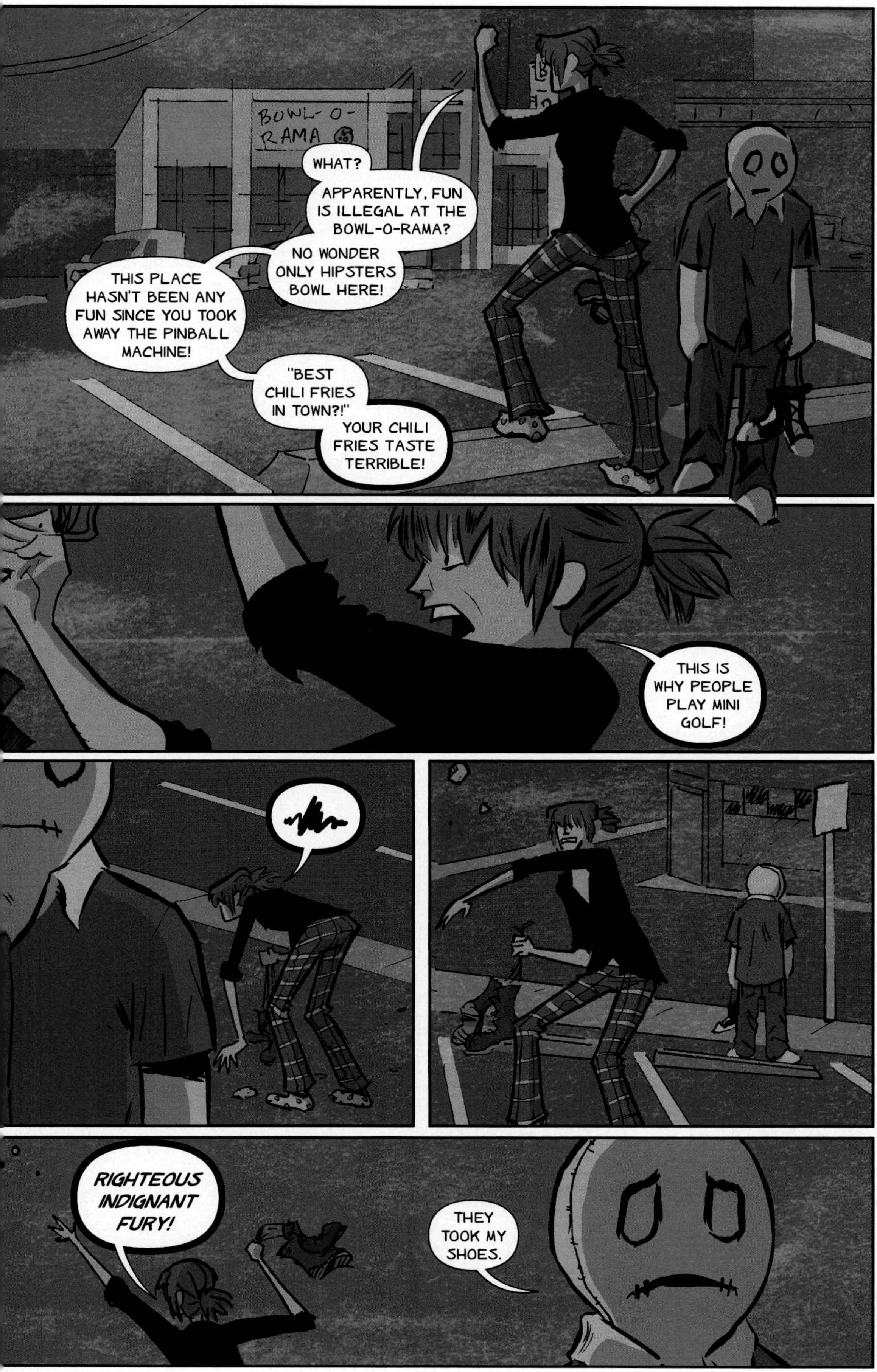
BOWL-O-RAMA
WHAT?
APPARENTLY, FUN IS ILLEGAL AT THE BOWL-O-RAMA?
NO WONDER ONLY HIPSTERS BOWL HERE!
THIS PLACE HASN'T BEEN ANY FUN SINCE YOU TOOK AWAY THE PINBALL MACHINE!
"BEST CHILI FRIES IN TOWN?!"
YOUR CHILI FRIES TASTE TERRIBLE!
THIS IS WHY PEOPLE PLAY MINI GOLF!
RIGHTEOUS INDIGNANT FURY!
THEY TOOK MY SHOES.

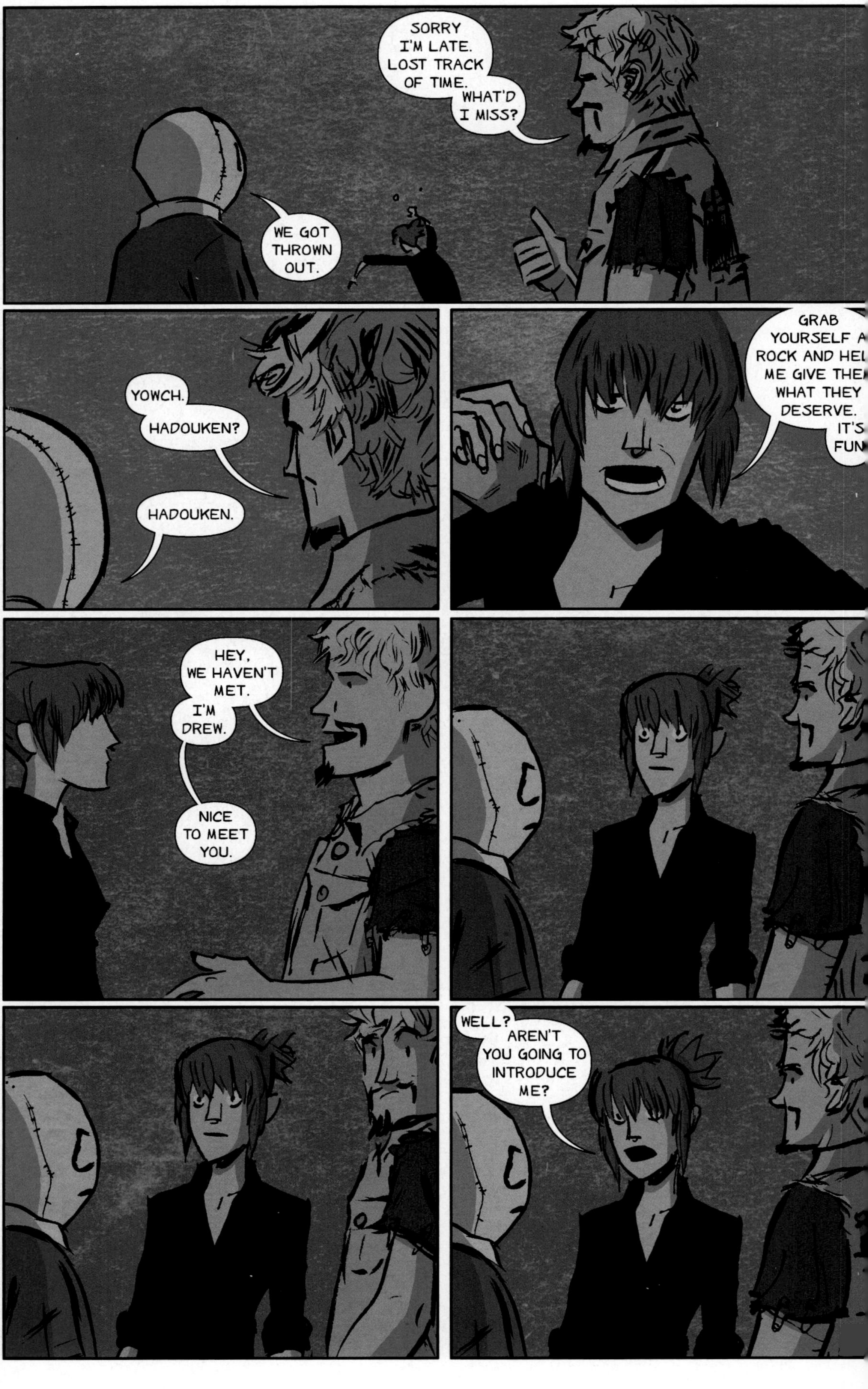
SORRY I'M LATE. LOST TRACK OF TIME.
WHAT'D I MISS?
WE GOT THROWN OUT.
YOWCH.
HADOUKEN?
HADOUKEN.
GRAB YOURSELF A ROCK AND HEL ME GIVE THE WHAT THEY DESERVE.
IT'S FUN
HEY, WE HAVEN'T MET.
I'M DREW.
NICE TO MEET YOU.
WELL?
AREN'T YOU GOING TO INTRODUCE ME?

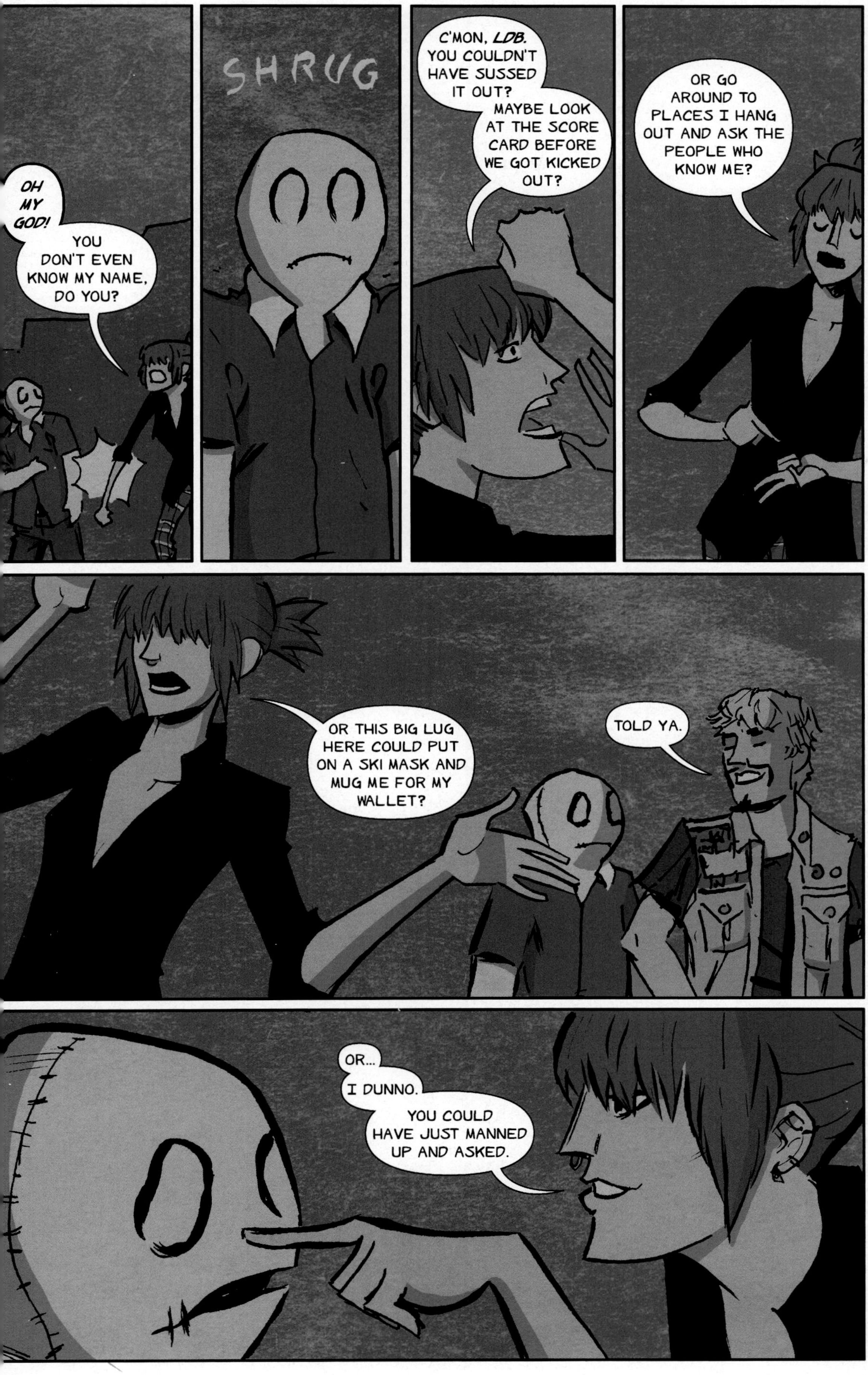
OH MY GOD!
YOU DON'T EVEN KNOW MY NAME, DO YOU?
SHRUG
C'MON, *LDB.* YOU COULDN'T HAVE SUSSED IT OUT?
MAYBE LOOK AT THE SCORE CARD BEFORE WE GOT KICKED OUT?
OR GO AROUND TO PLACES I HANG OUT AND ASK THE PEOPLE WHO KNOW ME?
OR THIS BIG LUG HERE COULD PUT ON A SKI MASK AND MUG ME FOR MY WALLET?
TOLD YA.
OR...
I DUNNO.
YOU COULD HAVE JUST MANNED UP AND ASKED.

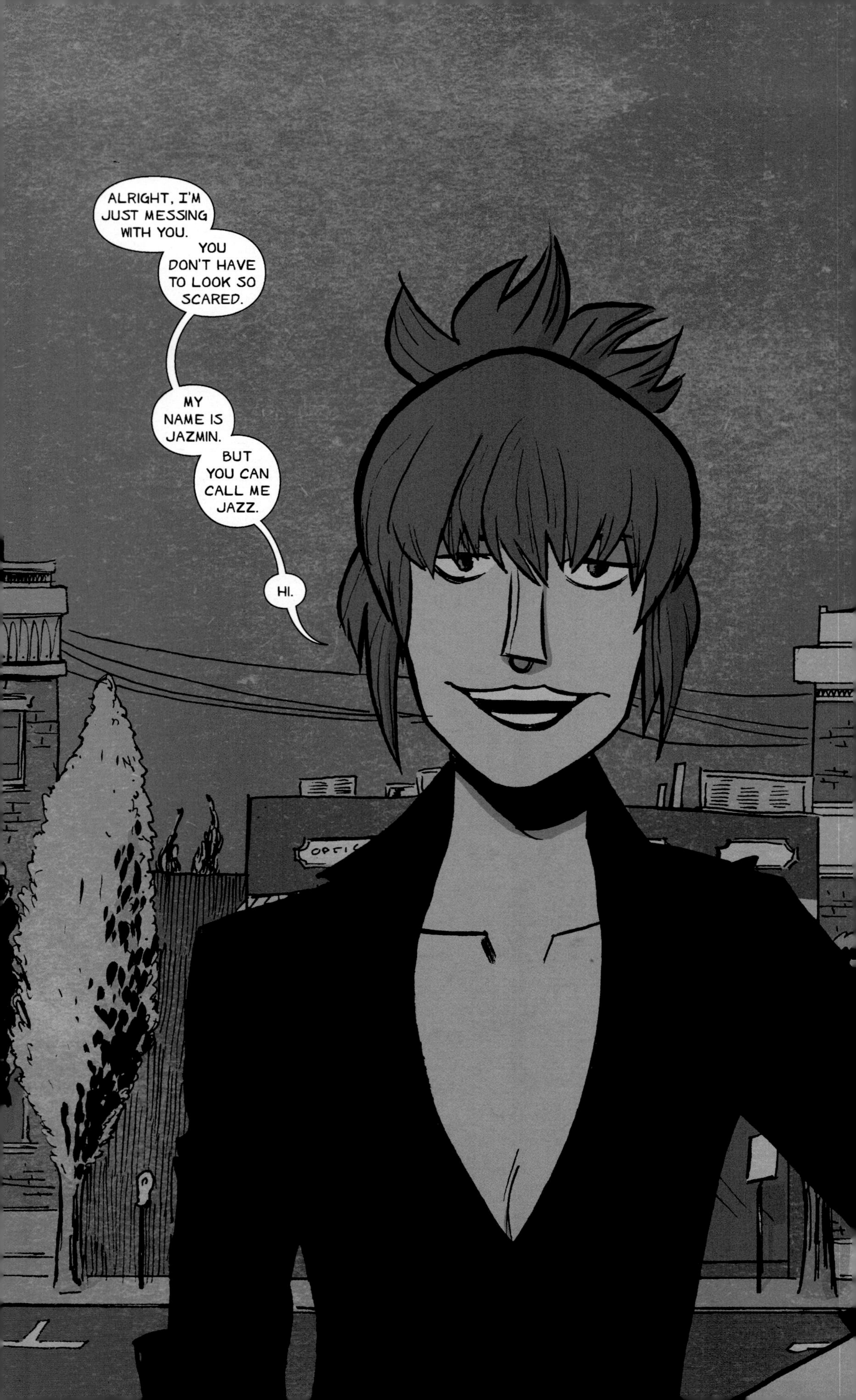
ALRIGHT, I'M JUST MESSING WITH YOU.
YOU DON'T HAVE TO LOOK SO SCARED.
MY NAME IS JAZMIN.
BUT YOU CAN CALL ME JAZZ.
HI.

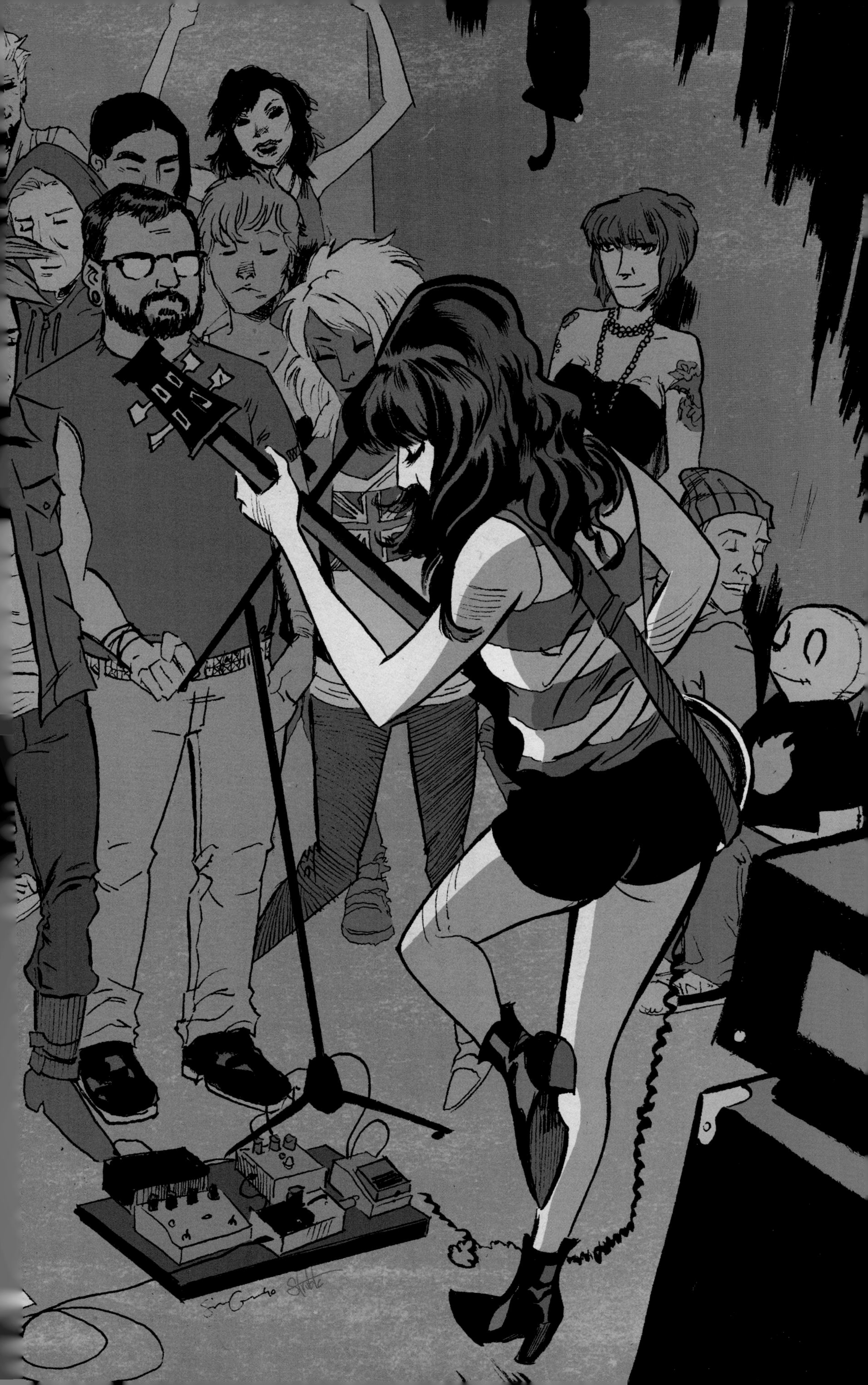

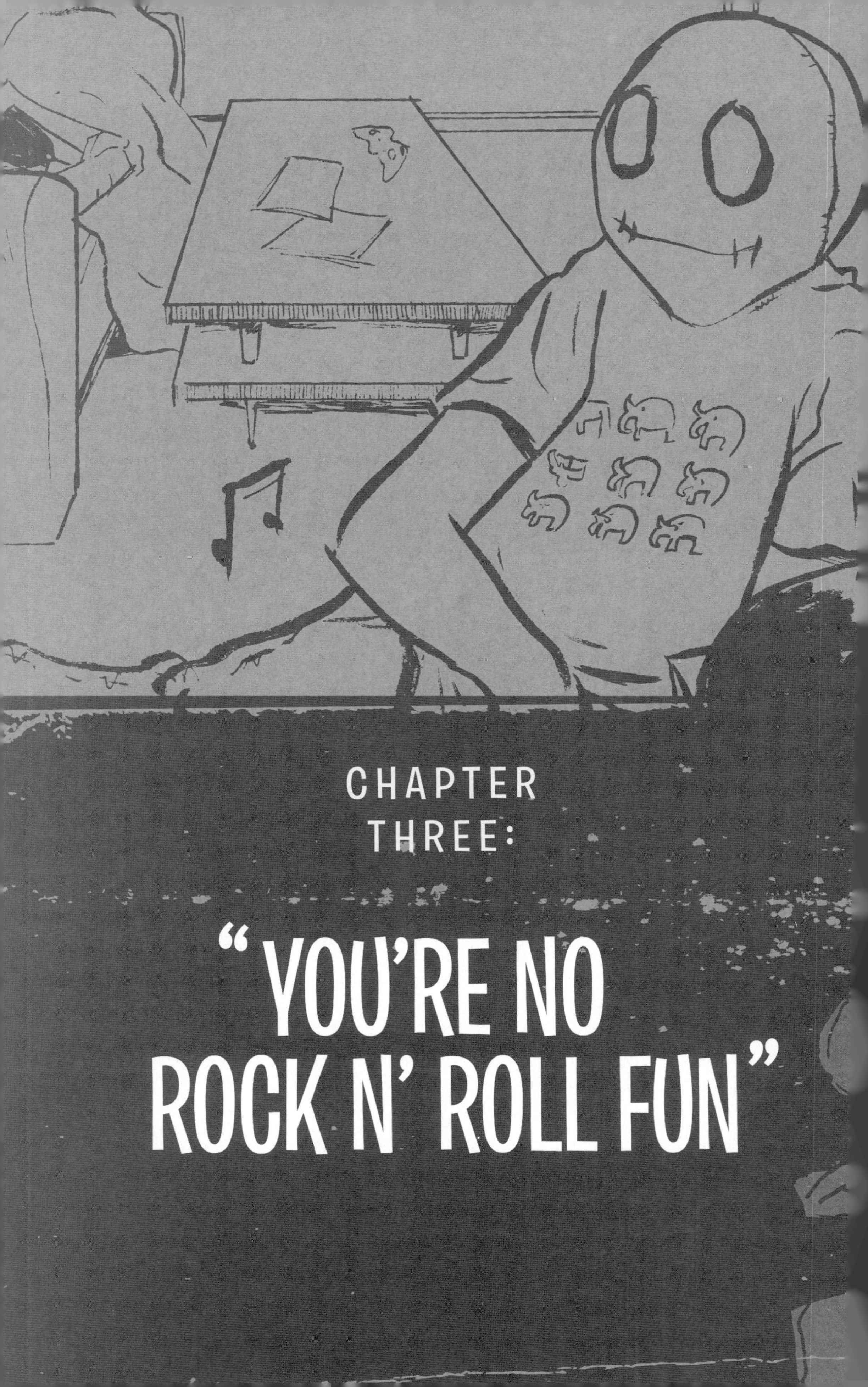

CHAPTER THREE:

"YOU'RE NO ROCK N' ROLL FUN"

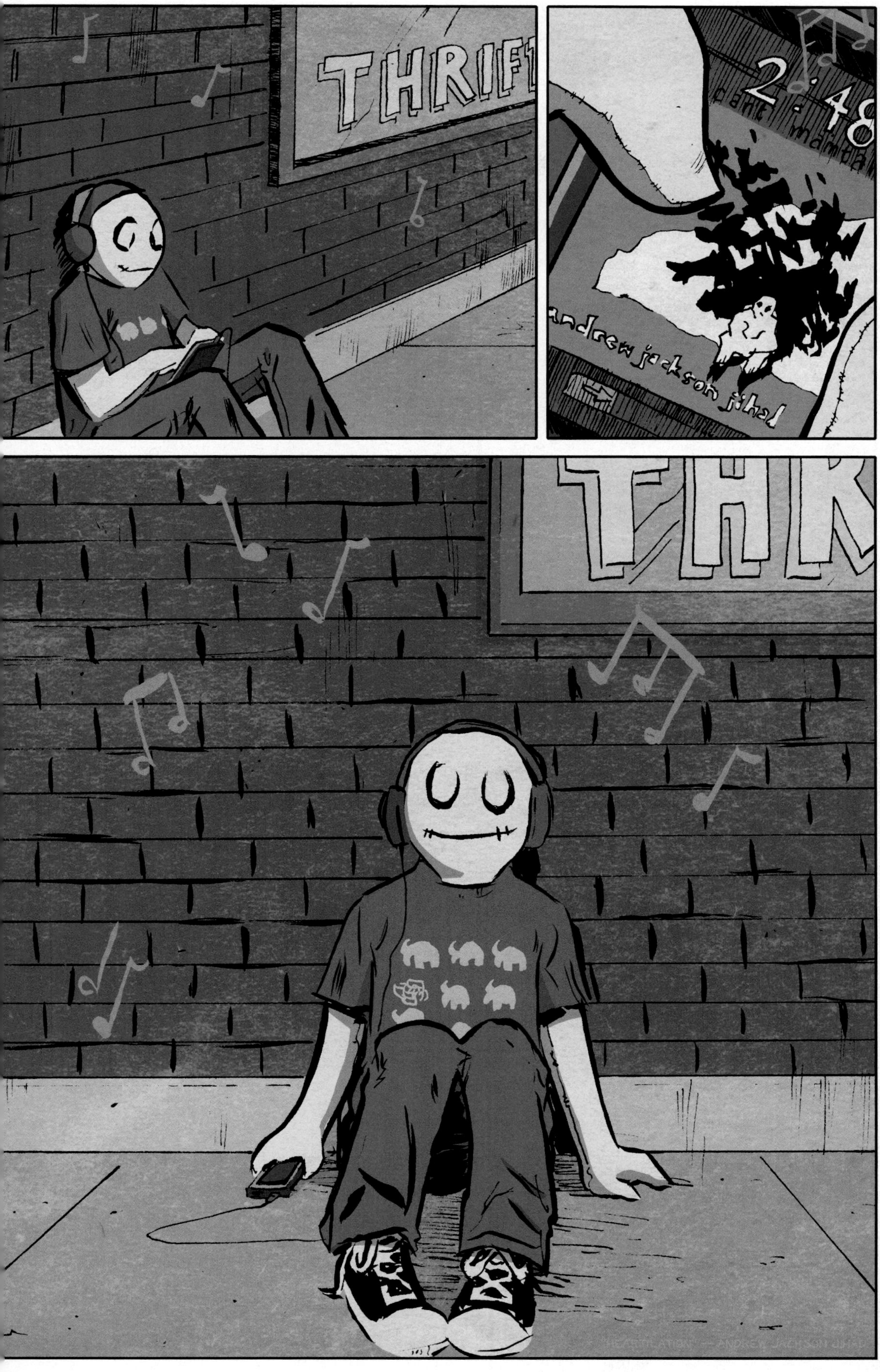
THRIFT
2:48
cant mamta
andrew jackson jihad
THR

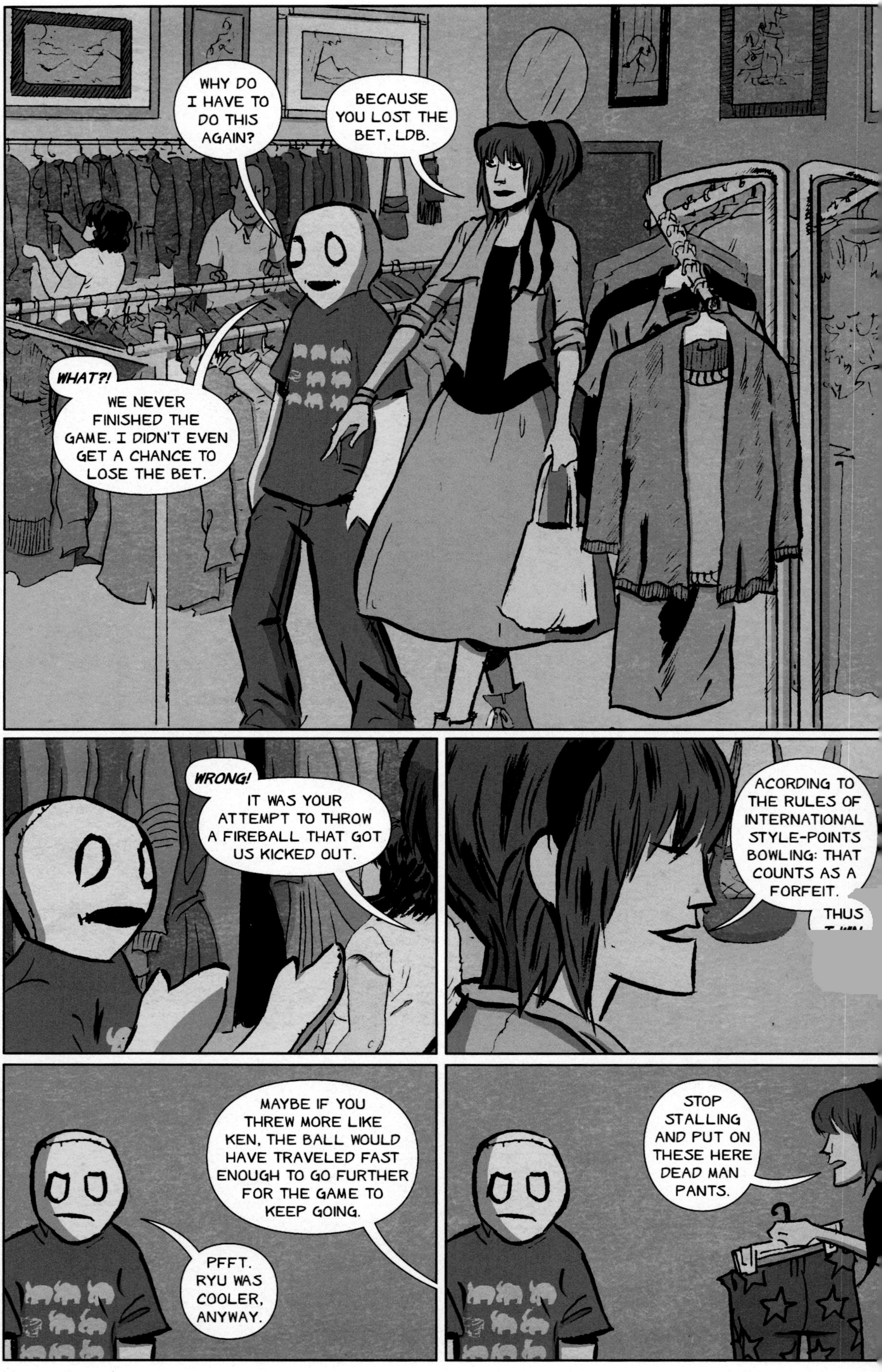

WHY DO I HAVE TO DO THIS AGAIN?
BECAUSE YOU LOST THE BET, LDB.
WHAT?! WE NEVER FINISHED THE GAME. I DIDN'T EVEN GET A CHANCE TO LOSE THE BET.
WRONG! IT WAS YOUR ATTEMPT TO THROW A FIREBALL THAT GOT US KICKED OUT.
ACORDING TO THE RULES OF INTERNATIONAL STYLE-POINTS BOWLING: THAT COUNTS AS A FORFEIT.
THUS
MAYBE IF YOU THREW MORE LIKE KEN, THE BALL WOULD HAVE TRAVELED FAST ENOUGH TO GO FURTHER FOR THE GAME TO KEEP GOING.
PFFT. RYU WAS COOLER, ANYWAY.
STOP STALLING AND PUT ON THESE HERE DEAD MAN PANTS.

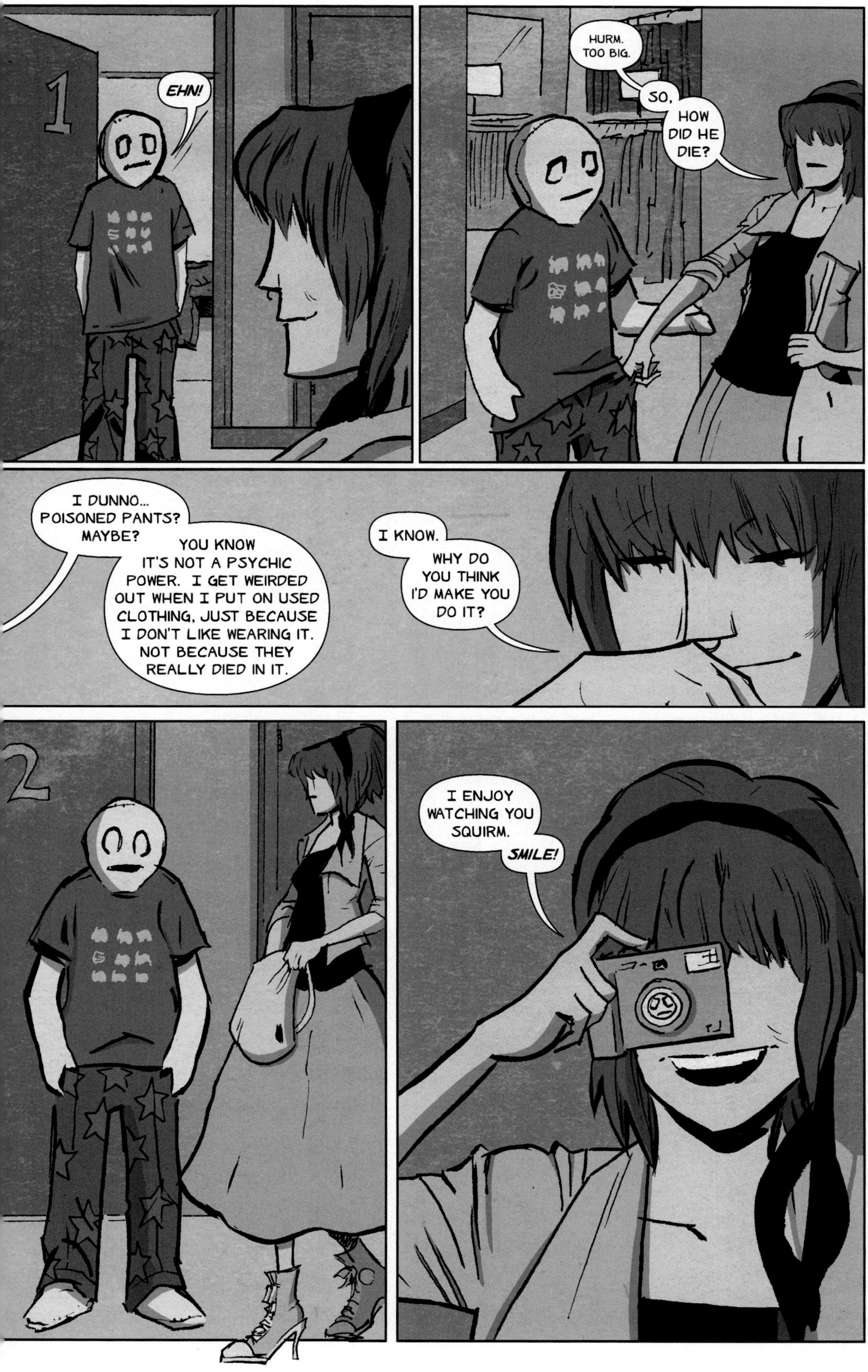
EHN!
HURM. TOO BIG.
SO,
HOW DID HE DIE?
I DUNNO... POISONED PANTS? MAYBE?
YOU KNOW IT'S NOT A PSYCHIC POWER. I GET WEIRDED OUT WHEN I PUT ON USED CLOTHING, JUST BECAUSE I DON'T LIKE WEARING IT. NOT BECAUSE THEY REALLY DIED IN IT.
I KNOW.
WHY DO YOU THINK I'D MAKE YOU DO IT?
I ENJOY WATCHING YOU SQUIRM.
SMILE!

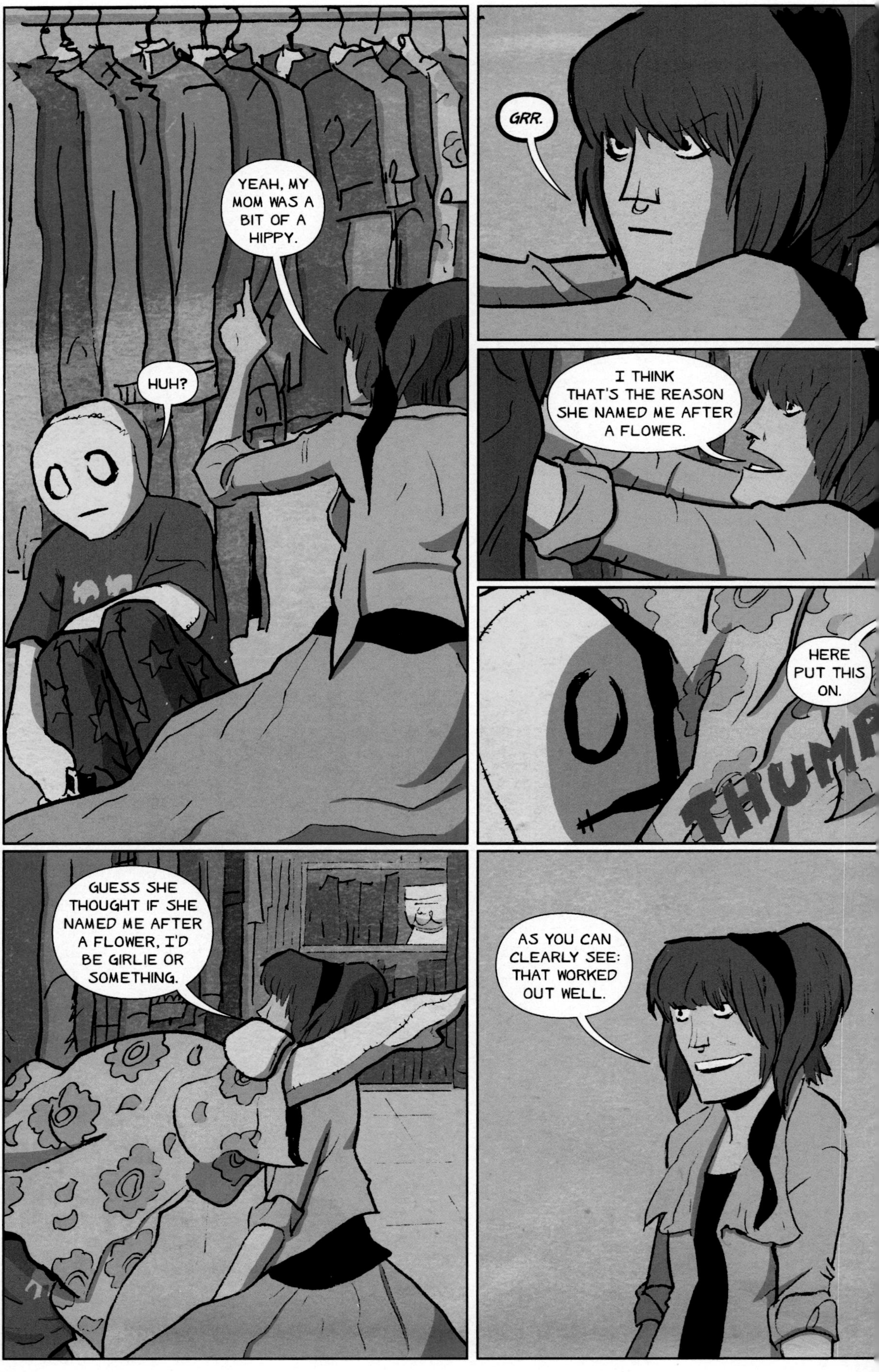
YEAH, MY MOM WAS A BIT OF A HIPPY.
HUH?
GRR.
I THINK THAT'S THE REASON SHE NAMED ME AFTER A FLOWER.
HERE PUT THIS ON.
THUMP
GUESS SHE THOUGHT IF SHE NAMED ME AFTER A FLOWER, I'D BE GIRLIE OR SOMETHING.
AS YOU CAN CLEARLY SEE: THAT WORKED OUT WELL.

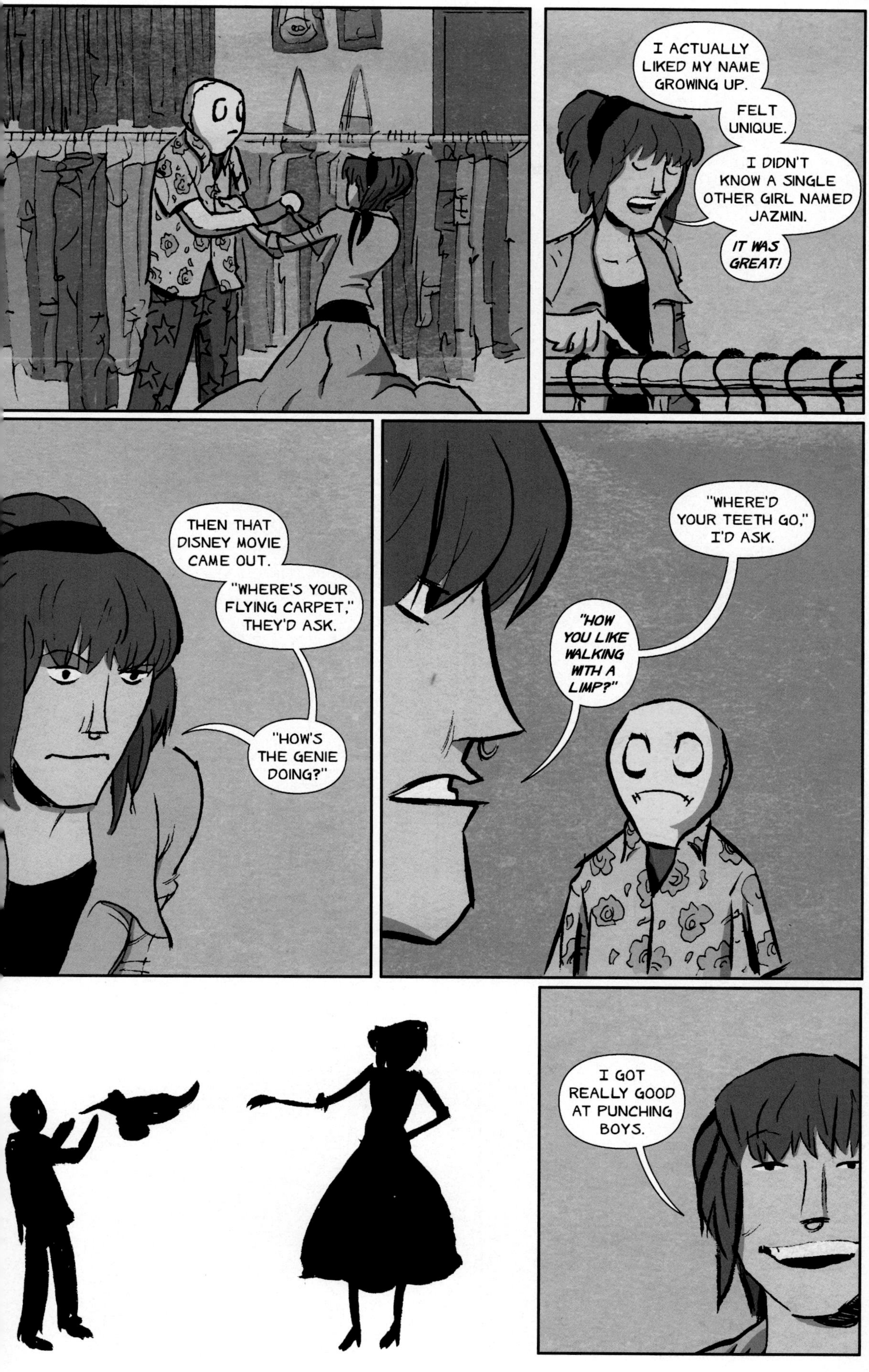

I ACTUALLY LIKED MY NAME GROWING UP.
FELT UNIQUE.
I DIDN'T KNOW A SINGLE OTHER GIRL NAMED JAZMIN.
IT WAS GREAT!
THEN THAT DISNEY MOVIE CAME OUT.
"WHERE'S YOUR FLYING CARPET," THEY'D ASK.
"HOW'S THE GENIE DOING?"
"WHERE'D YOUR TEETH GO," I'D ASK.
"HOW YOU LIKE WALKING WITH A LIMP?"
I GOT REALLY GOOD AT PUNCHING BOYS.

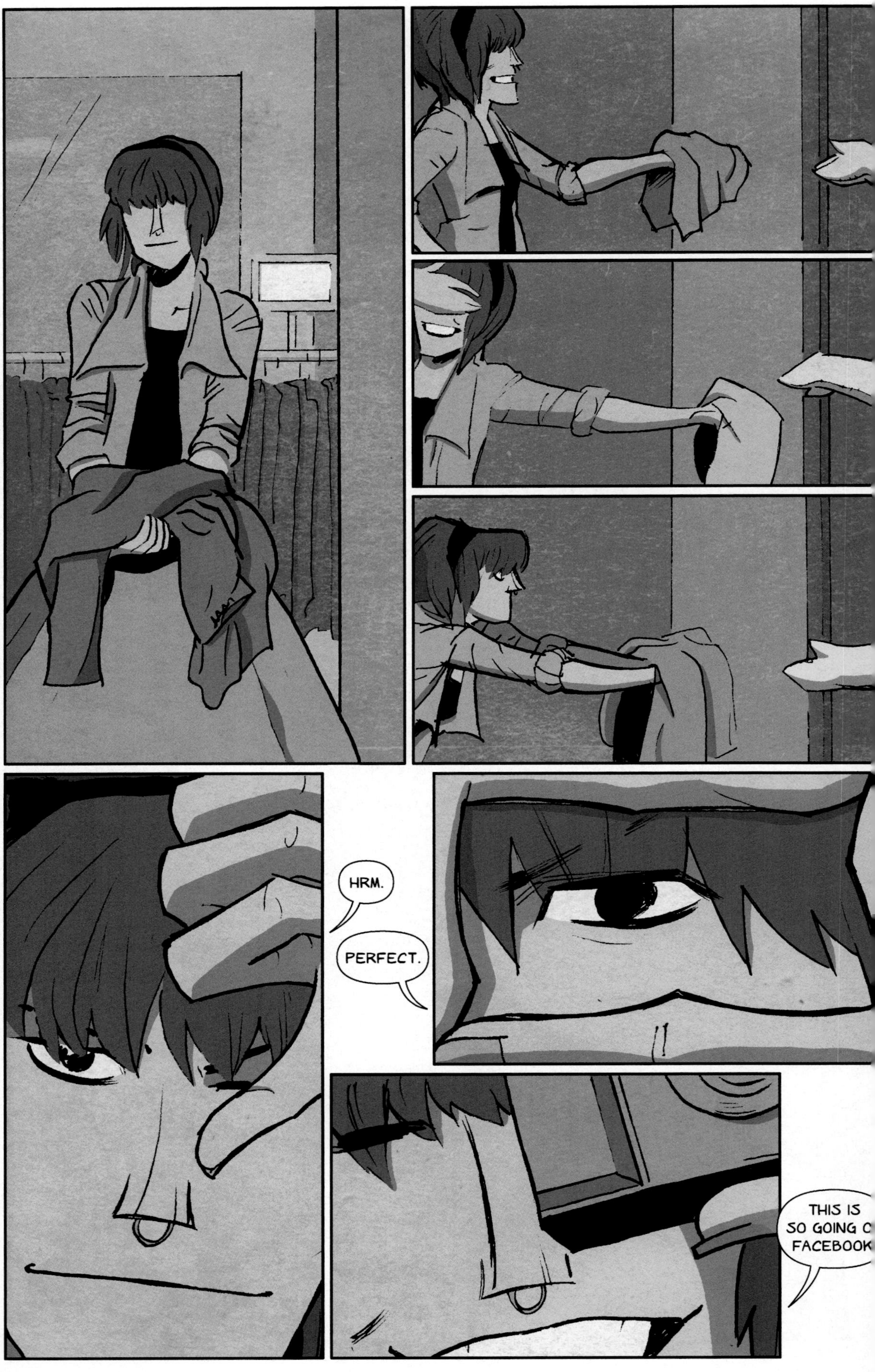
HRM.
PERFECT.
THIS IS
SO GOING
FACEBOOK

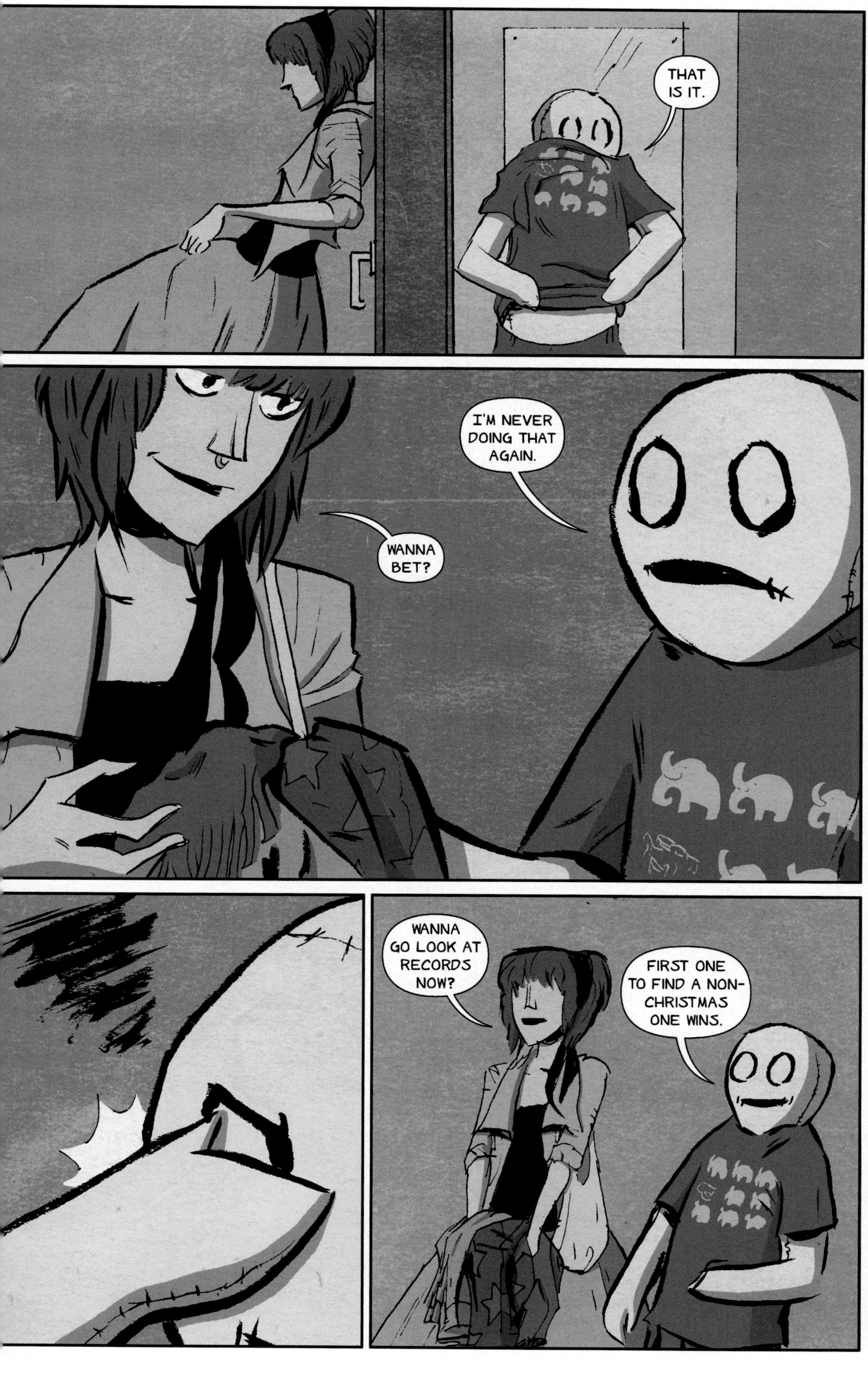
THAT IS IT.
I'M NEVER DOING THAT AGAIN.
WANNA BET?
WANNA GO LOOK AT RECORDS NOW?
FIRST ONE TO FIND A NON-CHRISTMAS ONE WINS.

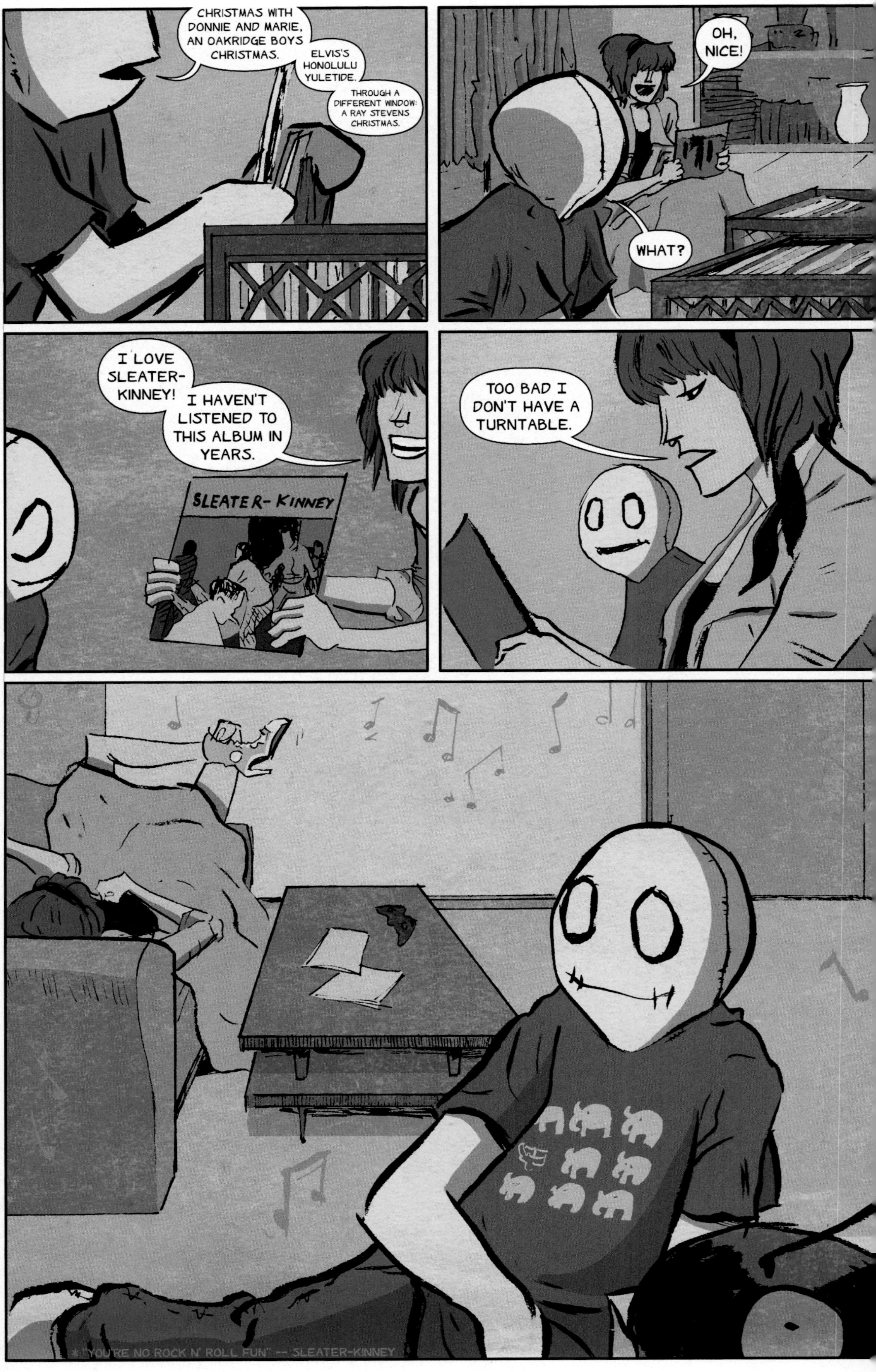
CHRISTMAS WITH DONNIE AND MARIE, AN OAKRIDGE BOYS CHRISTMAS.
ELVIS'S HONOLULU YULETIDE.
THROUGH A DIFFERENT WINDOW: A RAY STEVENS CHRISTMAS.
OH, NICE!
WHAT?
I LOVE SLEATER-KINNEY!
I HAVEN'T LISTENED TO THIS ALBUM IN YEARS.
SLEATER-KINNEY
TOO BAD I DON'T HAVE A TURNTABLE.
* "YOU'RE NO ROCK N' ROLL FUN" -- SLEATER-KINNEY

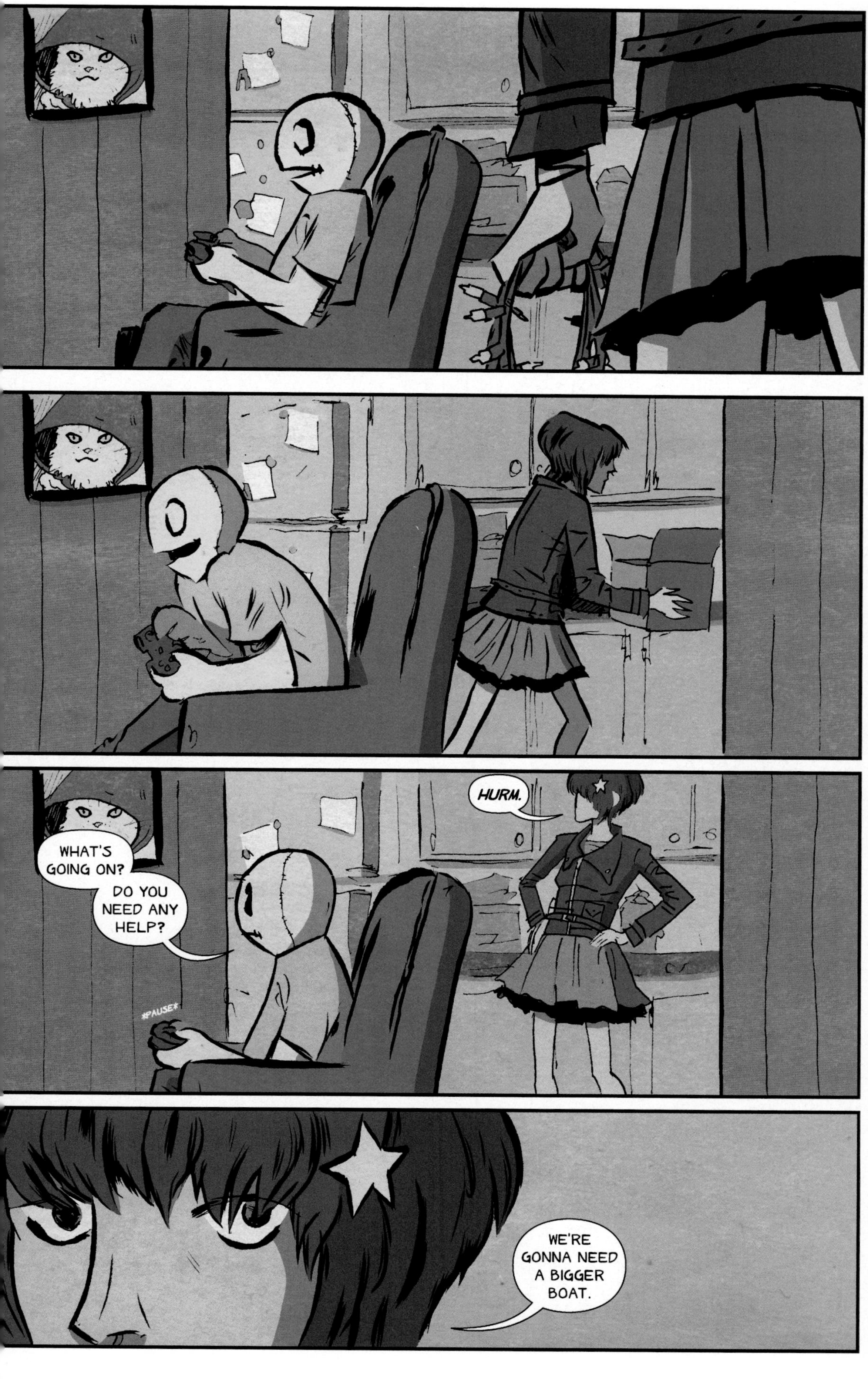
HURM.
WHAT'S GOING ON?
DO YOU NEED ANY HELP?
PAUSE
WE'RE GONNA NEED A BIGGER BOAT.

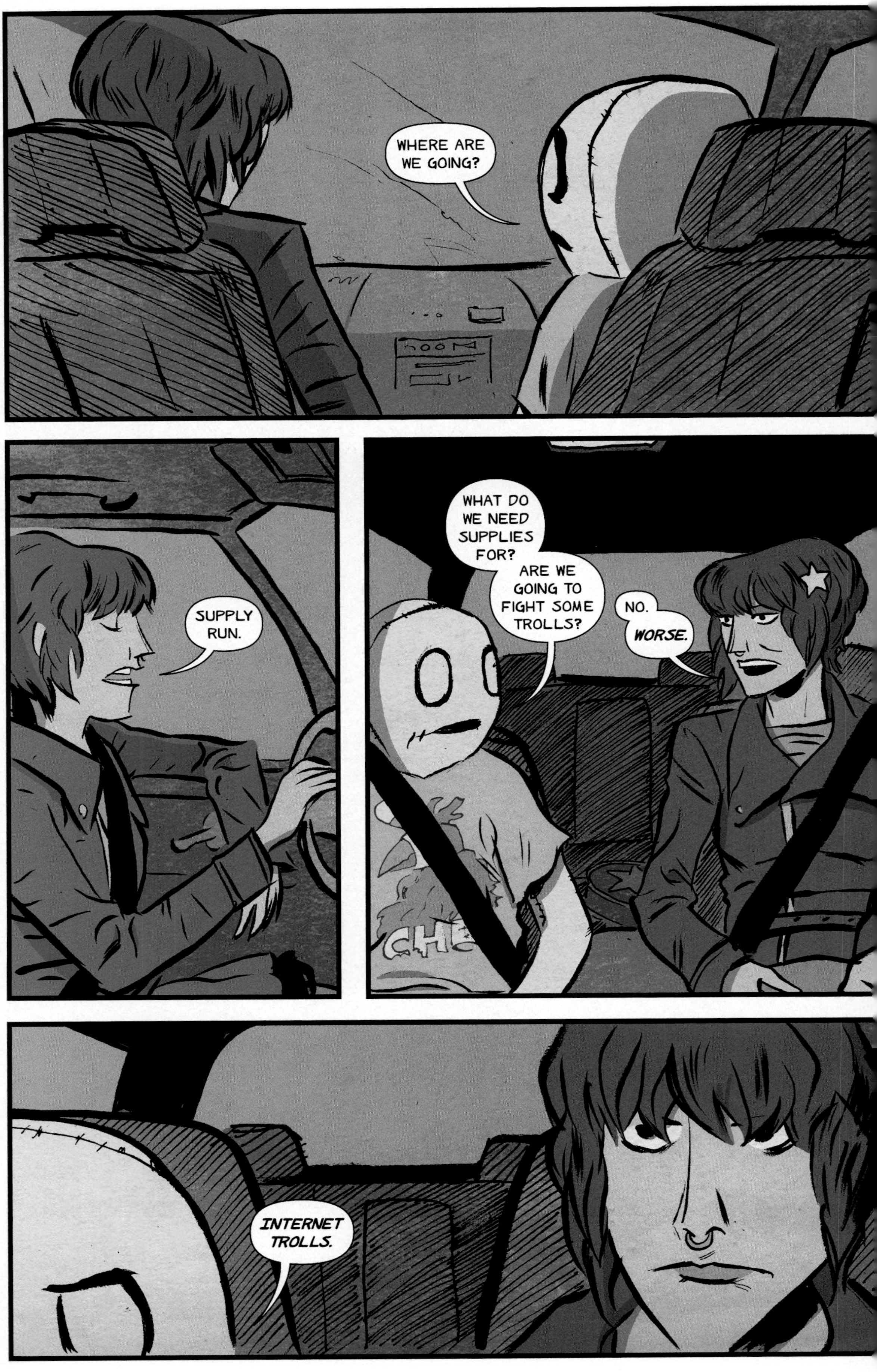
WHERE ARE WE GOING?
SUPPLY RUN.
WHAT DO WE NEED SUPPLIES FOR?
ARE WE GOING TO FIGHT SOME TROLLS?
NO. *WORSE.*
INTERNET TROLLS.

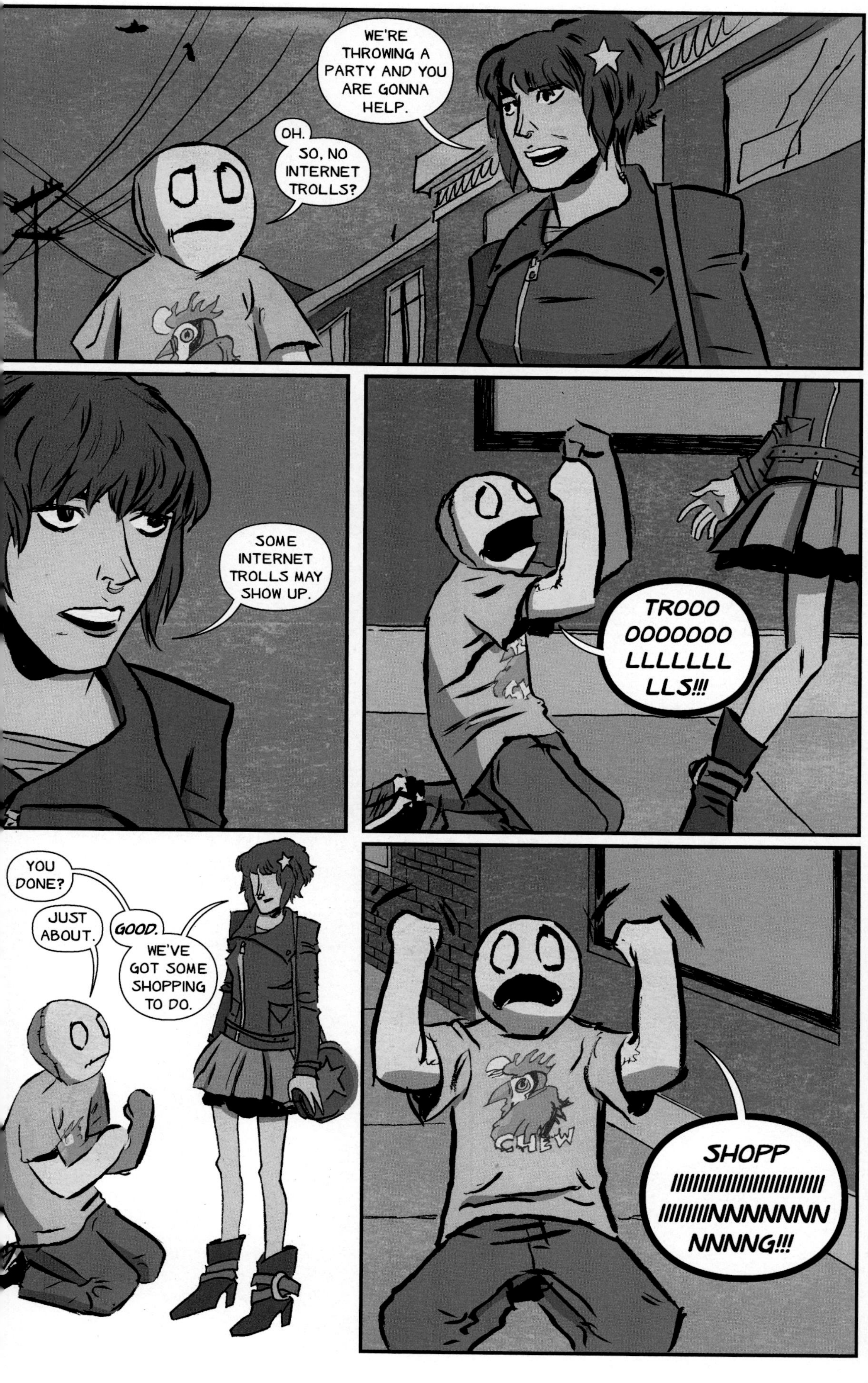
WE'RE THROWING A PARTY AND YOU ARE GONNA HELP.
OH. SO, NO INTERNET TROLLS?
SOME INTERNET TROLLS MAY SHOW UP.
TROOOOOOOOOLLLLLLLLLS!!!
YOU DONE?
JUST ABOUT.
GOOD. WE'VE GOT SOME SHOPPING TO DO.
CHEW
SHOPPIIIIIIIIIIIIIIIIIIIIIIIIIIIIIIIIIIIIIIIIIIIIINNNNNNNNNNNG!!!

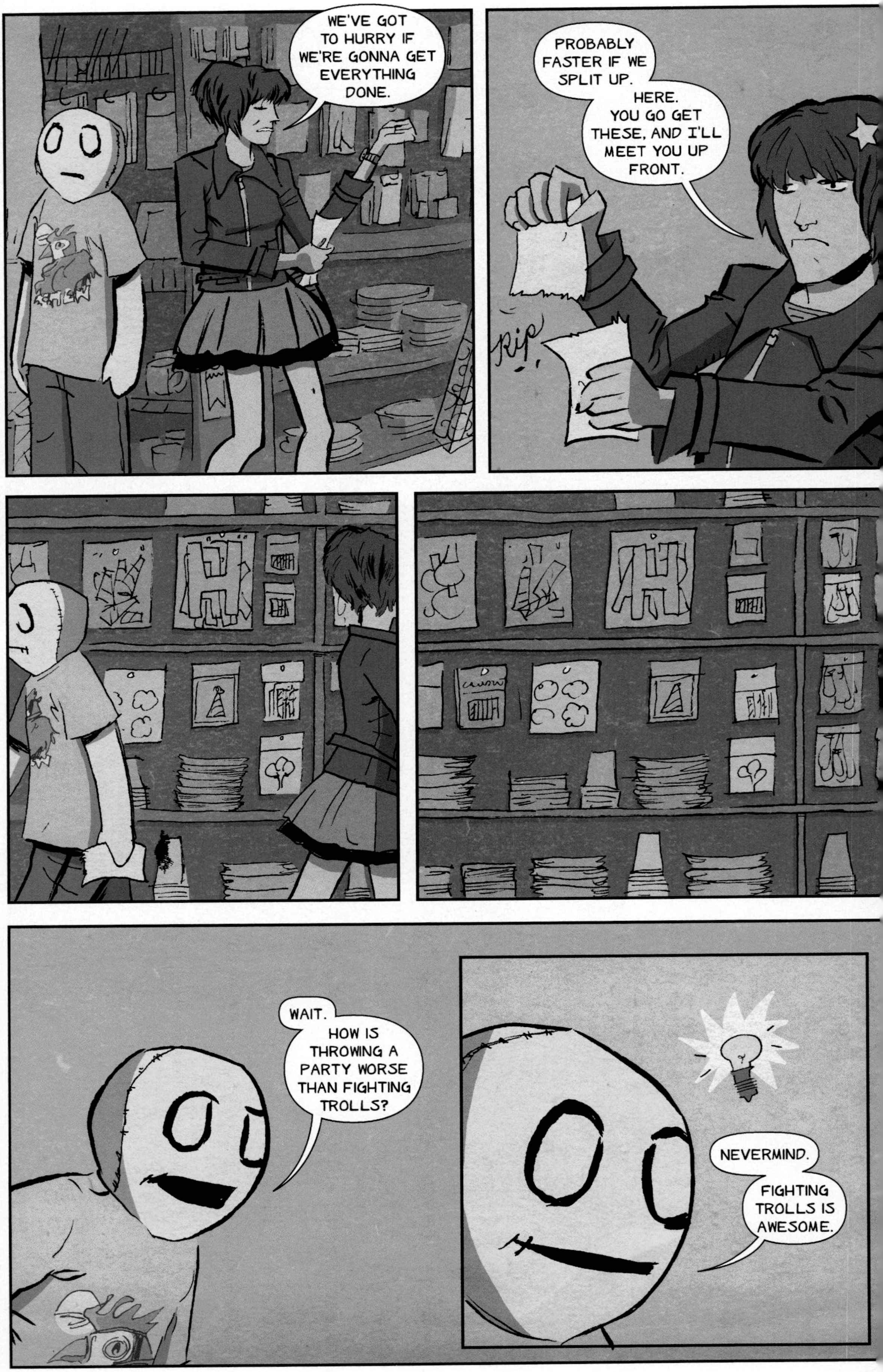
WE'VE GOT TO HURRY IF WE'RE GONNA GET EVERYTHING DONE.
PROBABLY FASTER IF WE SPLIT UP.
HERE. YOU GO GET THESE, AND I'LL MEET YOU UP FRONT.
RIP
WAIT.
HOW IS THROWING A PARTY WORSE THAN FIGHTING TROLLS?
NEVERMIND.
FIGHTING TROLLS IS AWESOME.

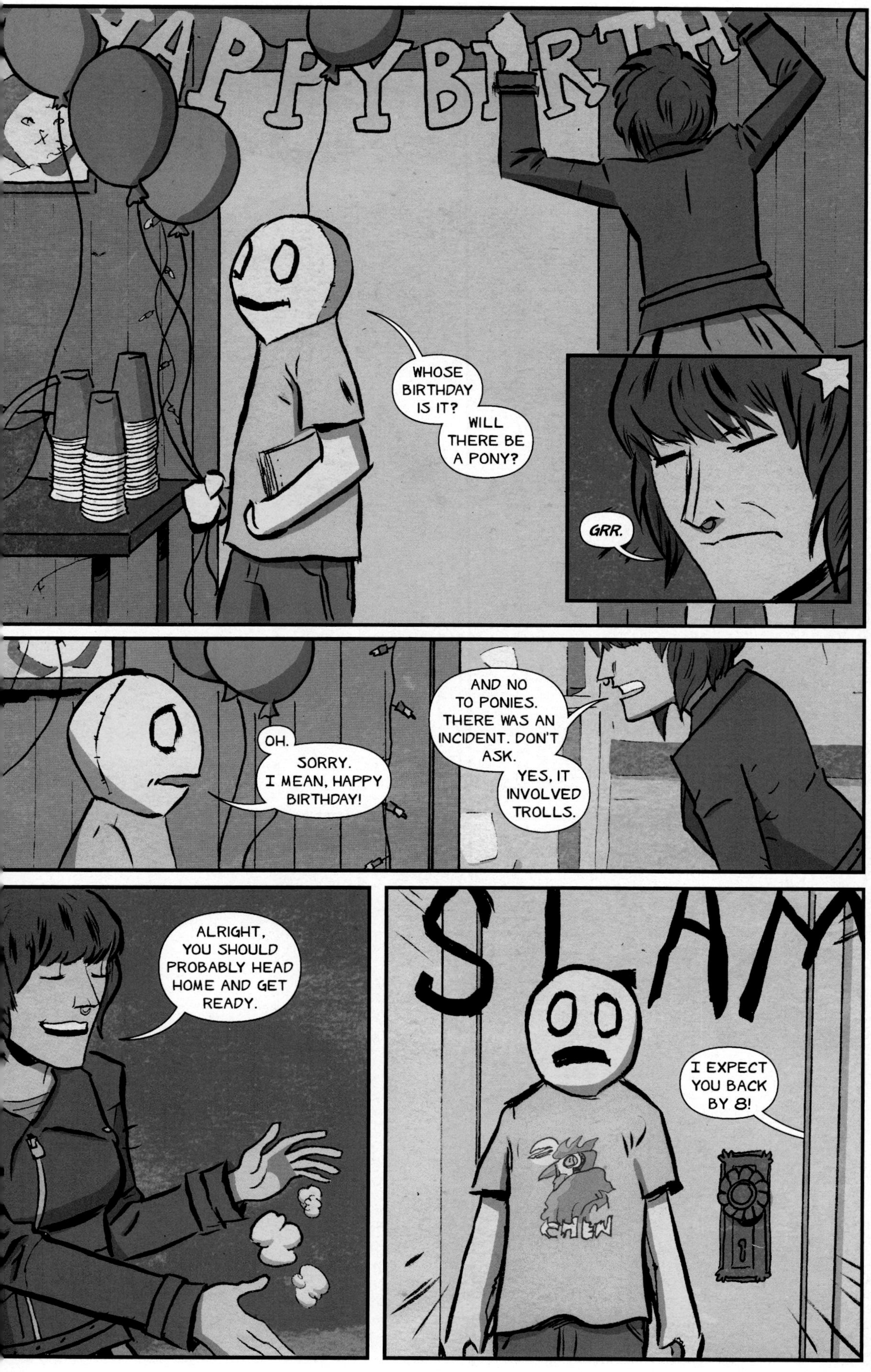

YAPPY BIRTH
WHOSE BIRTHDAY IS IT?
WILL THERE BE A PONY?
GRR.
OH.
SORRY. I MEAN, HAPPY BIRTHDAY!
AND NO TO PONIES. THERE WAS AN INCIDENT. DON'T ASK.
YES, IT INVOLVED TROLLS.
ALRIGHT, YOU SHOULD PROBABLY HEAD HOME AND GET READY.
SLAM
I EXPECT YOU BACK BY 8!
CHEW

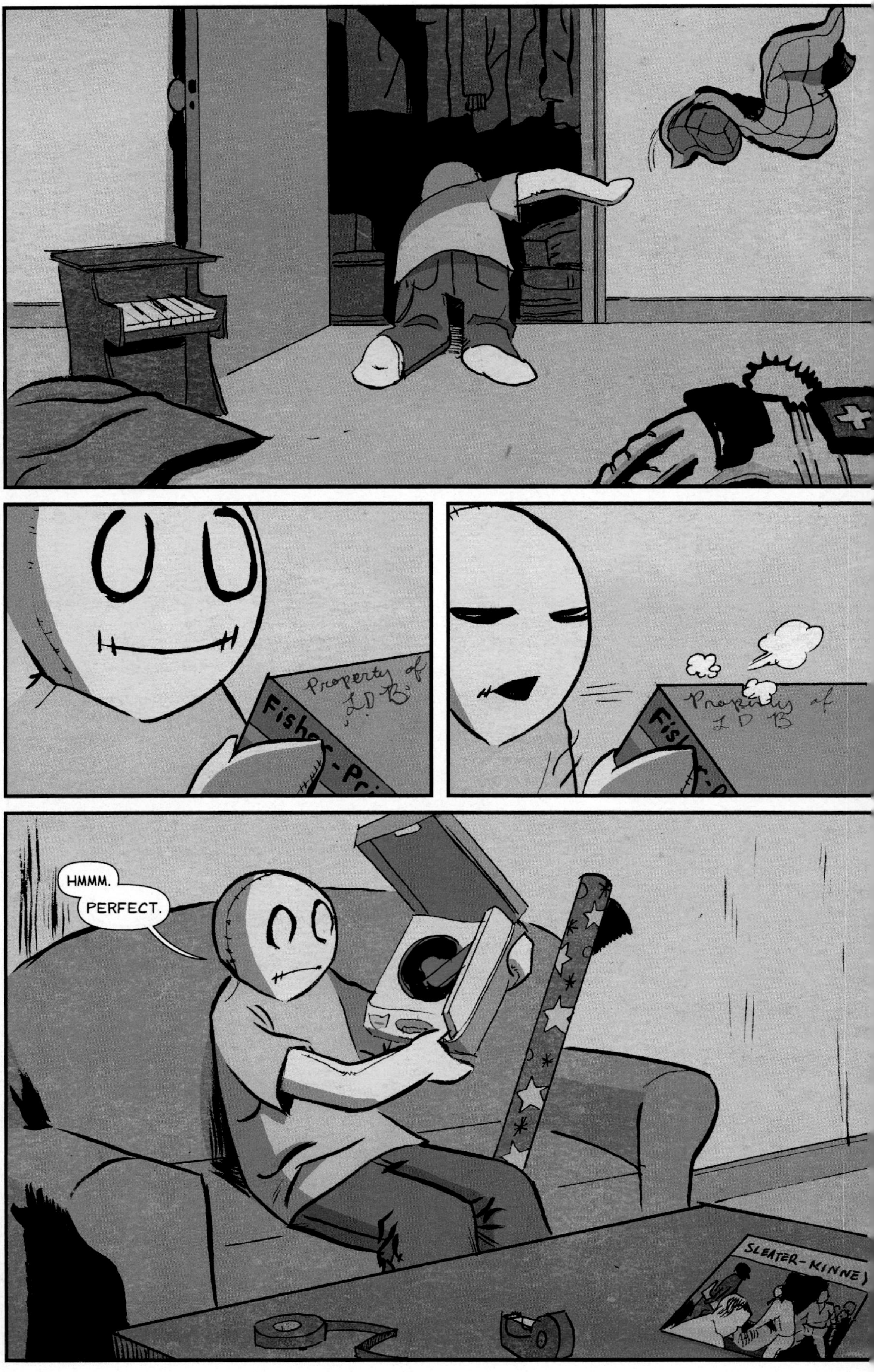

Property of L D B
HMMM.
PERFECT.
SLEATER-KINNE

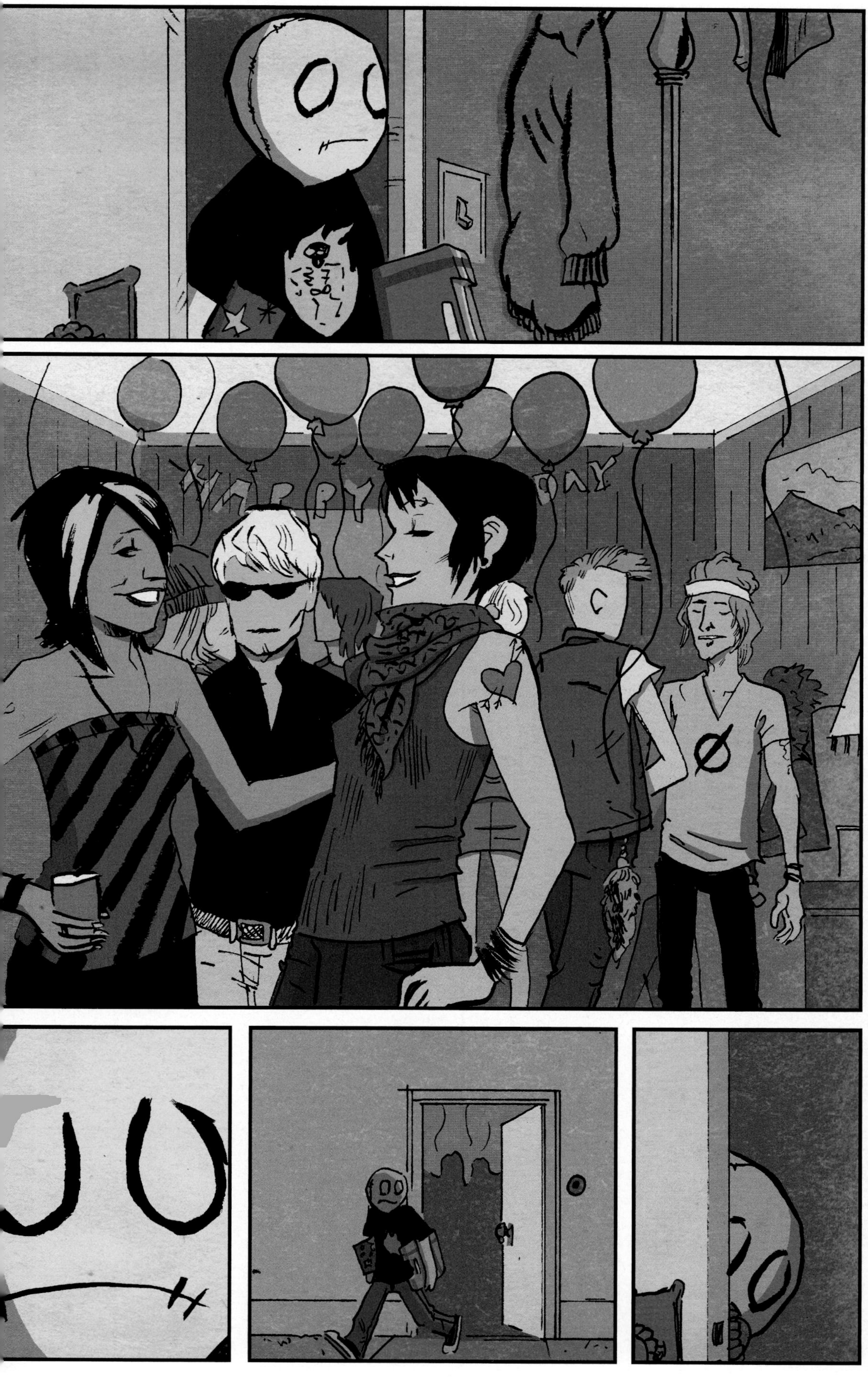

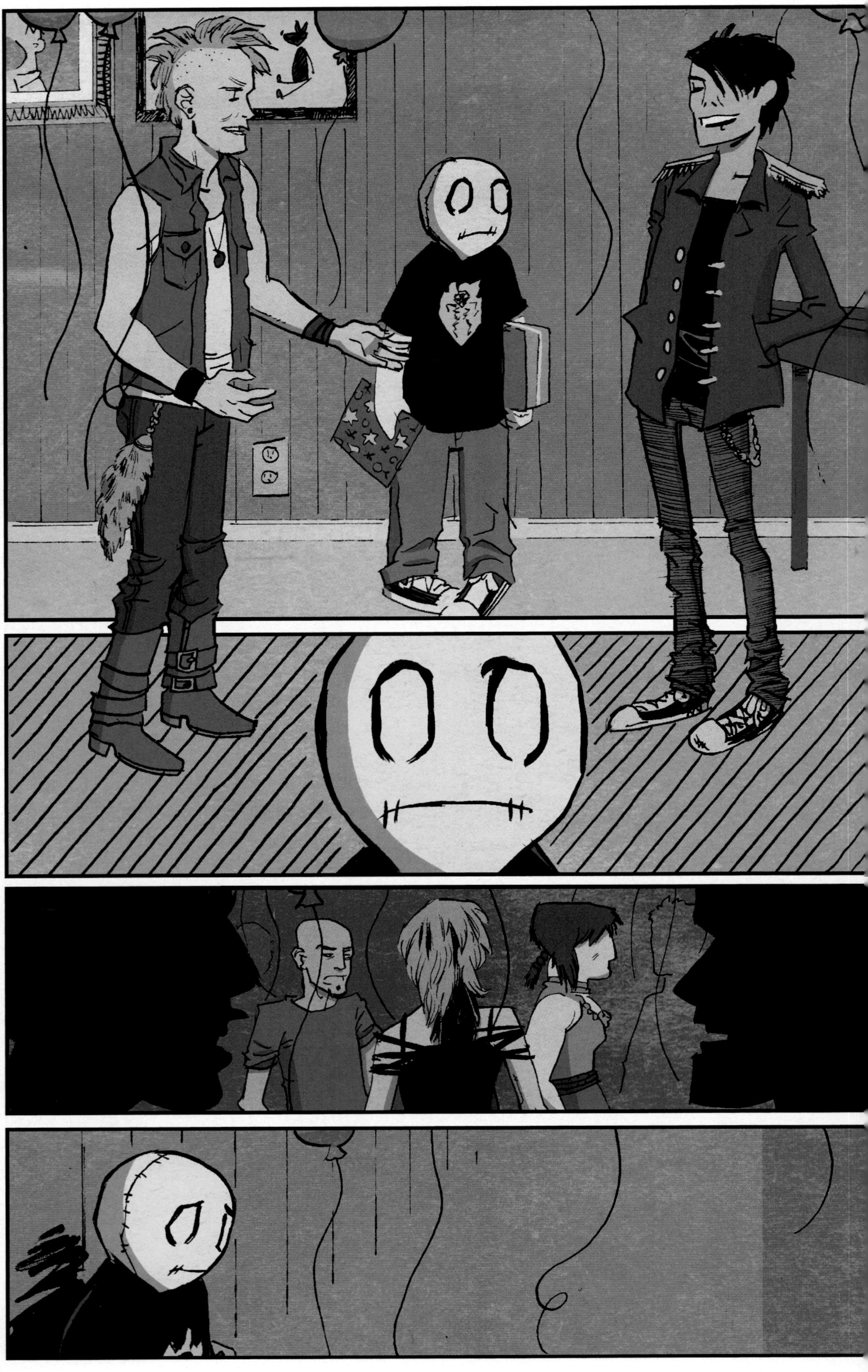

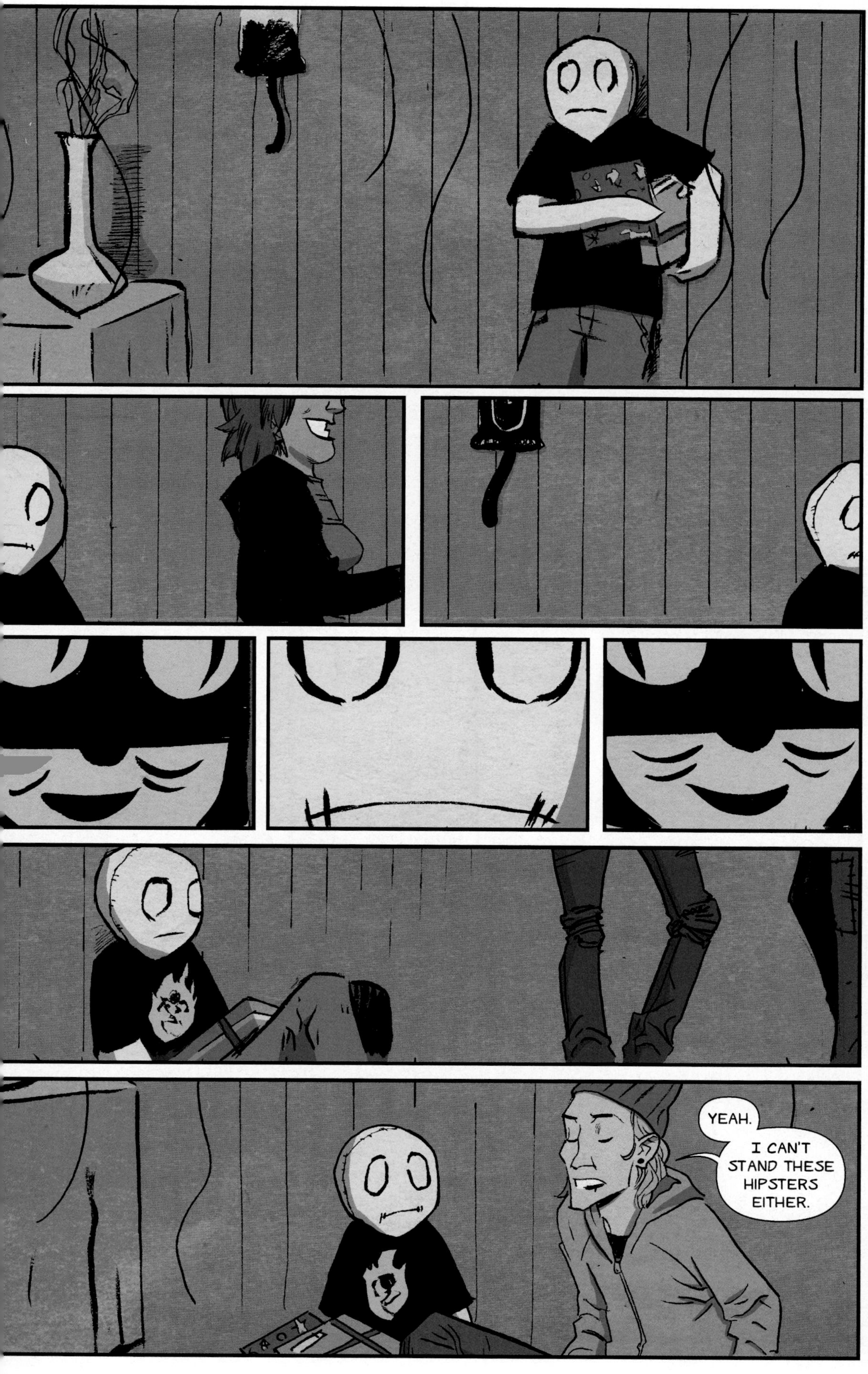
YEAH.
I CAN'T STAND THESE HIPSTERS EITHER.

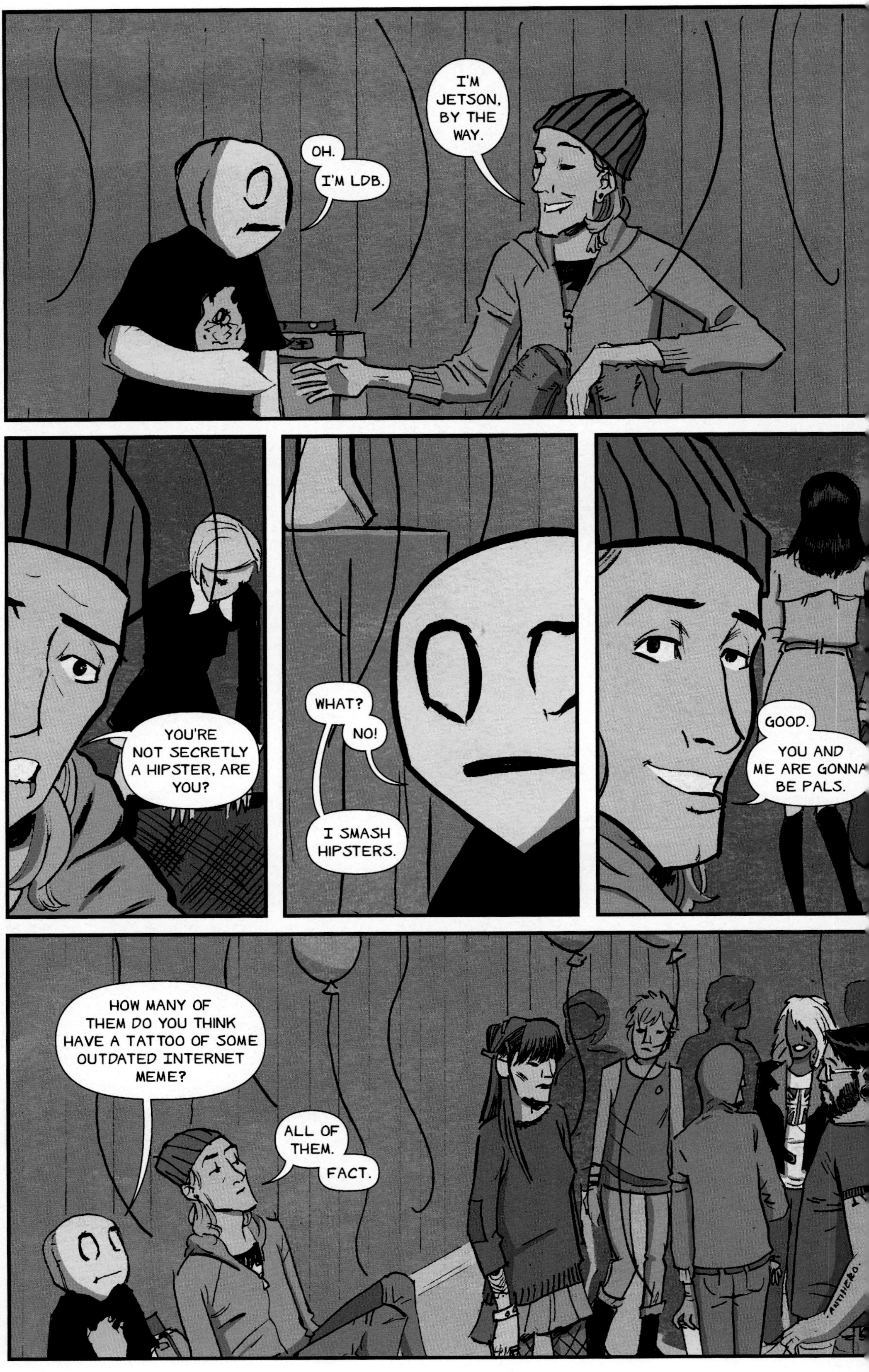
I'M JETSON, BY THE WAY.
OH.
I'M LDB.
YOU'RE NOT SECRETLY A HIPSTER, ARE YOU?
WHAT?
NO!
I SMASH HIPSTERS.
GOOD.
YOU AND ME ARE GONNA BE PALS.
HOW MANY OF THEM DO YOU THINK HAVE A TATTOO OF SOME OUTDATED INTERNET MEME?
ALL OF THEM.
FACT.

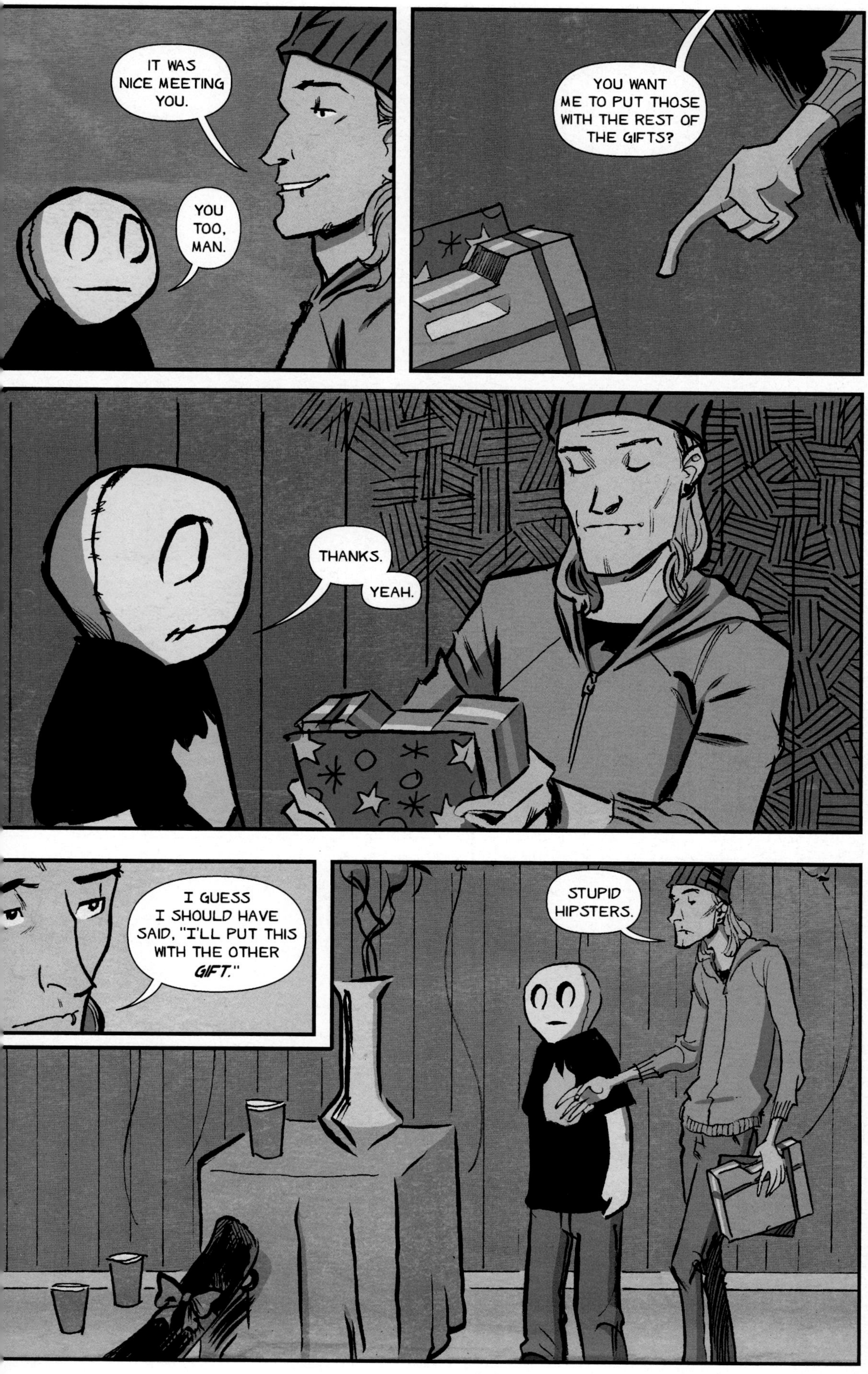
IT WAS NICE MEETING YOU.
YOU TOO, MAN.
YOU WANT ME TO PUT THOSE WITH THE REST OF THE GIFTS?
THANKS.
YEAH.
I GUESS I SHOULD HAVE SAID, "I'LL PUT THIS WITH THE OTHER *GIFT*."
STUPID HIPSTERS.

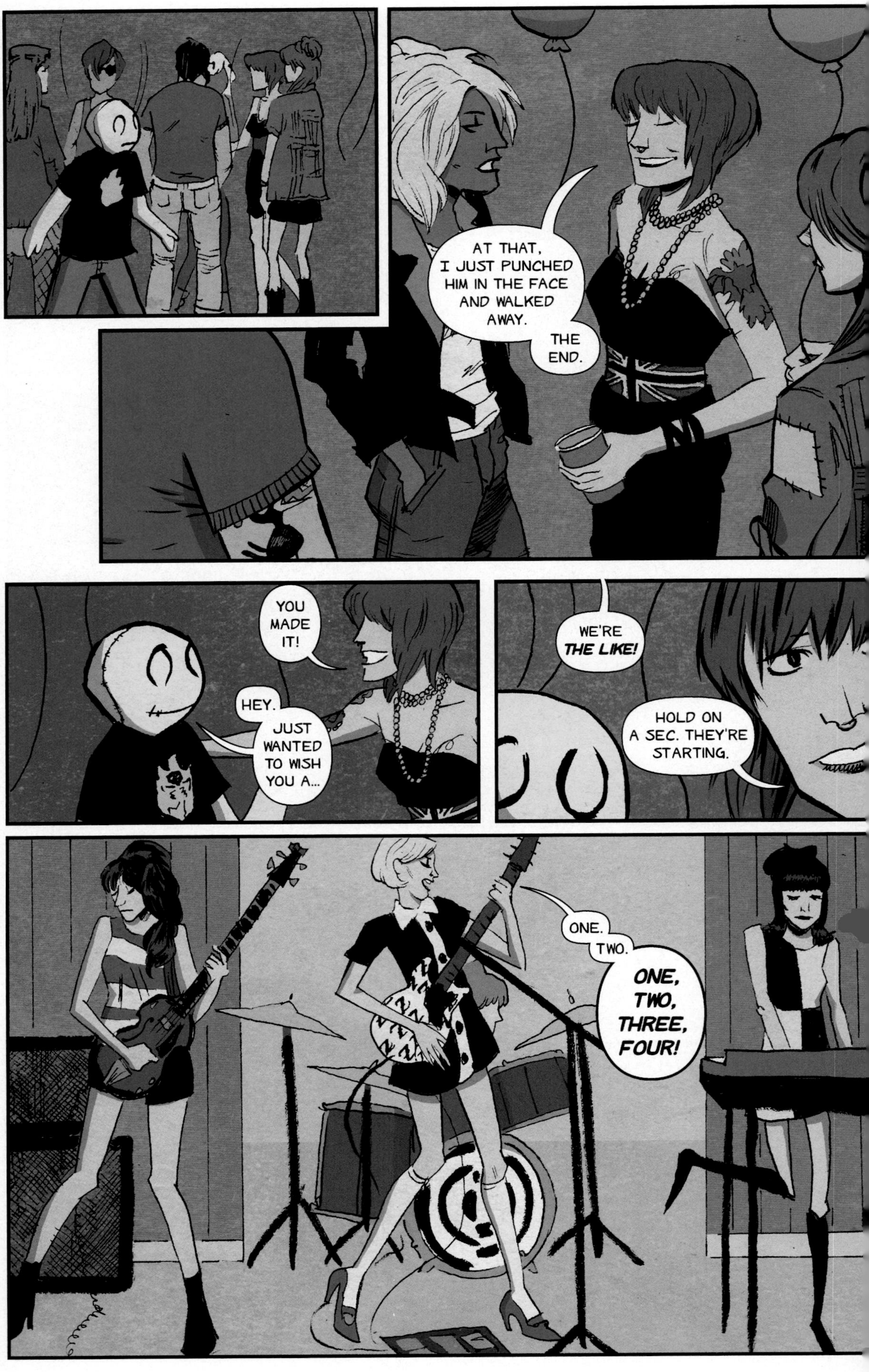
AT THAT, I JUST PUNCHED HIM IN THE FACE AND WALKED AWAY.
THE END.
YOU MADE IT!
HEY.
JUST WANTED TO WISH YOU A...
WE'RE *THE LIKE!*
HOLD ON A SEC. THEY'RE STARTING.
ONE.
TWO.
ONE, TWO, THREE, FOUR!

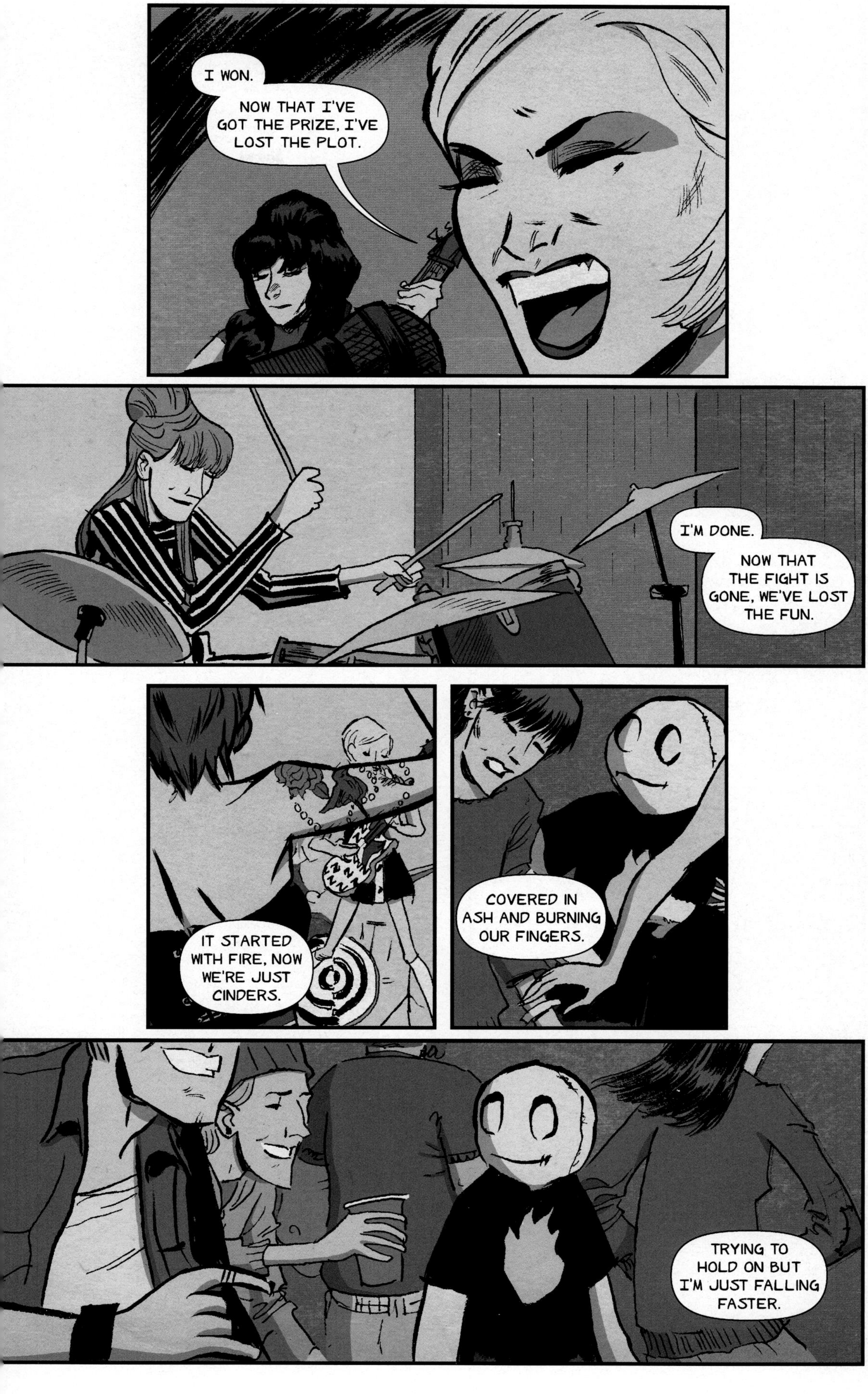
I WON.
NOW THAT I'VE GOT THE PRIZE, I'VE LOST THE PLOT.
I'M DONE.
NOW THAT THE FIGHT IS GONE, WE'VE LOST THE FUN.
IT STARTED WITH FIRE, NOW WE'RE JUST CINDERS.
COVERED IN ASH AND BURNING OUR FINGERS.
TRYING TO HOLD ON BUT I'M JUST FALLING FASTER.

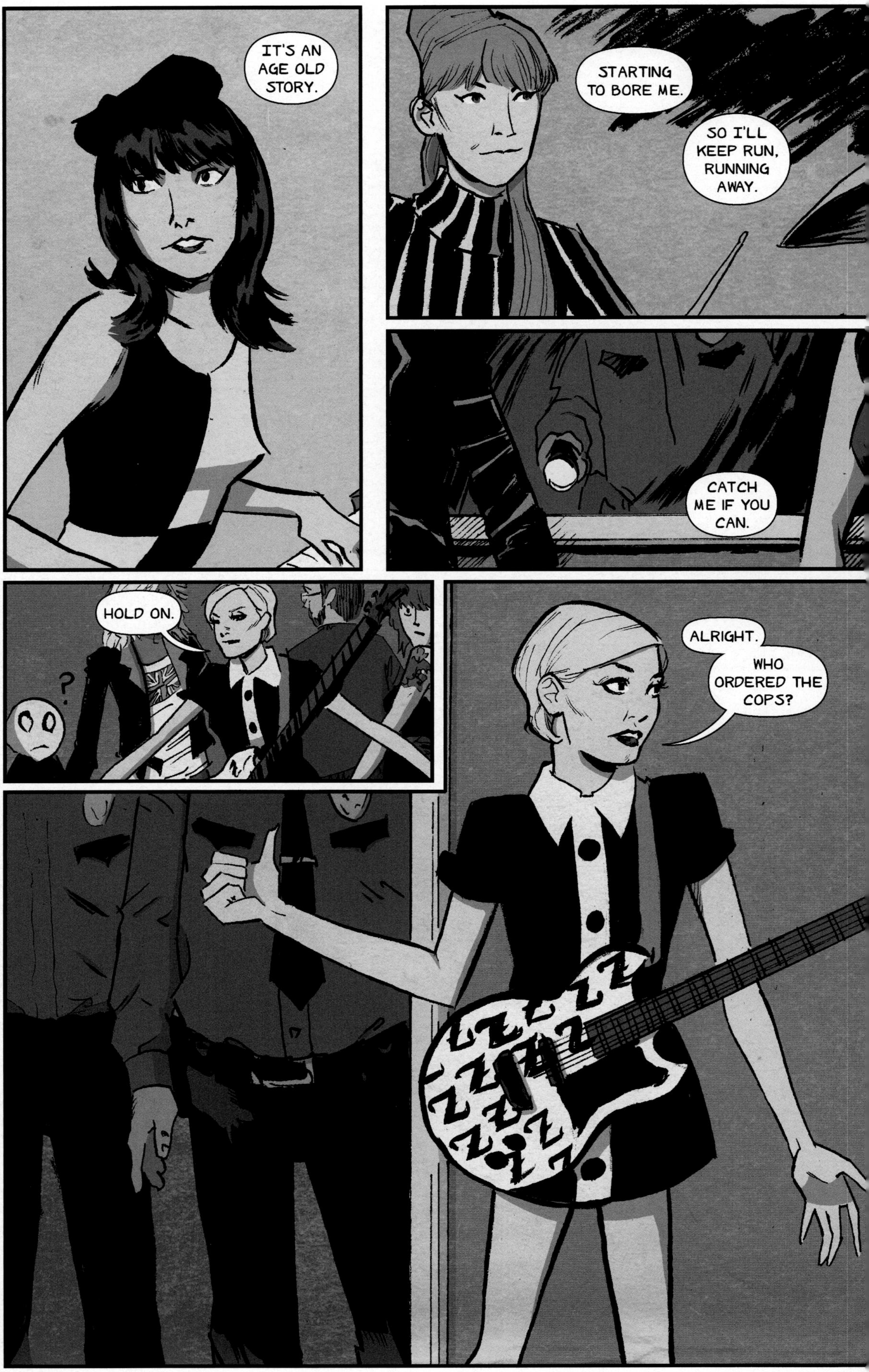
IT'S AN AGE OLD STORY.
STARTING TO BORE ME.
SO I'LL KEEP RUN, RUNNING AWAY.
CATCH ME IF YOU CAN.
HOLD ON.
?
ALRIGHT.
WHO ORDERED THE COPS?

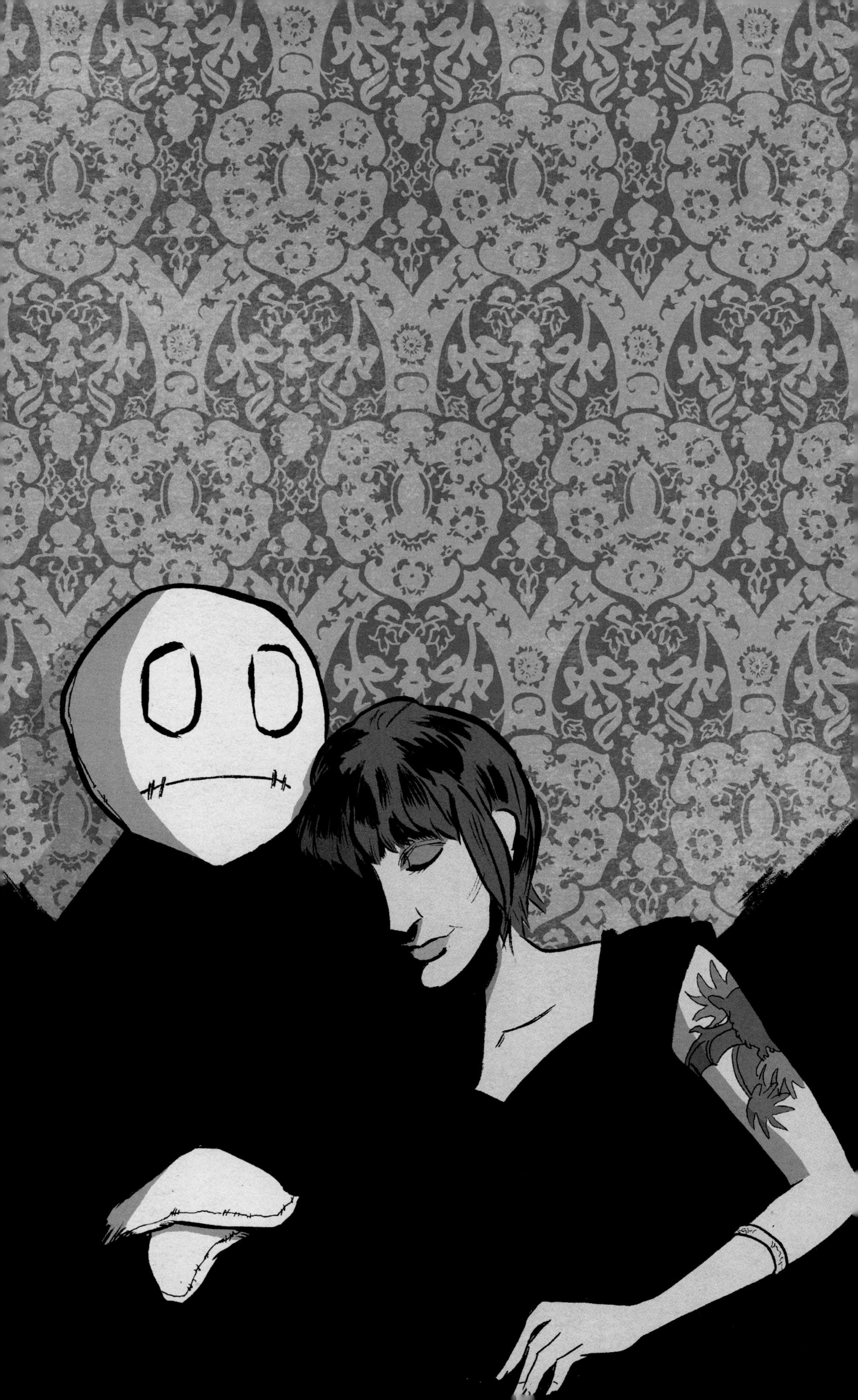

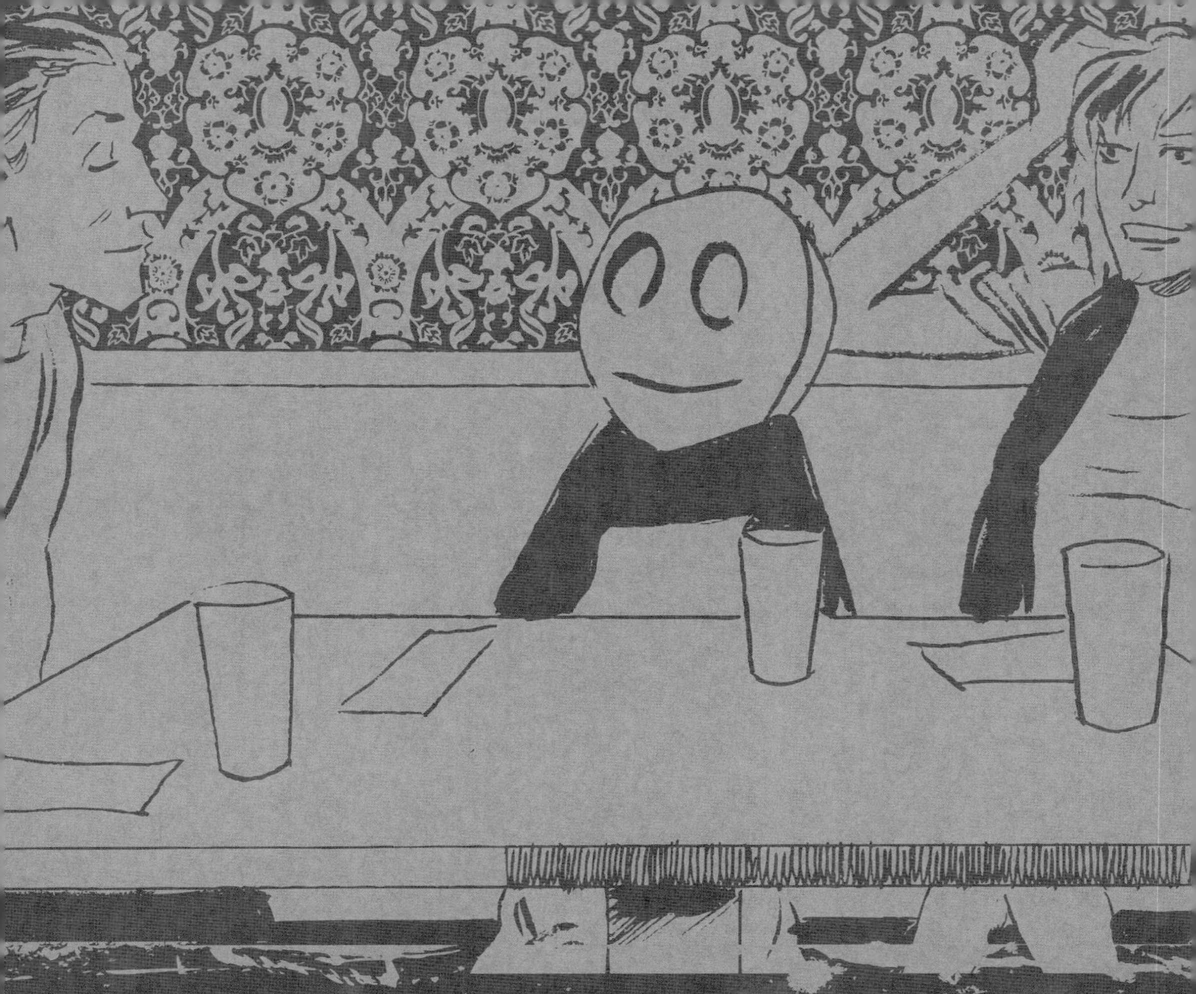

CHAPTER FOUR:

“THERE IS A LIGHT THAT NEVER GOES OUT”

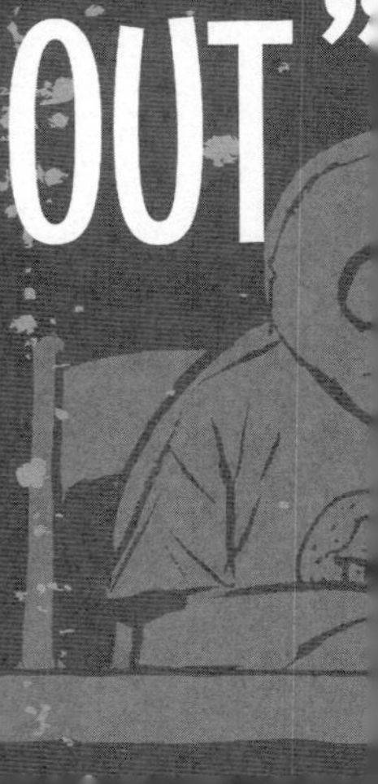

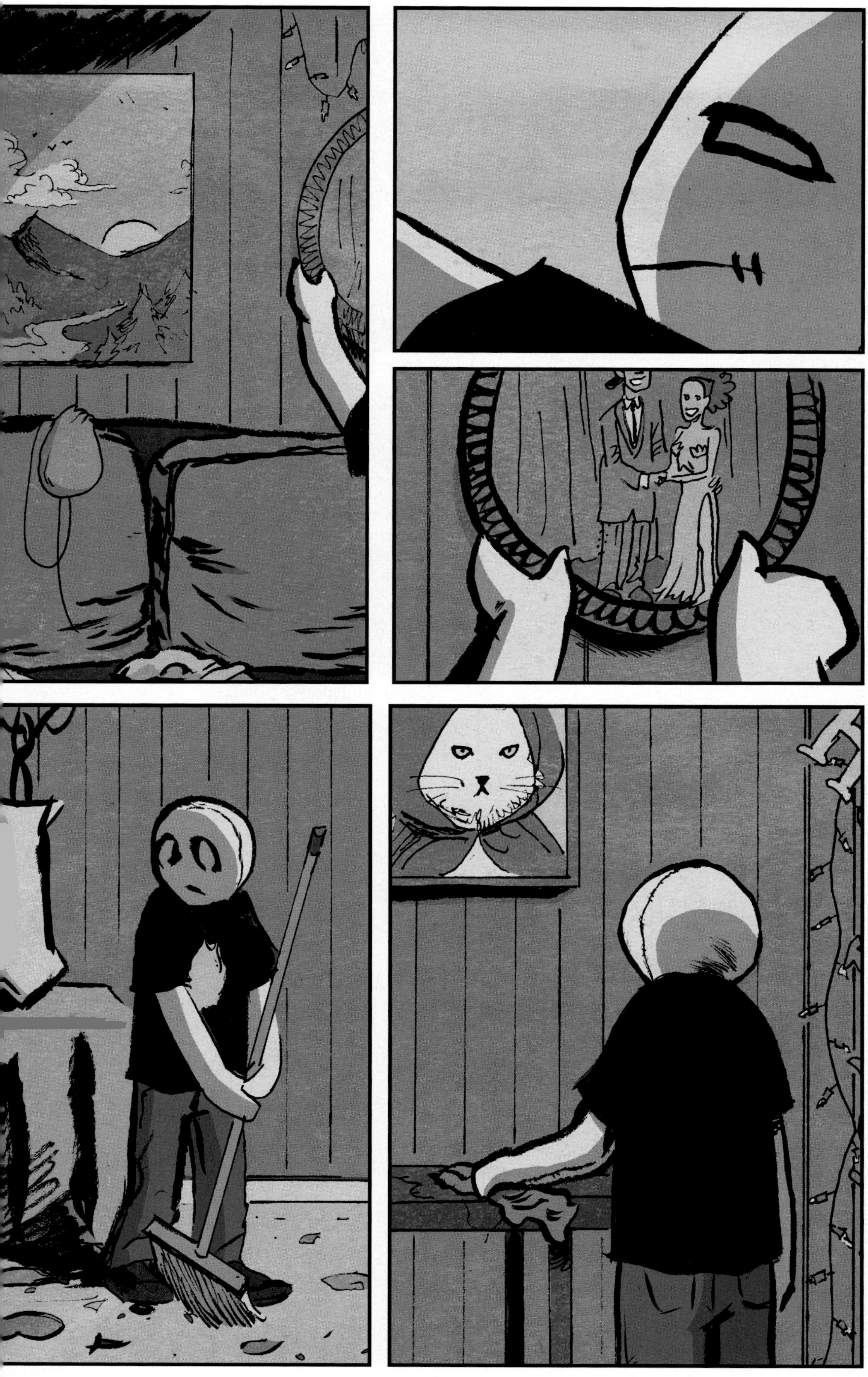

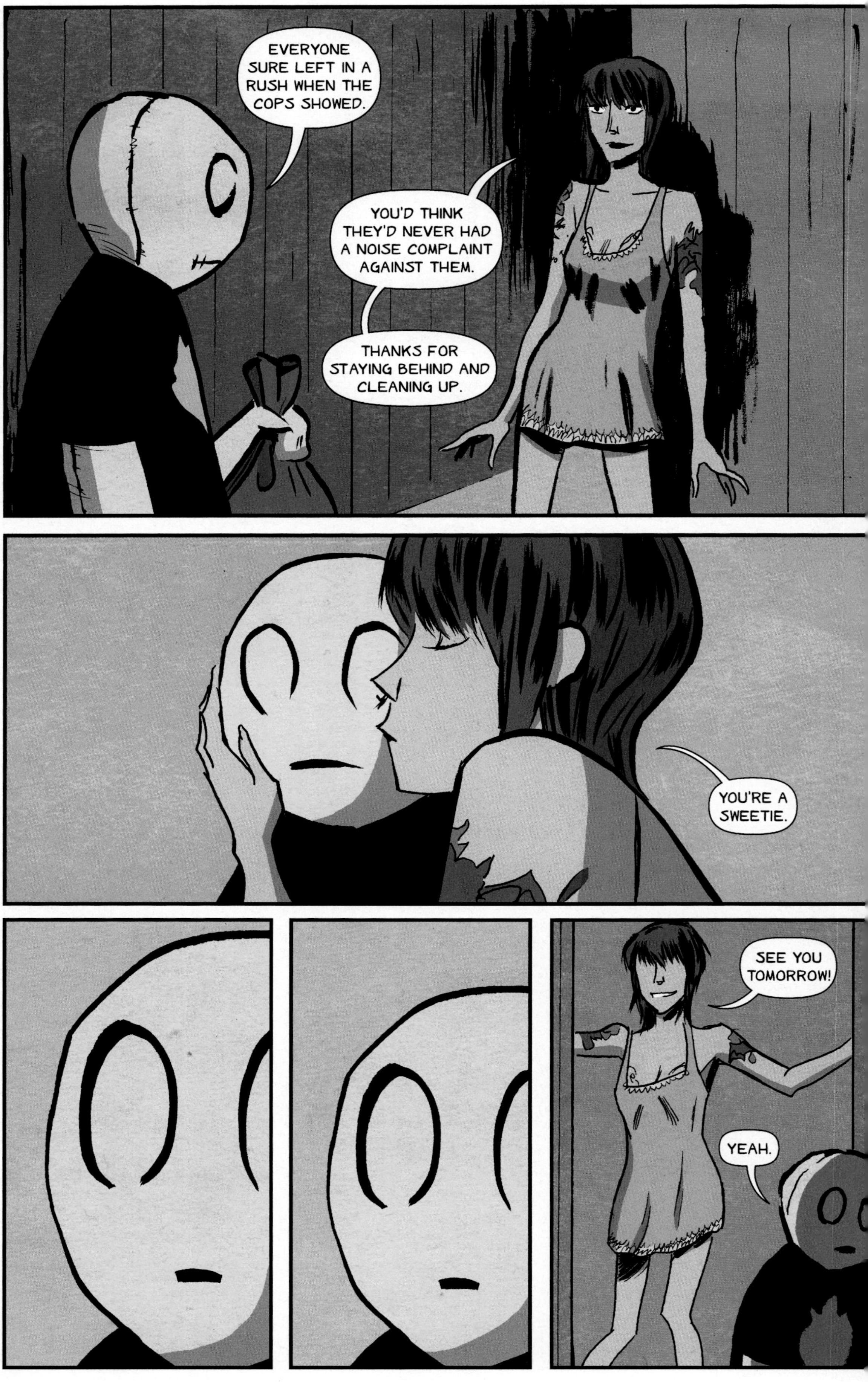
EVERYONE SURE LEFT IN A RUSH WHEN THE COPS SHOWED.
YOU'D THINK THEY'D NEVER HAD A NOISE COMPLAINT AGAINST THEM.
THANKS FOR STAYING BEHIND AND CLEANING UP.
YOU'RE A SWEETIE.
SEE YOU TOMORROW!
YEAH.

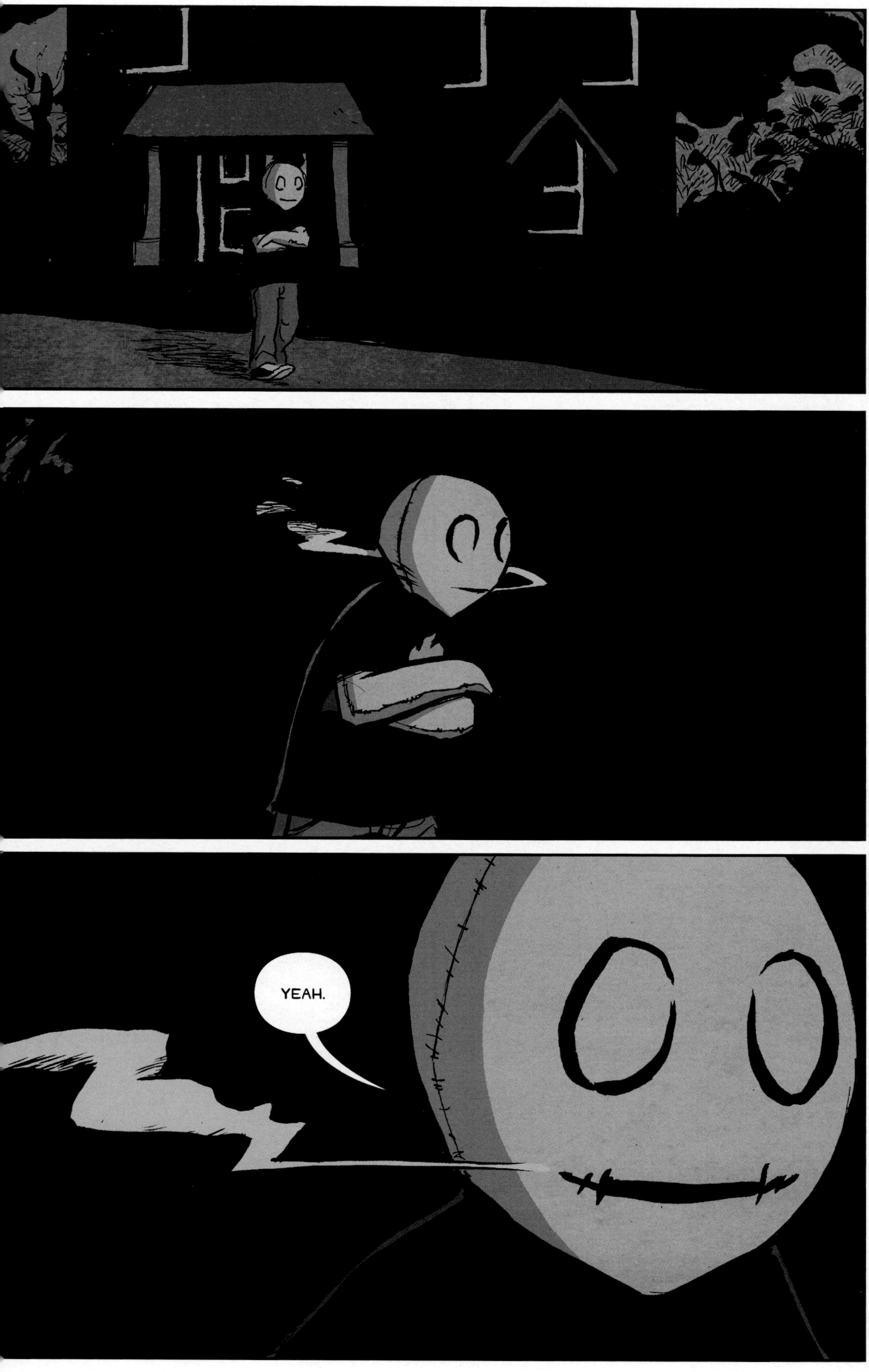
YEAH.

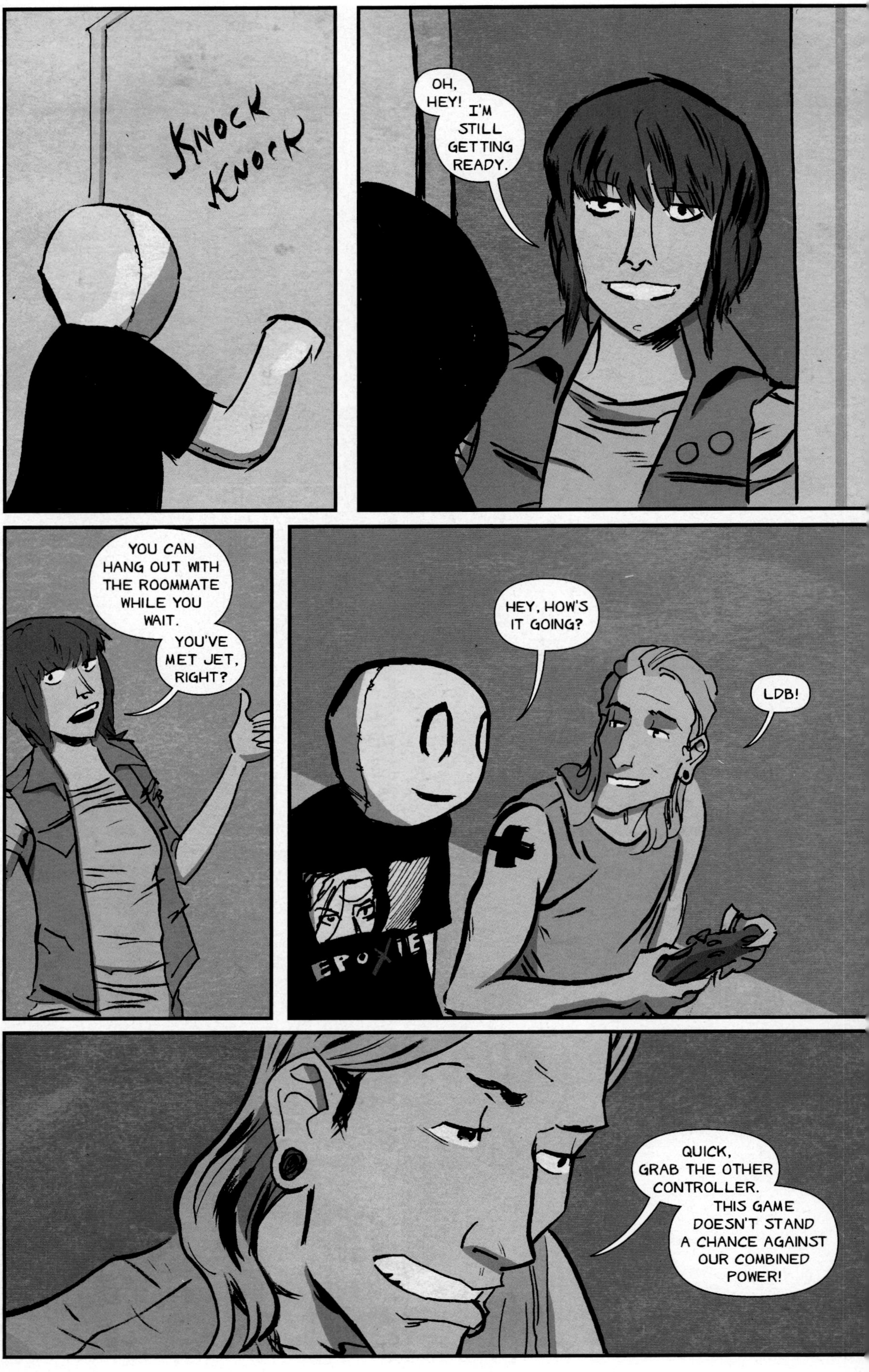
KNOCK KNOCK
OH, HEY!
I'M STILL GETTING READY.
YOU CAN HANG OUT WITH THE ROOMMATE WHILE YOU WAIT.
YOU'VE MET JET, RIGHT?
HEY, HOW'S IT GOING?
LDB!
EPOXIE
QUICK, GRAB THE OTHER CONTROLLER.
THIS GAME DOESN'T STAND A CHANCE AGAINST OUR COMBINED POWER!

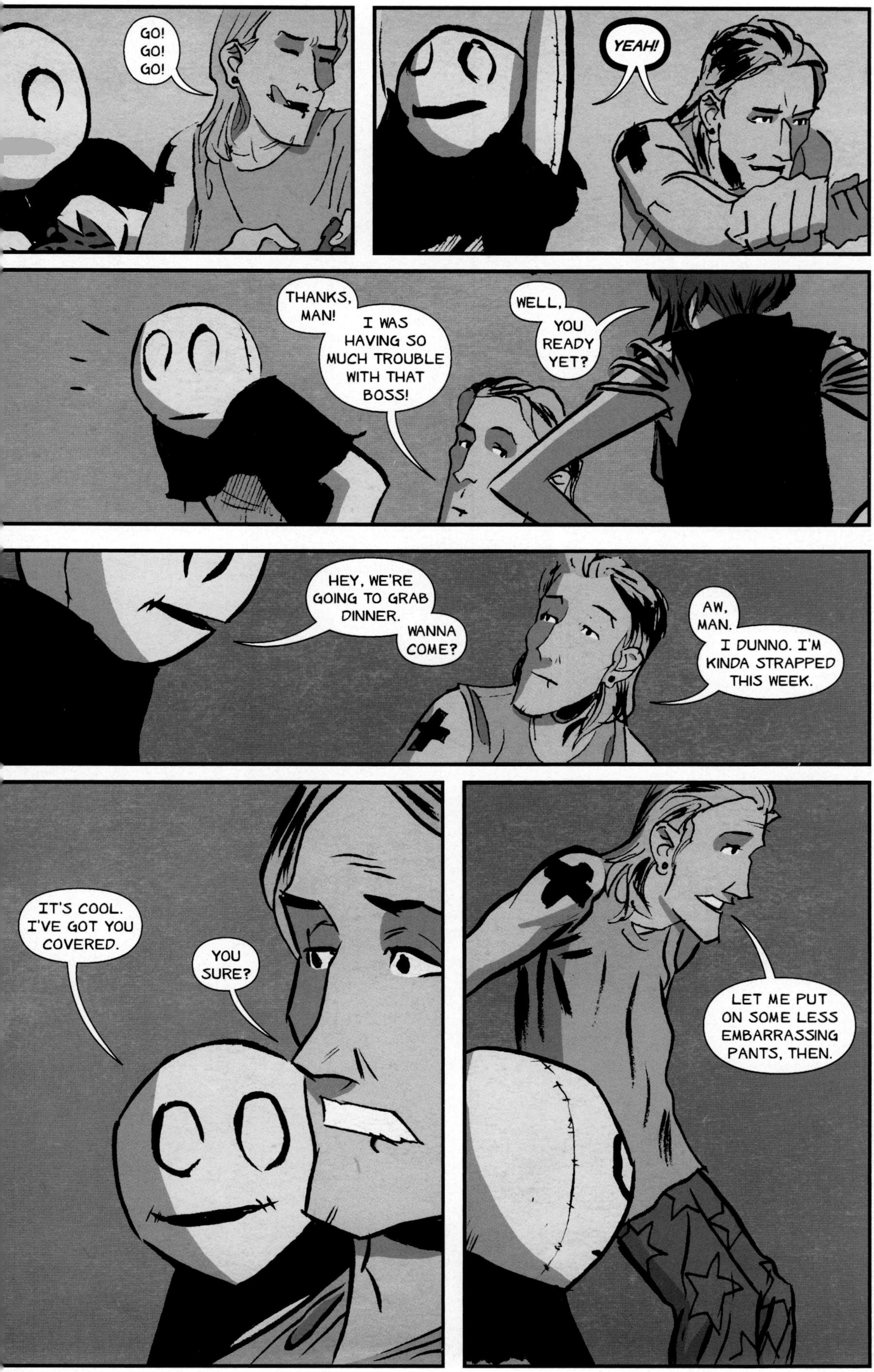
GO! GO! GO!
YEAH!
THANKS, MAN!
I WAS HAVING SO MUCH TROUBLE WITH THAT BOSS!
WELL, YOU READY YET?
HEY, WE'RE GOING TO GRAB DINNER.
WANNA COME?
AW, MAN.
I DUNNO. I'M KINDA STRAPPED THIS WEEK.
IT'S COOL. I'VE GOT YOU COVERED.
YOU SURE?
LET ME PUT ON SOME LESS EMBARRASSING PANTS, THEN.

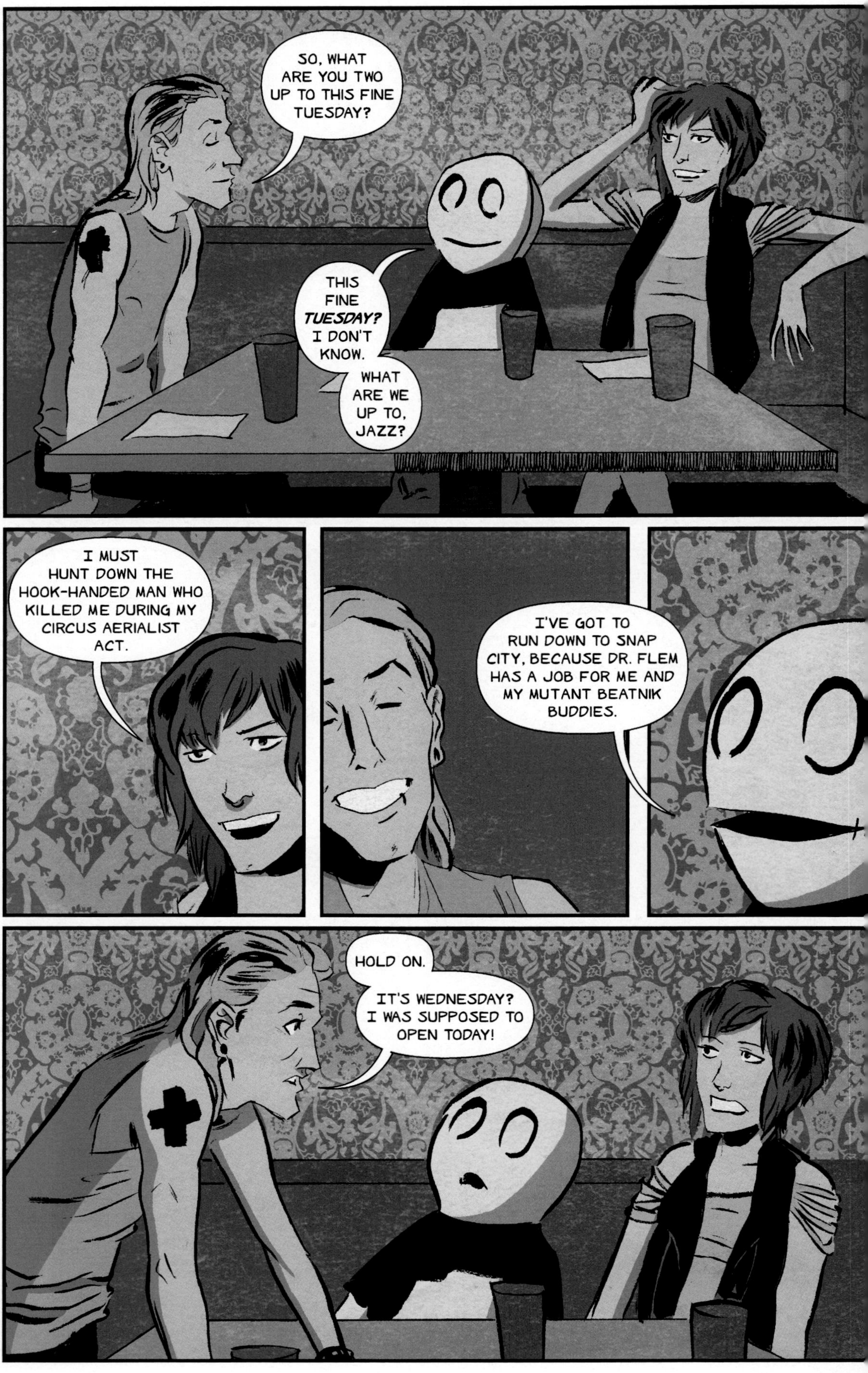
SO, WHAT ARE YOU TWO UP TO THIS FINE TUESDAY?
THIS FINE *TUESDAY?* I DON'T KNOW.
WHAT ARE WE UP TO, JAZZ?
I MUST HUNT DOWN THE HOOK-HANDED MAN WHO KILLED ME DURING MY CIRCUS AERIALIST ACT.
I'VE GOT TO RUN DOWN TO SNAP CITY, BECAUSE DR. FLEM HAS A JOB FOR ME AND MY MUTANT BEATNIK BUDDIES.
HOLD ON.
IT'S WEDNESDAY? I WAS SUPPOSED TO OPEN TODAY!

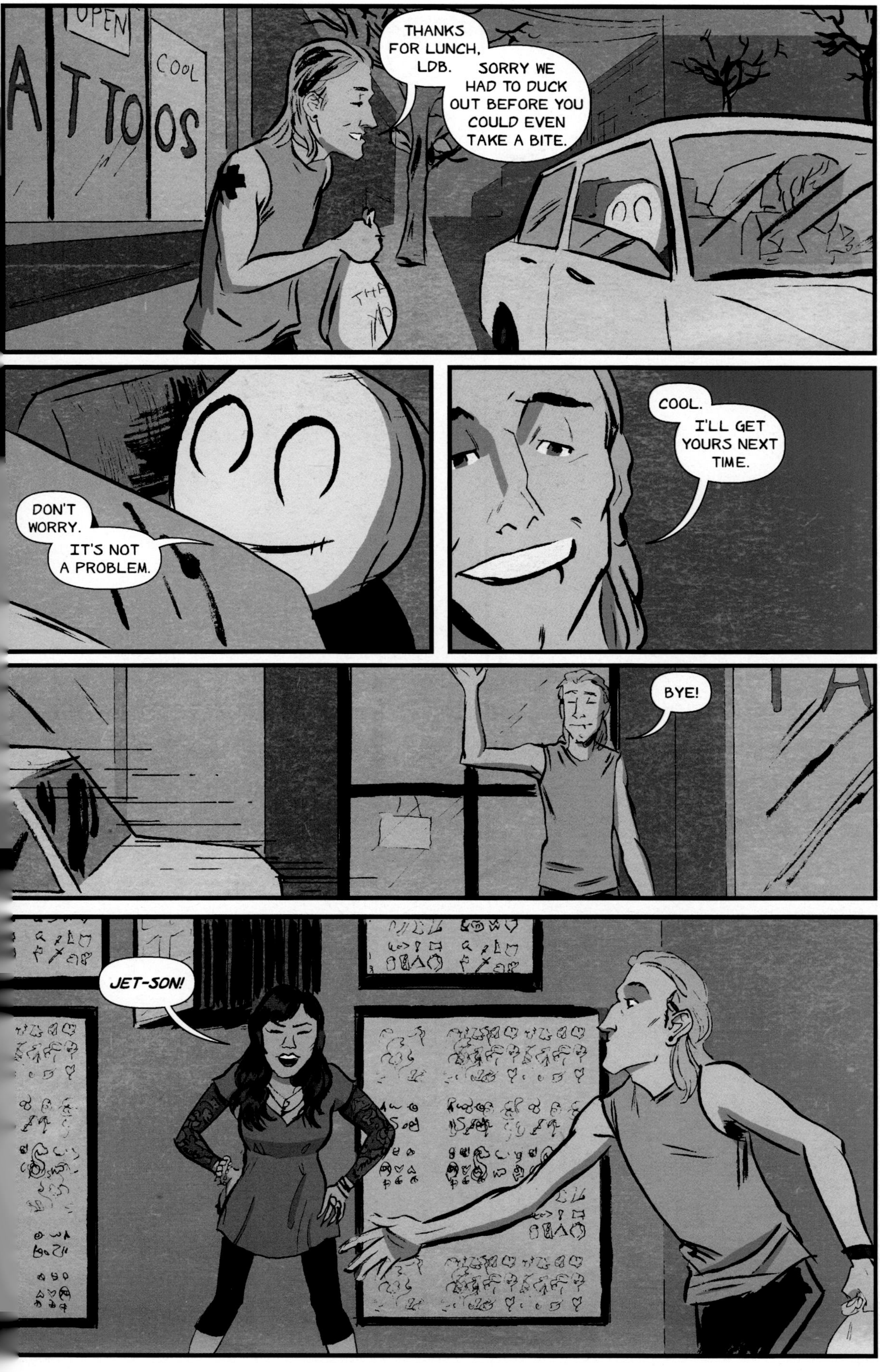

THANKS FOR LUNCH, LDB.
SORRY WE HAD TO DUCK OUT BEFORE YOU COULD EVEN TAKE A BITE.
DON'T WORRY.
IT'S NOT A PROBLEM.
COOL.
I'LL GET YOURS NEXT TIME.
BYE!
JET-SON!

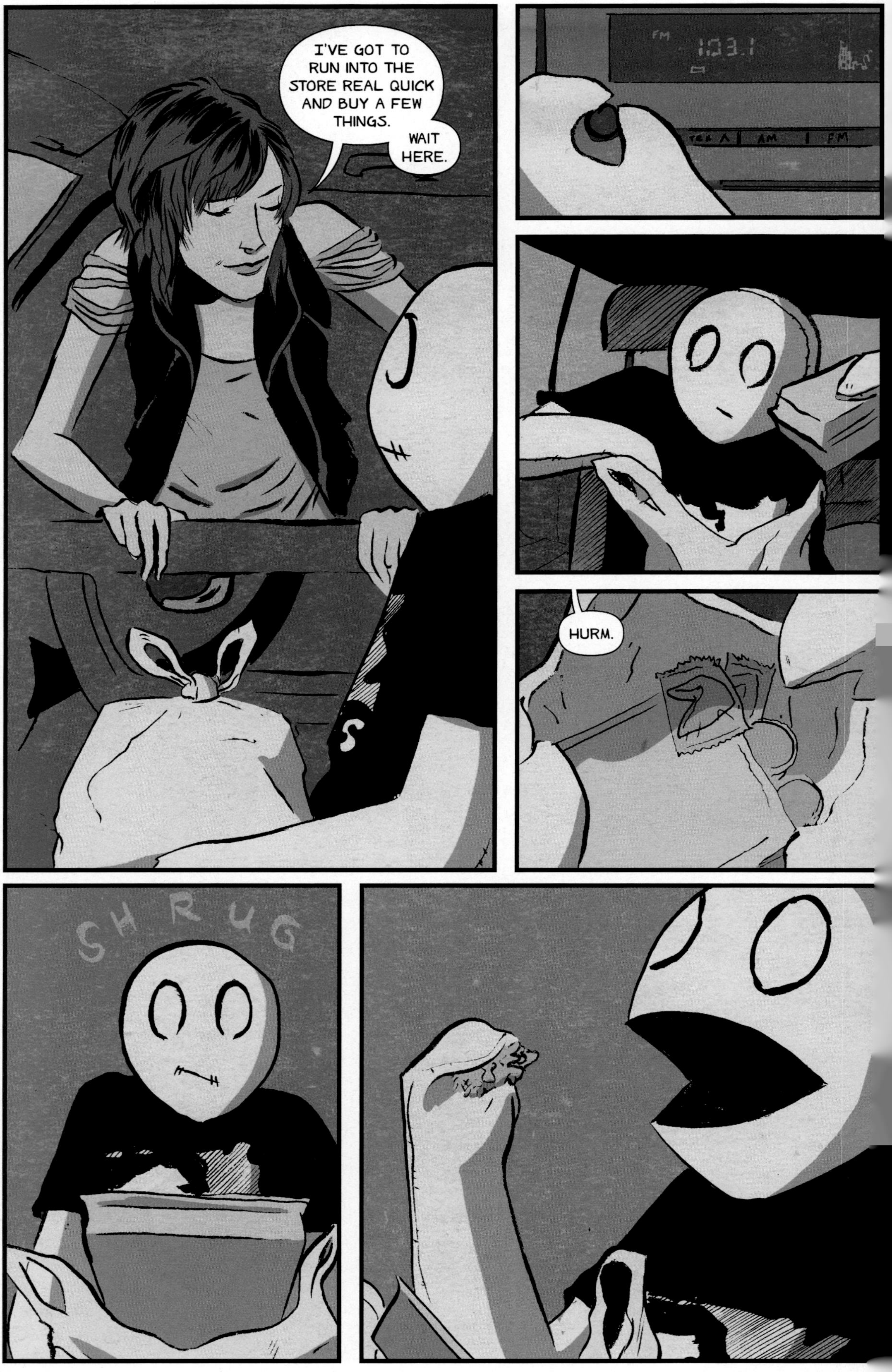
I'VE GOT TO RUN INTO THE STORE REAL QUICK AND BUY A FEW THINGS.
WAIT HERE.
FM 103.1
AM
FM
HURM.
SHRUG

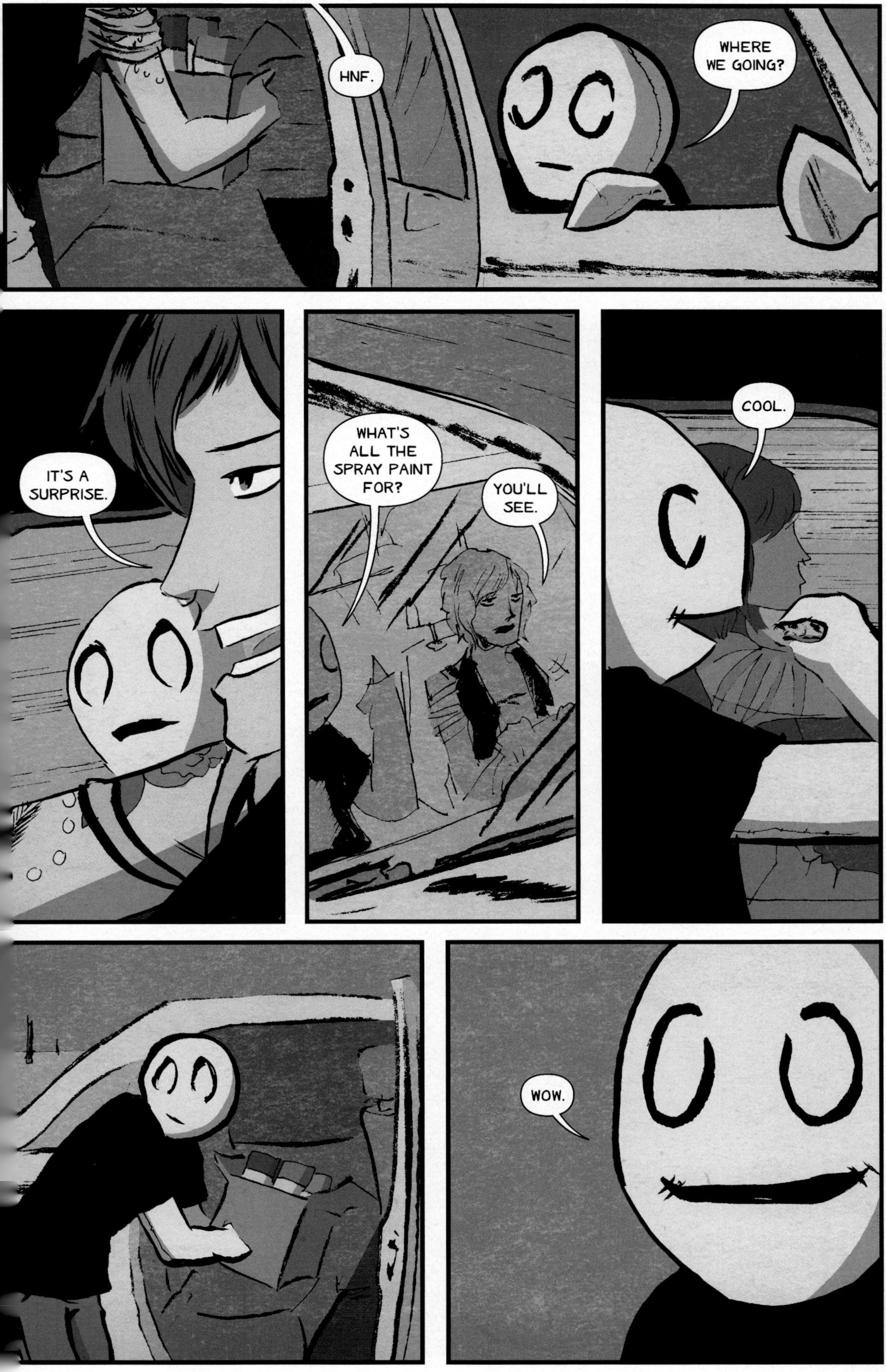
HNF.
WHERE WE GOING?
IT'S A SURPRISE.
WHAT'S ALL THE SPRAY PAINT FOR?
YOU'LL SEE.
COOL.
WOW.

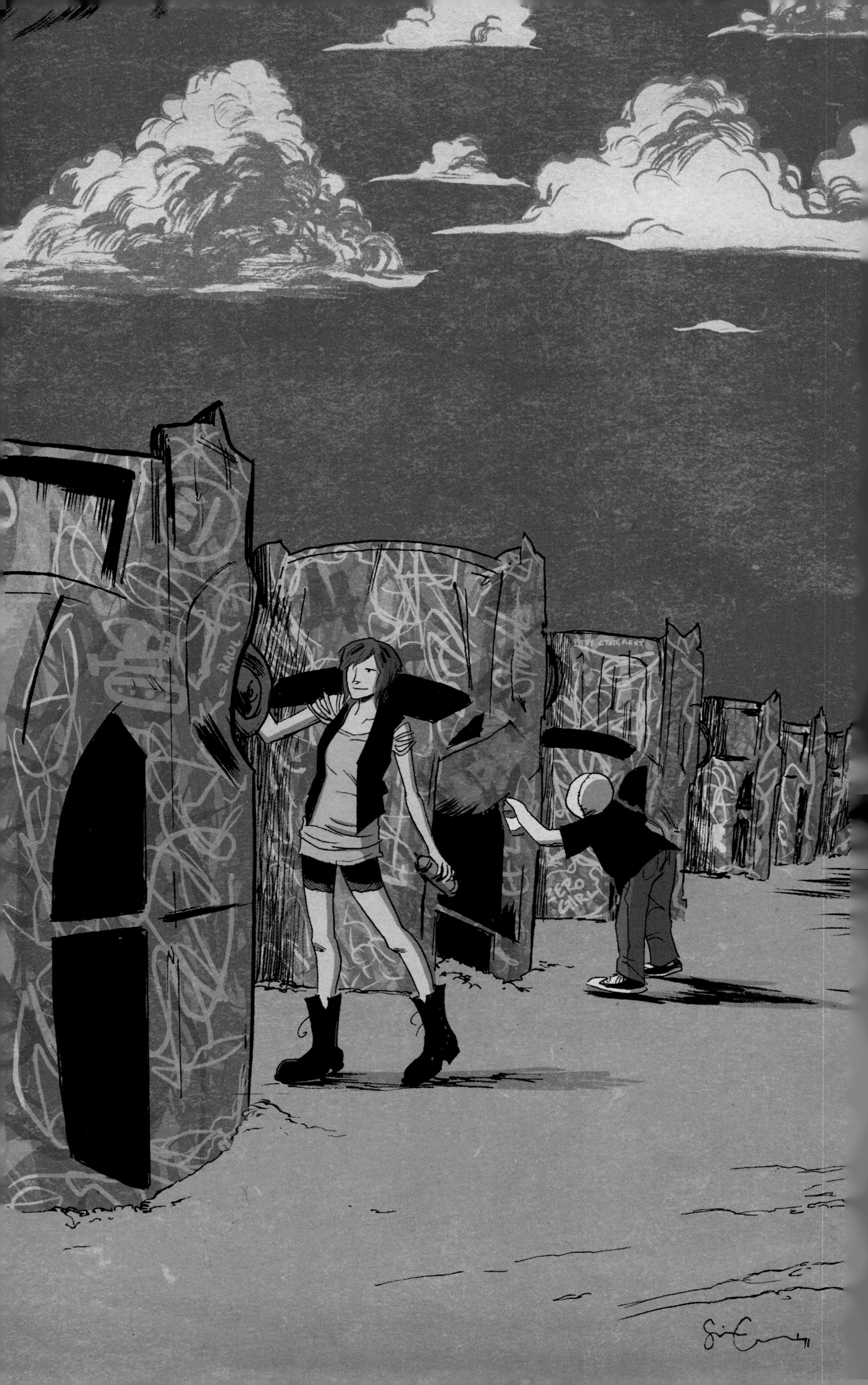
RAUL
PITHY STATEMENT
ZERO GIRL

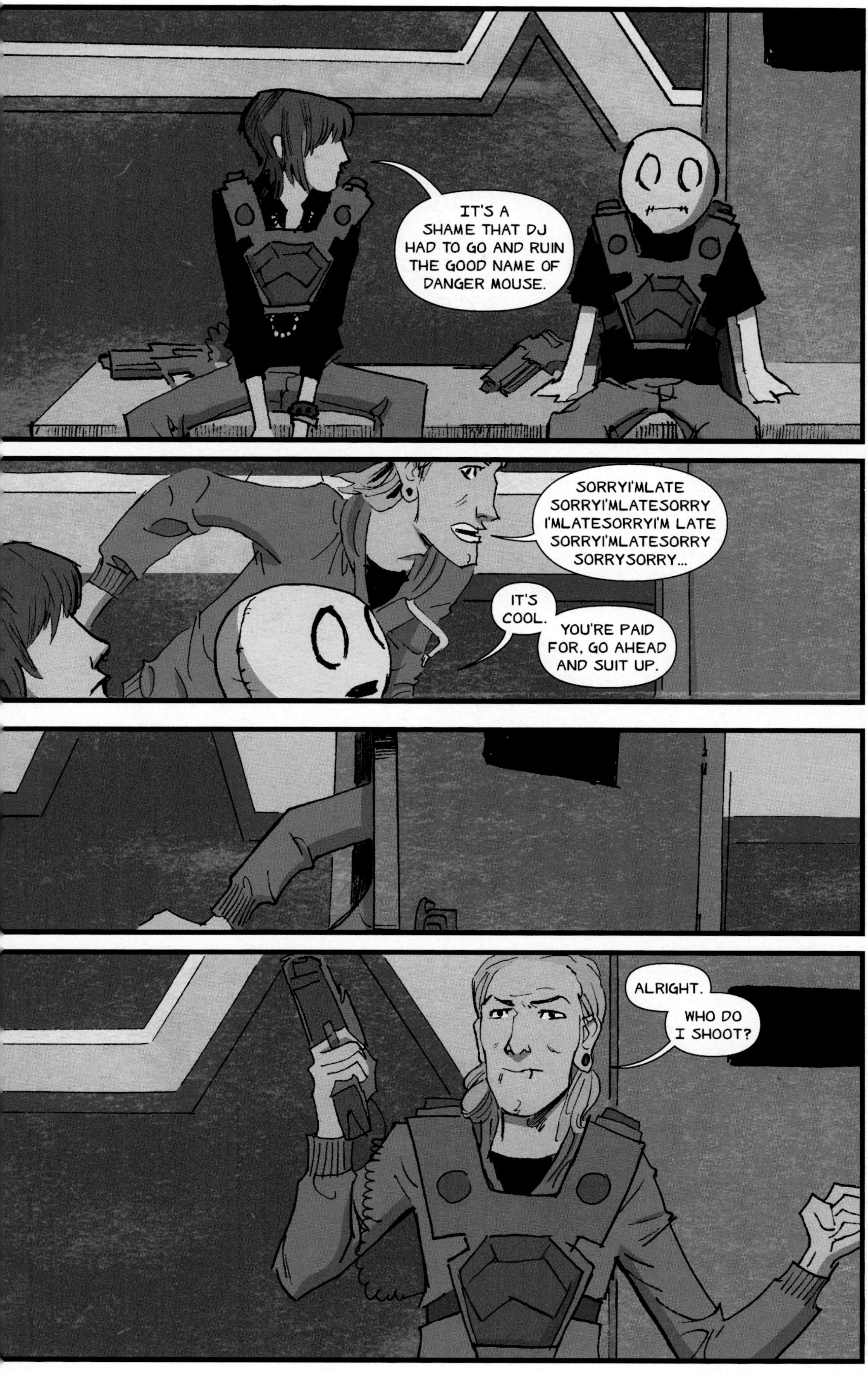
IT'S A SHAME THAT DJ HAD TO GO AND RUIN THE GOOD NAME OF DANGER MOUSE.
SORRYI'MLATE SORRYI'MLATESORRY I'MLATESORRYI'M LATE SORRYI'MLATESORRY SORRYSORRY...
IT'S COOL.
YOU'RE PAID FOR, GO AHEAD AND SUIT UP.
ALRIGHT.
WHO DO I SHOOT?

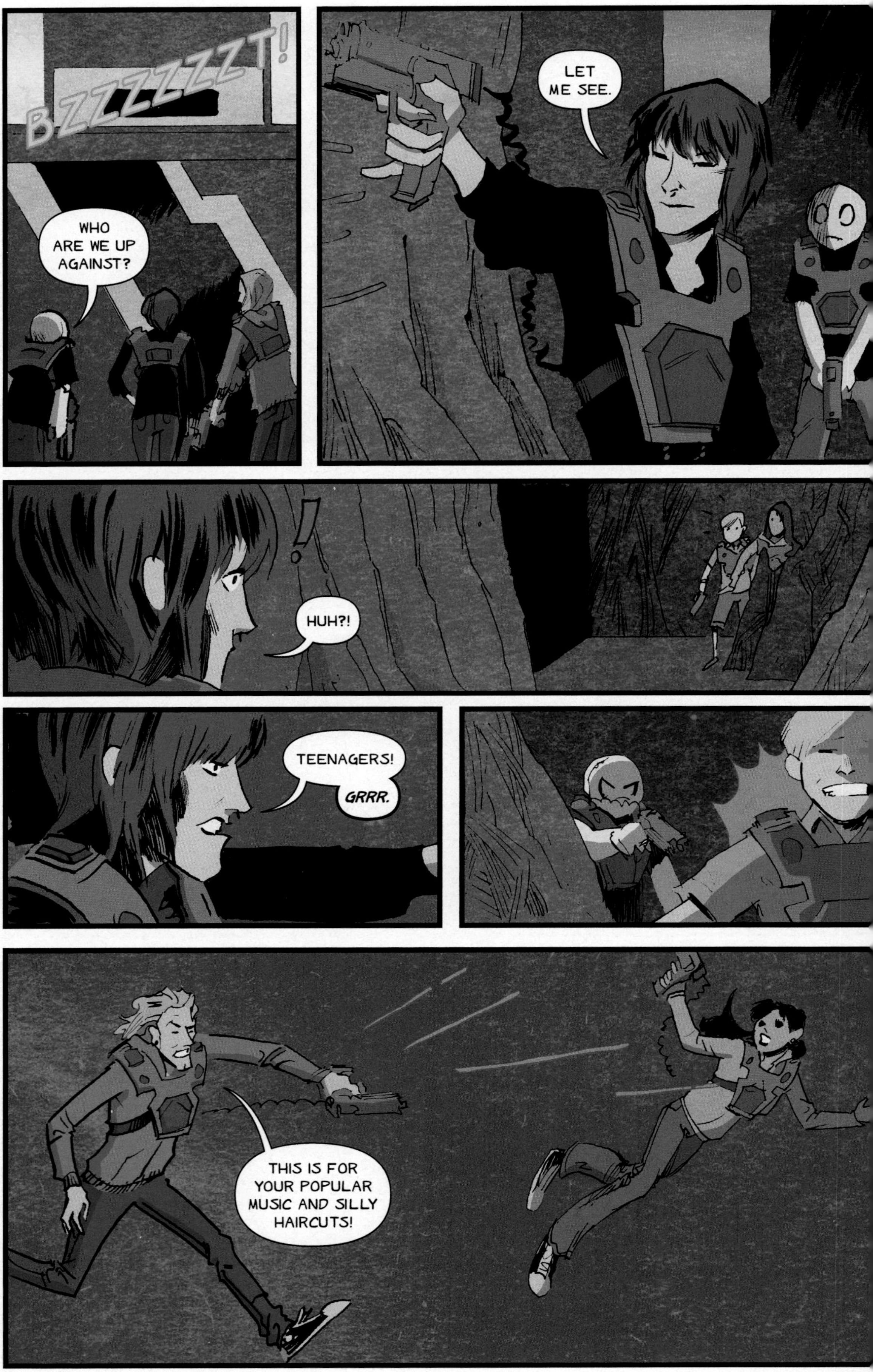
BZZZZZZZT!
WHO ARE WE UP AGAINST?
LET ME SEE.
!
HUH?!
TEENAGERS!
GRRR.
THIS IS FOR YOUR POPULAR MUSIC AND SILLY HAIRCUTS!

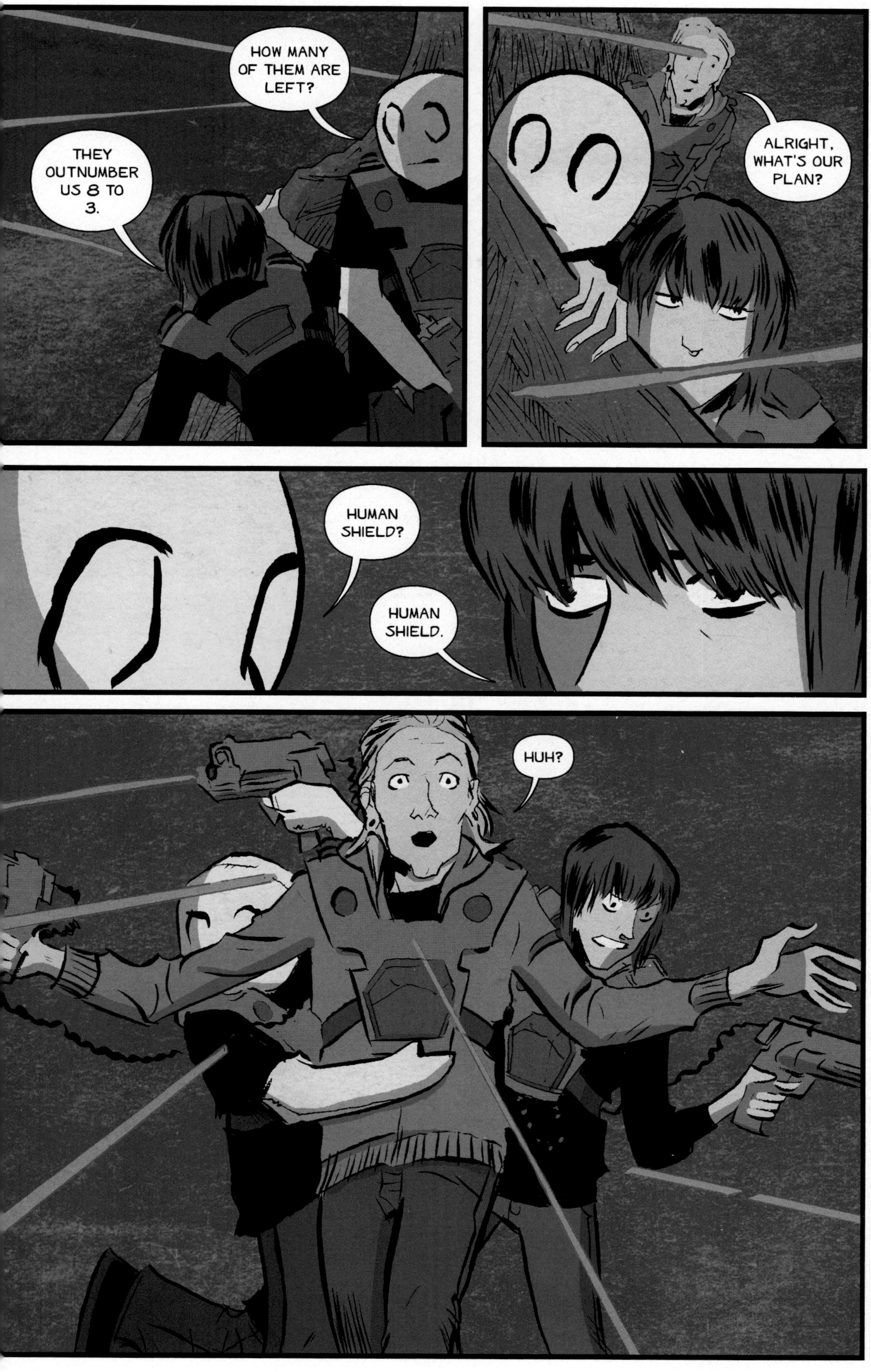
HOW MANY OF THEM ARE LEFT?
THEY OUTNUMBER US 8 TO 3.
ALRIGHT, WHAT'S OUR PLAN?
HUMAN SHIELD?
HUMAN SHIELD.
HUH?

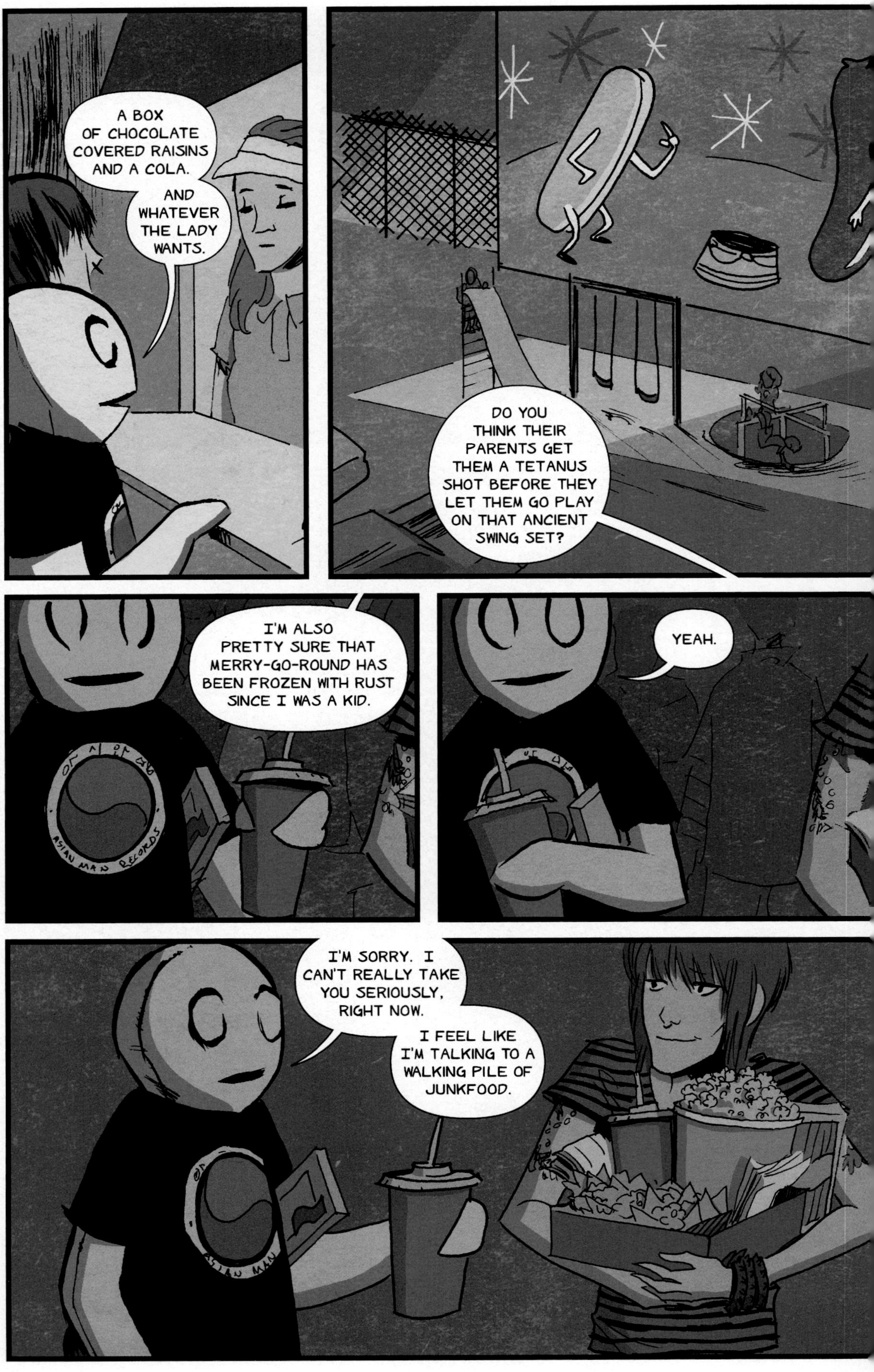
A BOX OF CHOCOLATE COVERED RAISINS AND A COLA.
AND WHATEVER THE LADY WANTS.
DO YOU THINK THEIR PARENTS GET THEM A TETANUS SHOT BEFORE THEY LET THEM GO PLAY ON THAT ANCIENT SWING SET?
I'M ALSO PRETTY SURE THAT MERRY-GO-ROUND HAS BEEN FROZEN WITH RUST SINCE I WAS A KID.
YEAH.
I'M SORRY. I CAN'T REALLY TAKE YOU SERIOUSLY, RIGHT NOW.
I FEEL LIKE I'M TALKING TO A WALKING PILE OF JUNKFOOD.
ASIAN MAN RECORDS

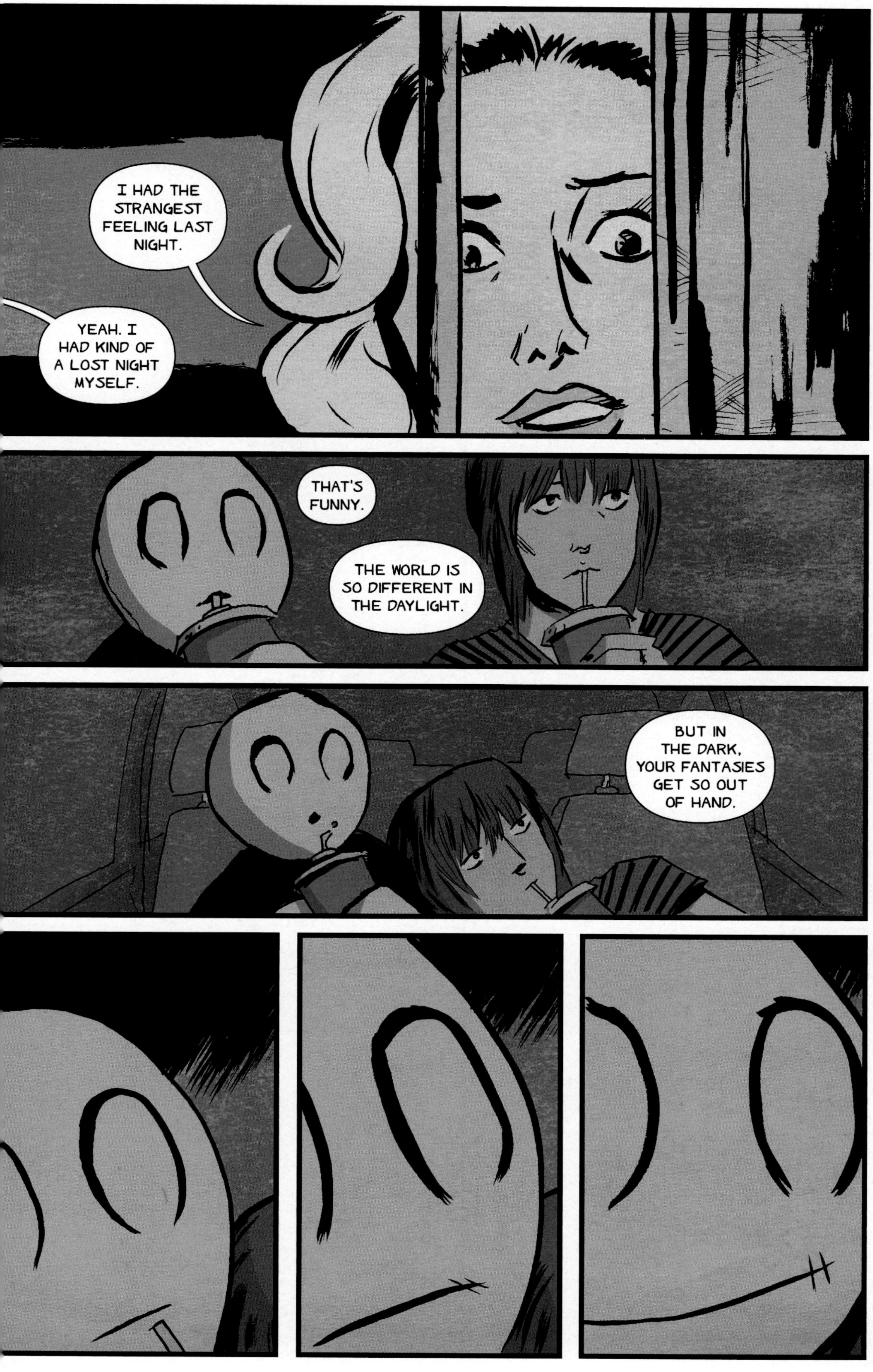
I HAD THE STRANGEST FEELING LAST NIGHT.
YEAH. I HAD KIND OF A LOST NIGHT MYSELF.
THAT'S FUNNY.
THE WORLD IS SO DIFFERENT IN THE DAYLIGHT.
BUT IN THE DARK, YOUR FANTASIES GET SO OUT OF HAND.

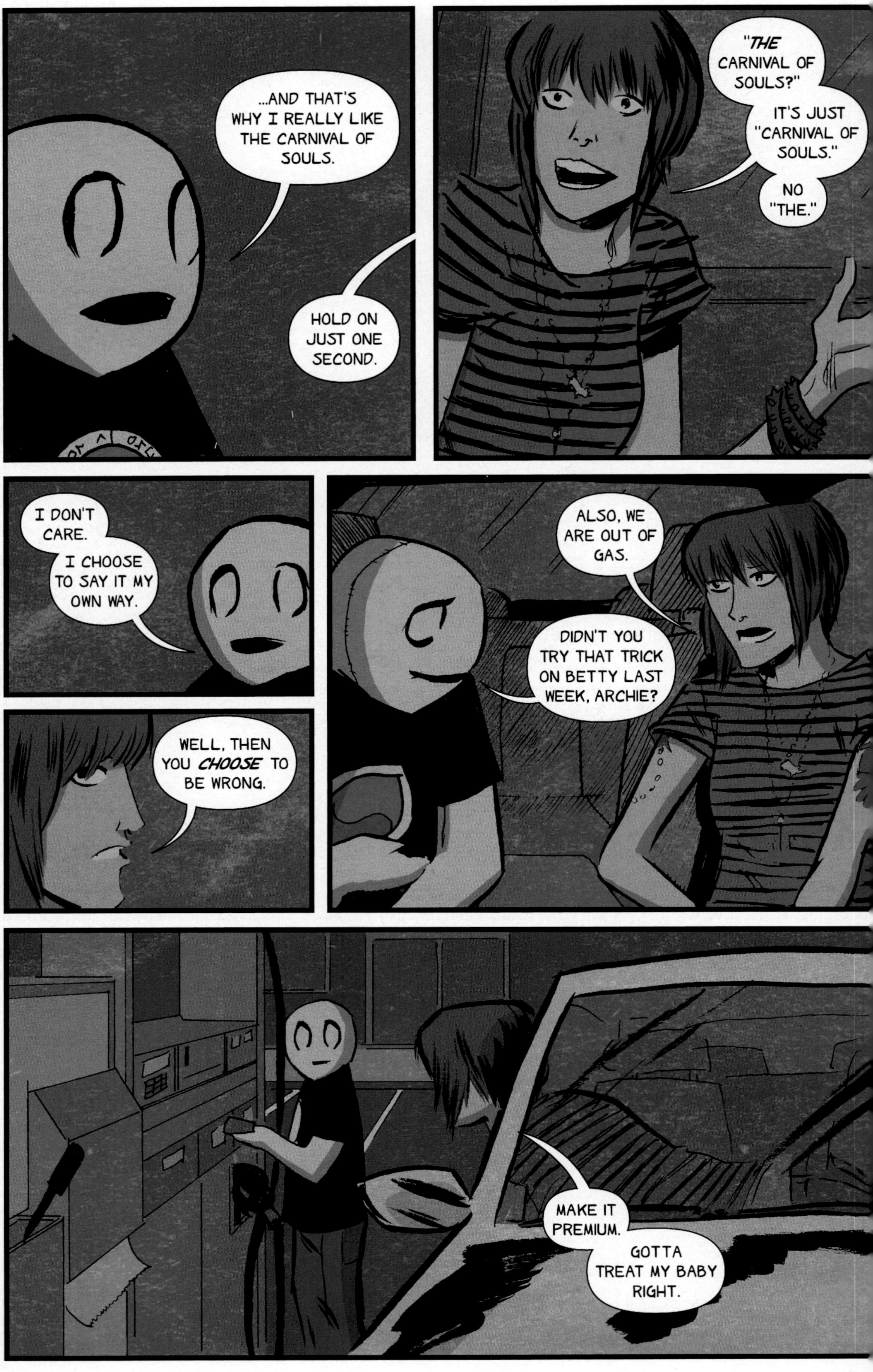
...AND THAT'S WHY I REALLY LIKE THE CARNIVAL OF SOULS.
HOLD ON JUST ONE SECOND.
"THE CARNIVAL OF SOULS?"
IT'S JUST "CARNIVAL OF SOULS."
NO "THE."
I DON'T CARE.
I CHOOSE TO SAY IT MY OWN WAY.
WELL, THEN YOU CHOOSE TO BE WRONG.
ALSO, WE ARE OUT OF GAS.
DIDN'T YOU TRY THAT TRICK ON BETTY LAST WEEK, ARCHIE?
MAKE IT PREMIUM.
GOTTA TREAT MY BABY RIGHT.

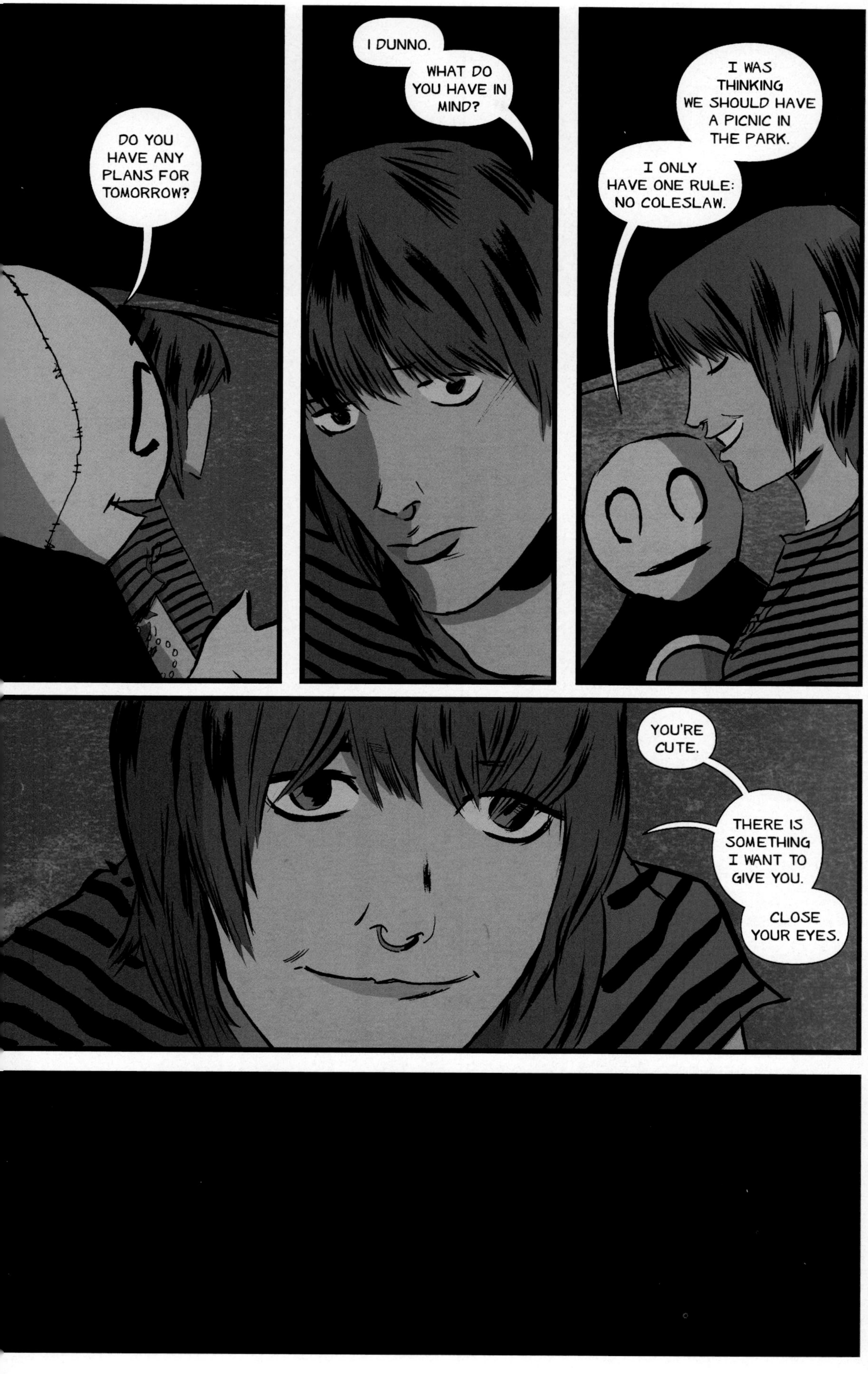

DO YOU HAVE ANY PLANS FOR TOMORROW?
I DUNNO.
WHAT DO YOU HAVE IN MIND?
I WAS THINKING WE SHOULD HAVE A PICNIC IN THE PARK.
I ONLY HAVE ONE RULE: NO COLESLAW.
YOU'RE CUTE.
THERE IS SOMETHING I WANT TO GIVE YOU.
CLOSE YOUR EYES.

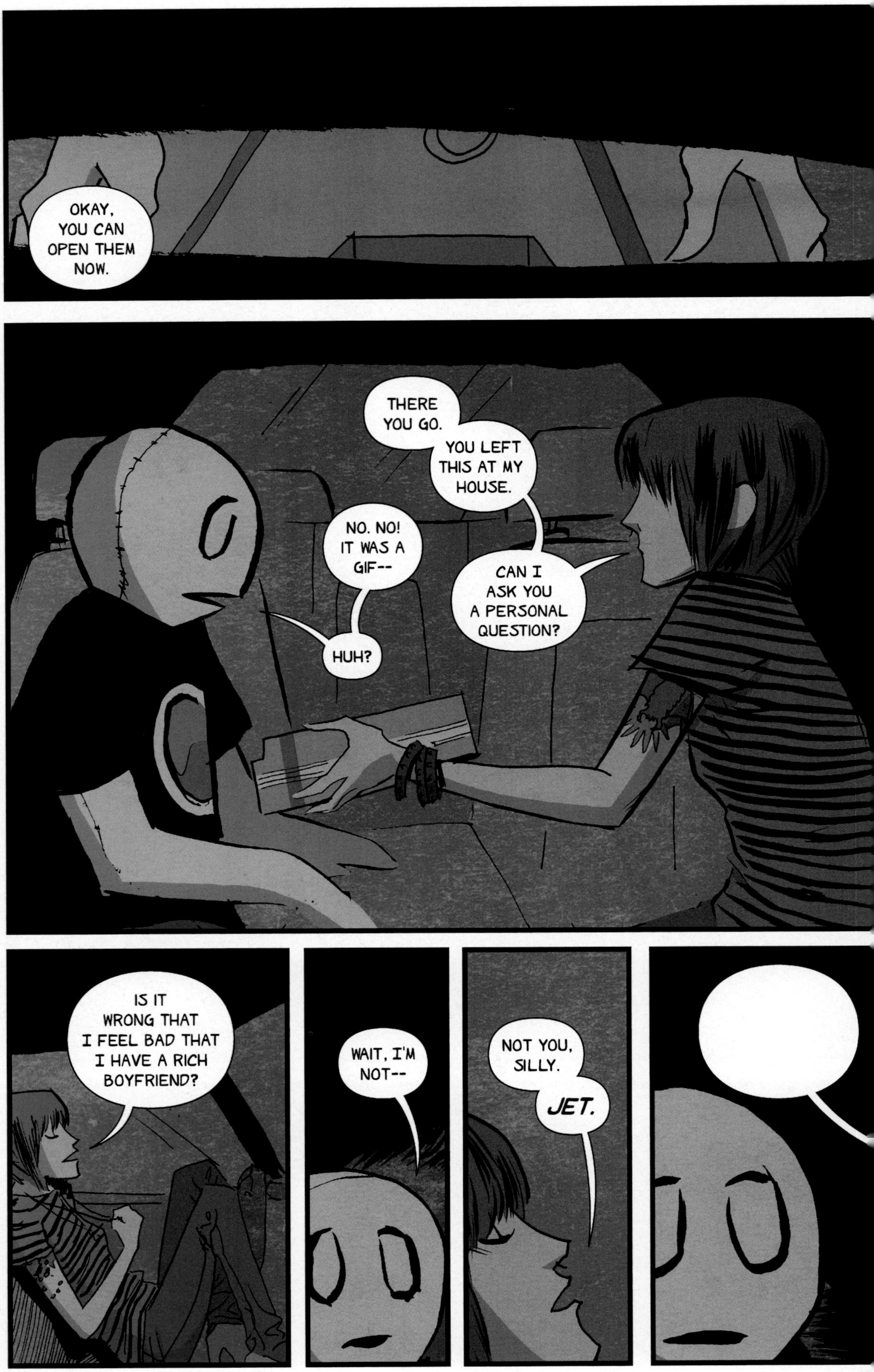
OKAY, YOU CAN OPEN THEM NOW.
THERE YOU GO.
YOU LEFT THIS AT MY HOUSE.
NO. NO! IT WAS A GIF--
HUH?
CAN I ASK YOU A PERSONAL QUESTION?
IS IT WRONG THAT I FEEL BAD THAT I HAVE A RICH BOYFRIEND?
WAIT, I'M NOT--
NOT YOU, SILLY.
JET.

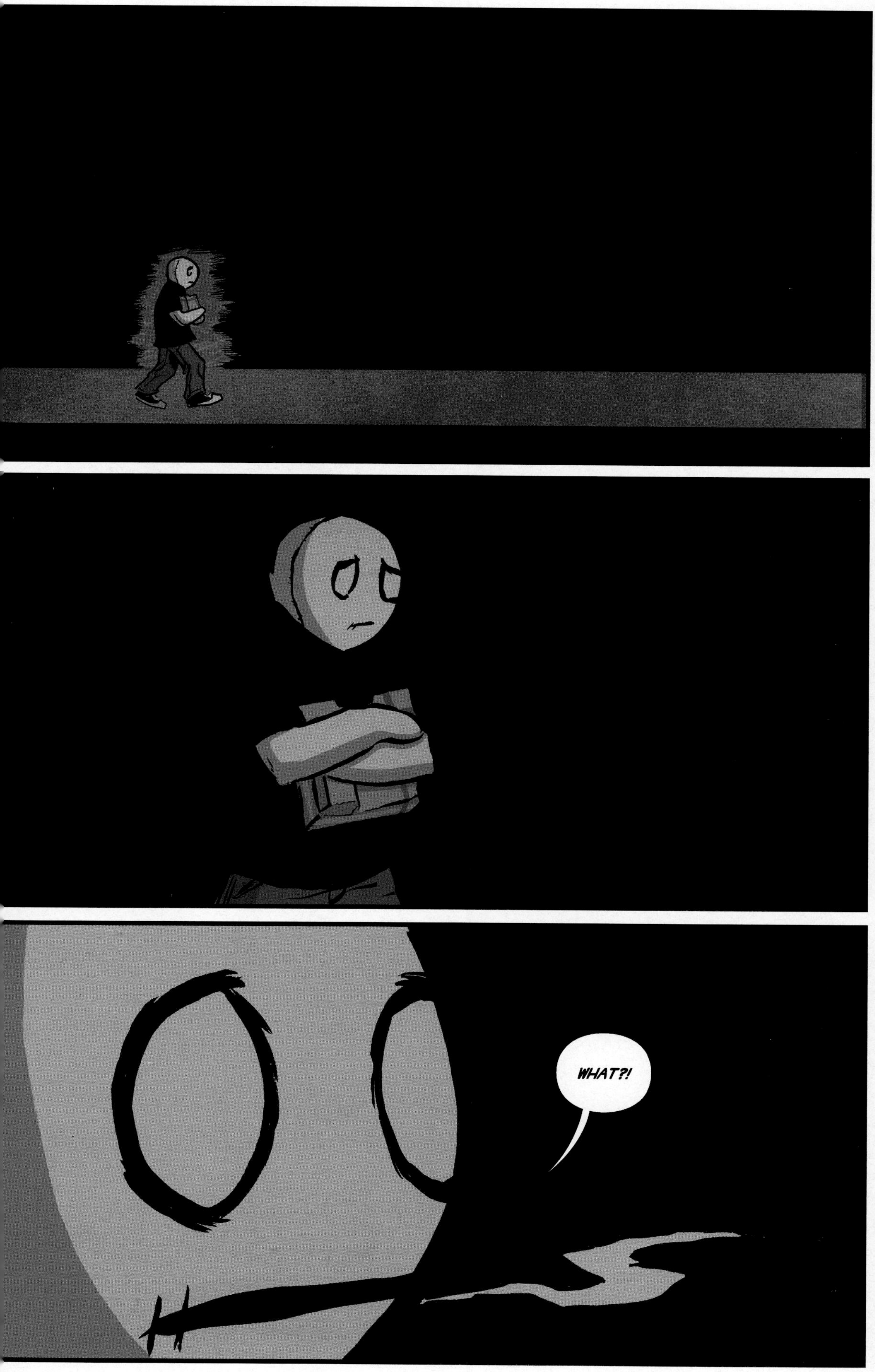
WHAT?!

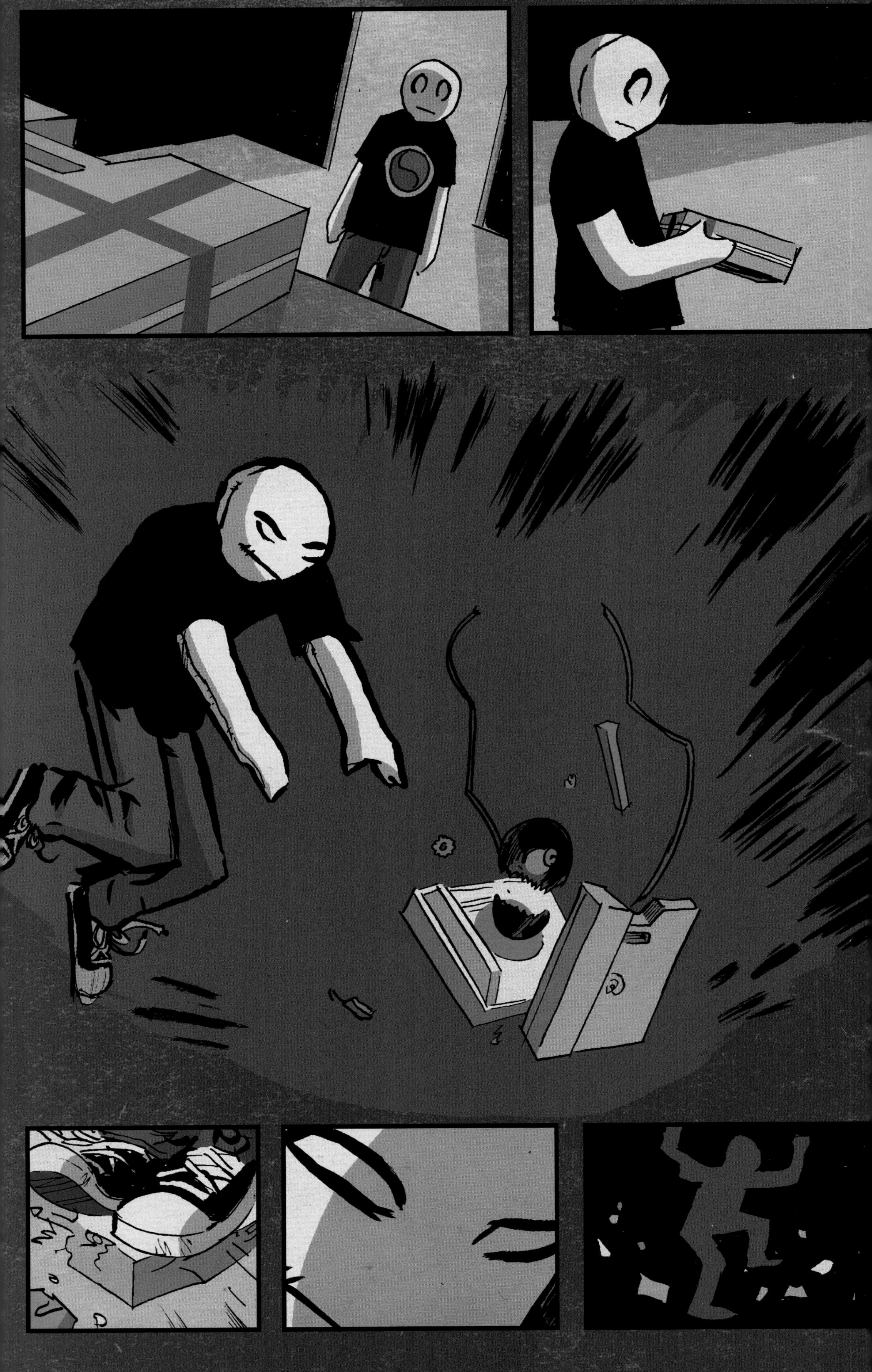

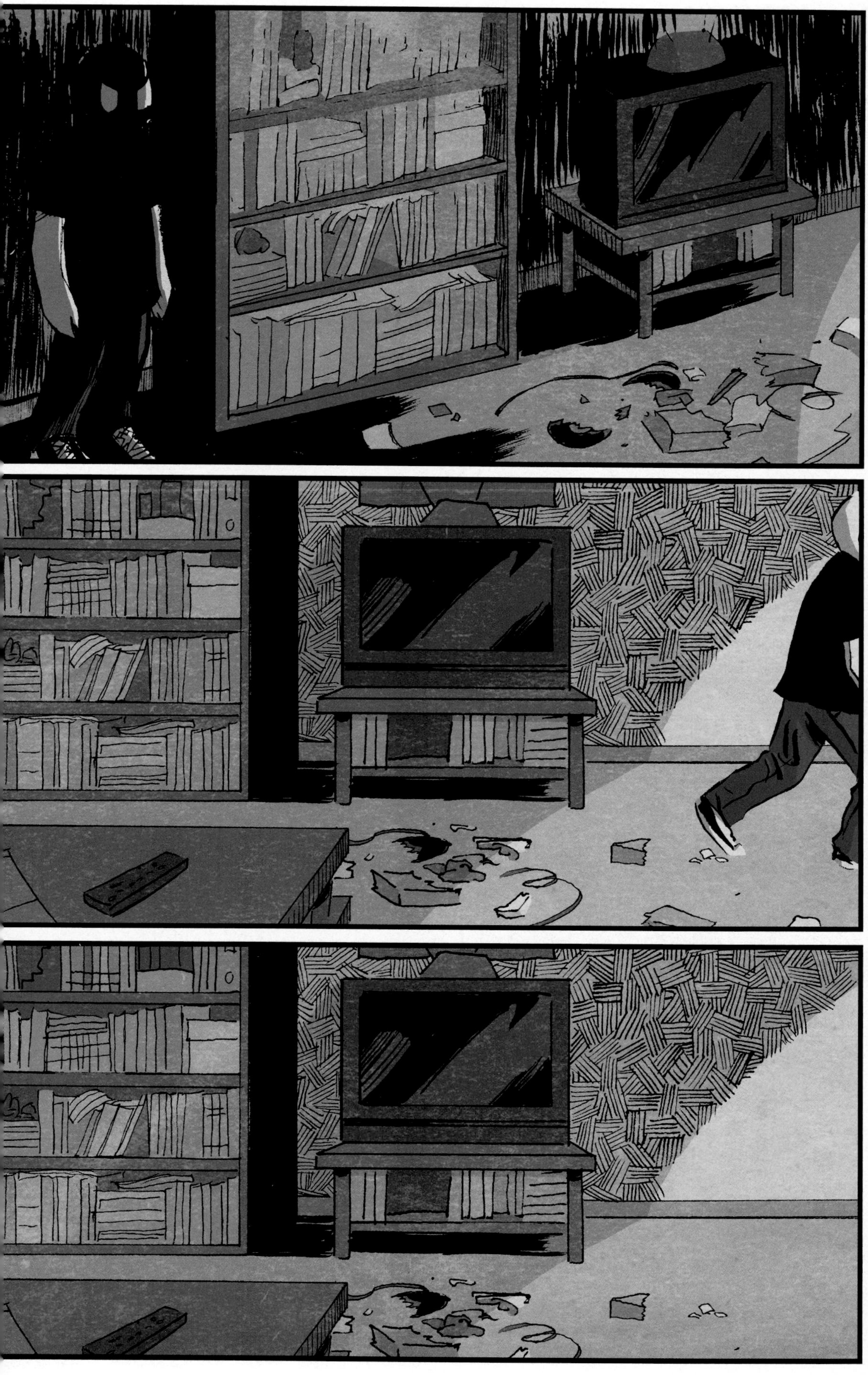

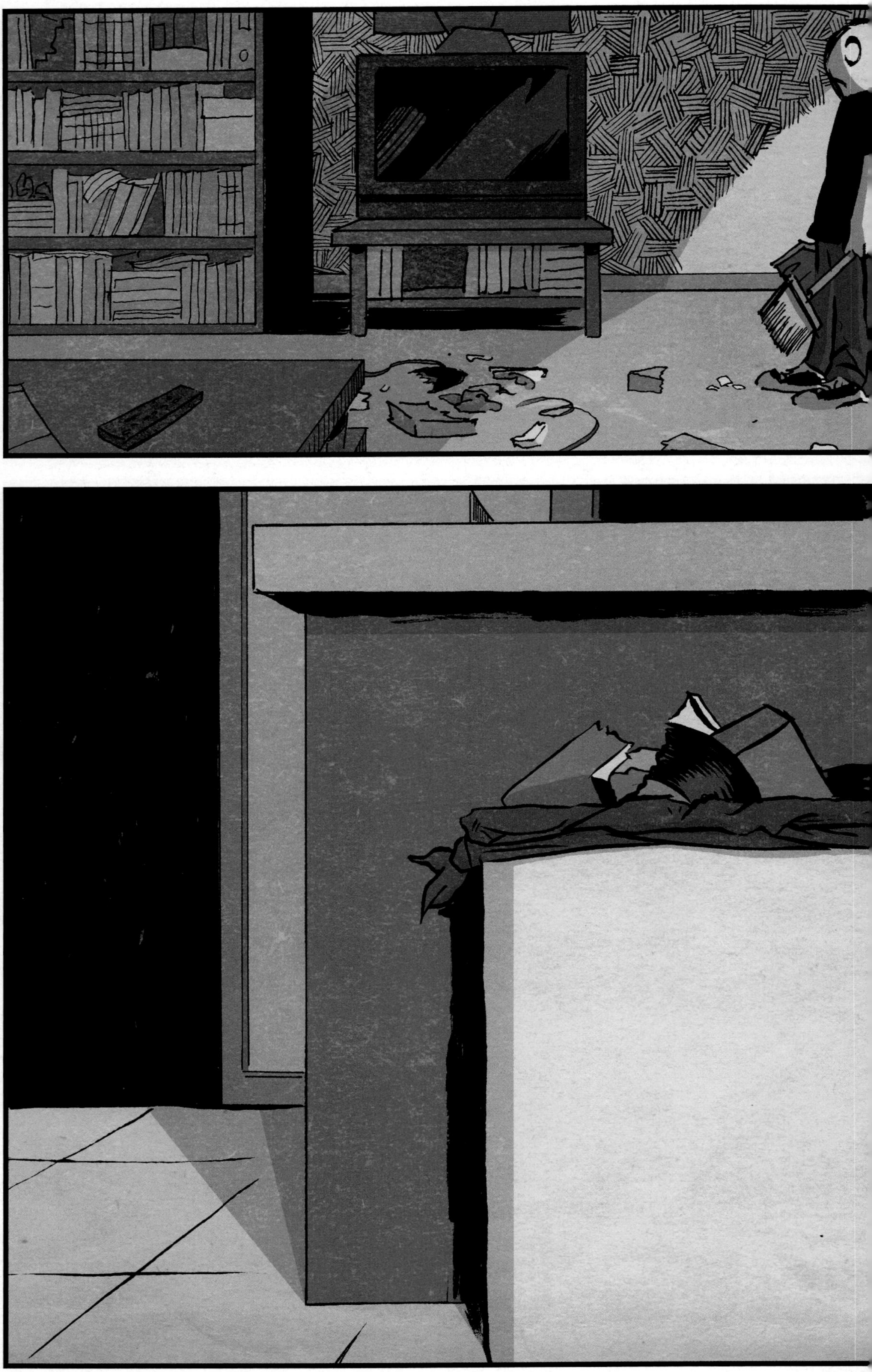

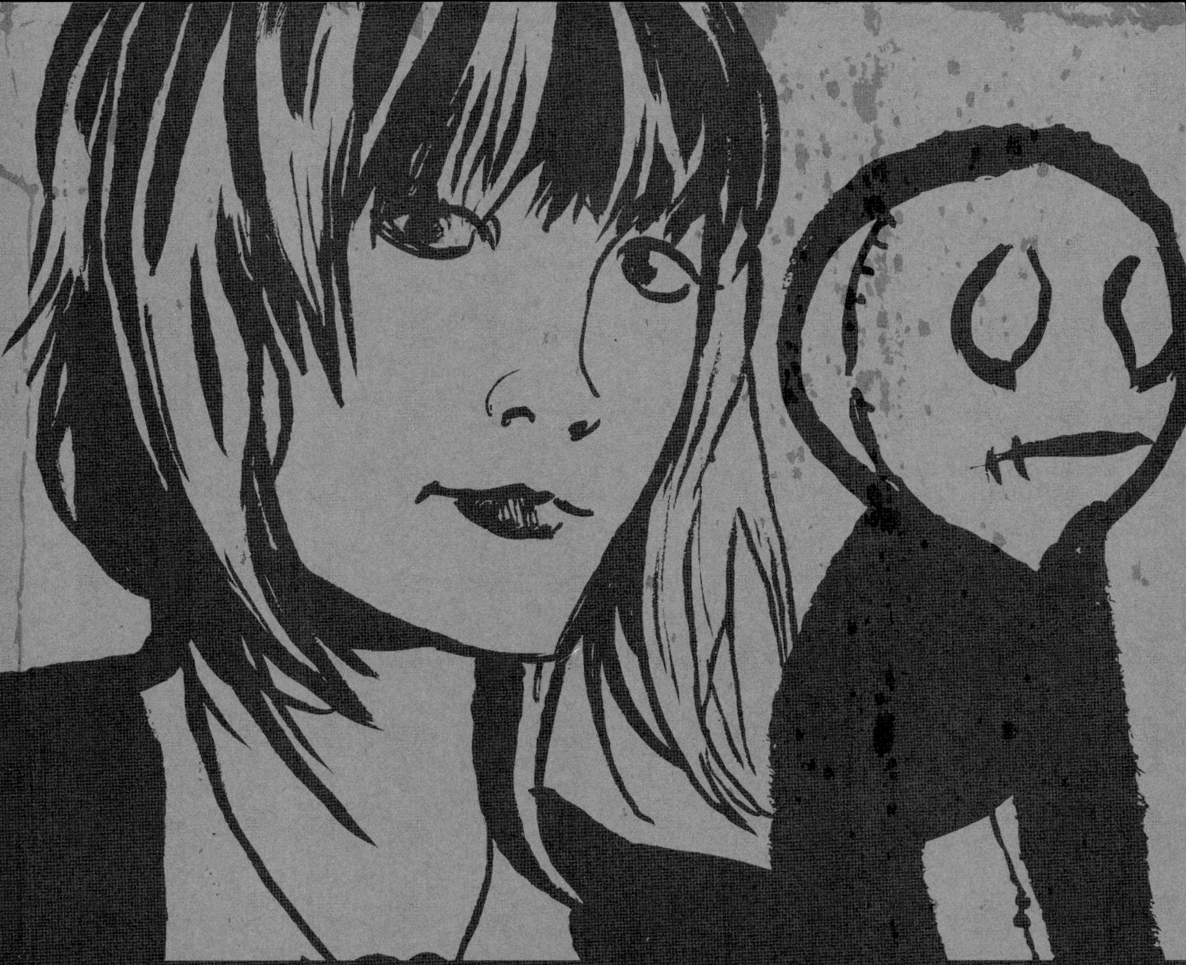

“EXPANSIVE HEART”

SKETCHES, PIN-UPS AND SURPRISES

Thank you so much for picking up our lovely trade paperback!

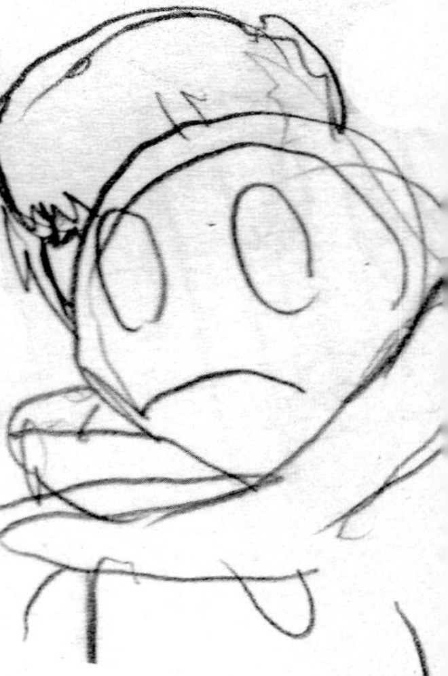

The best part of making comics for us is the collaboration aspect. Over the next few pages, we'll be sharing all the little things that readers don't think about when they get the final comic book: page layouts, outfit designs, funny doodles, so on and so forth.

Sina has dozens of notebooks full of random LDB scratches, and we've had a blast going through over two years' worth of chicken scratch, piecing together the more interesting tidbits.

The most exciting part of The Li'l Depressed Boy is that time right before a page- when there's a script ready, and we have to put our heads together to create the world that LDB lives in.

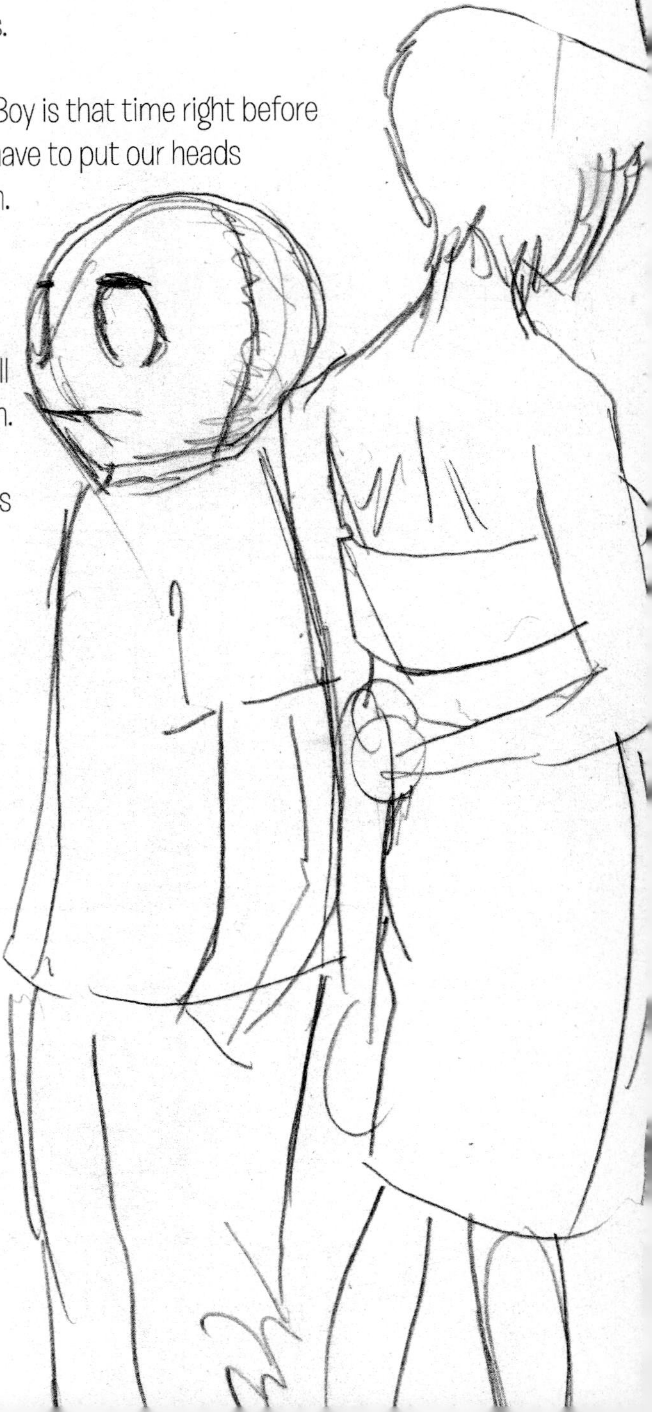

You'll also get to see how many cover ideas we go through before the final one ends up in your hands. Again: this is the most fun we'll have together- throwing ideas back and forth.

If only we could also share the text messages connected with these doodles!

Enjoy!

S&S

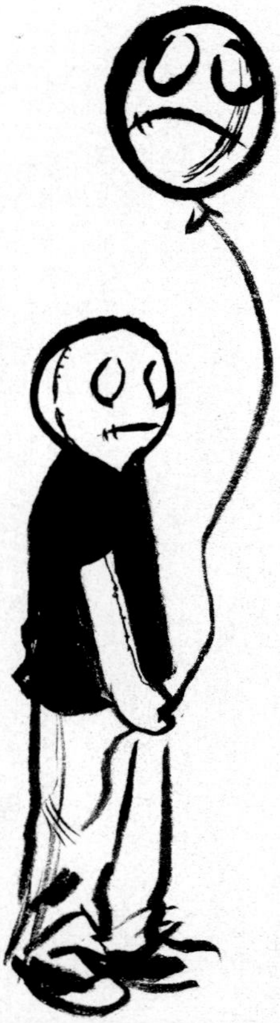

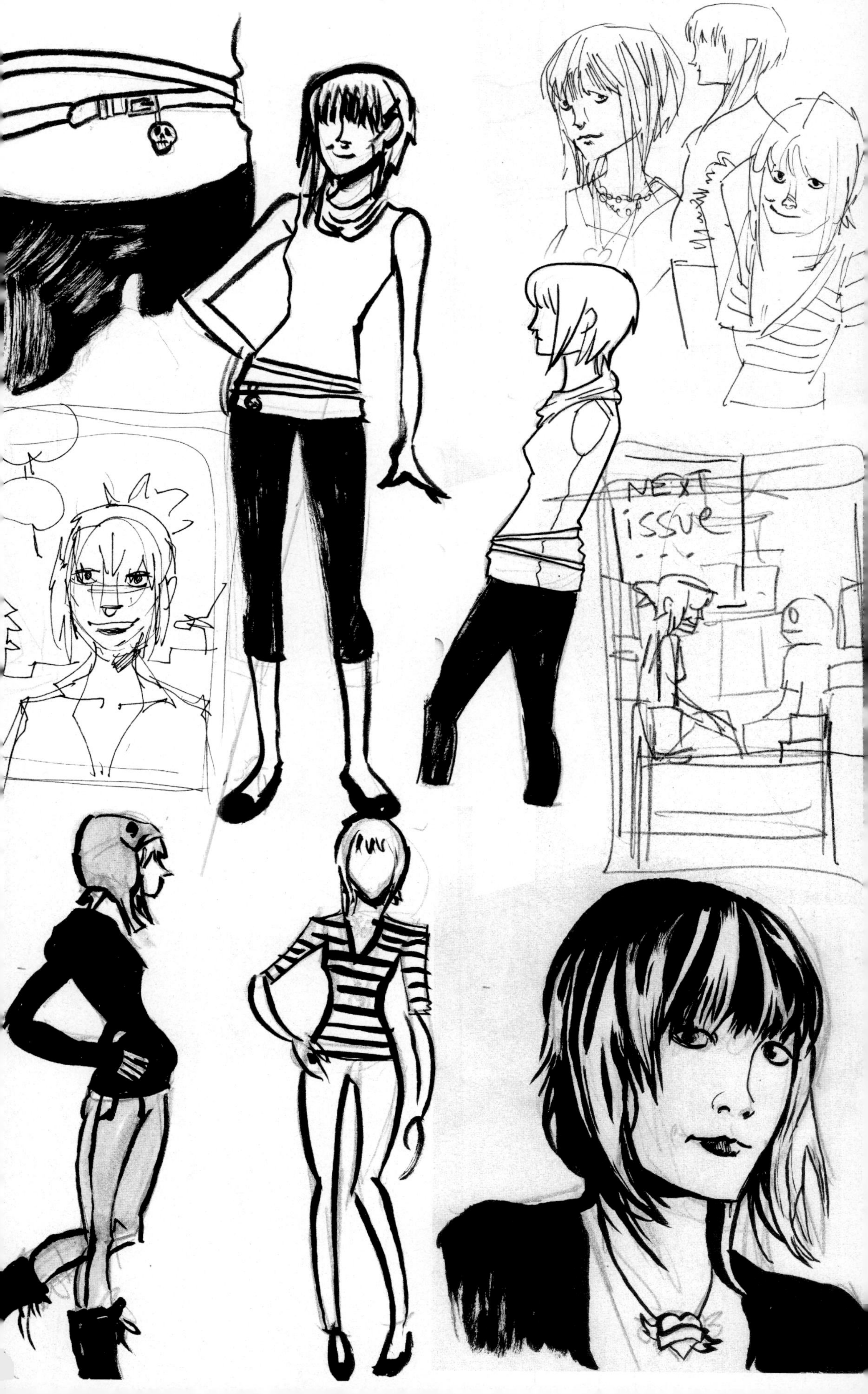

NEXT
issue

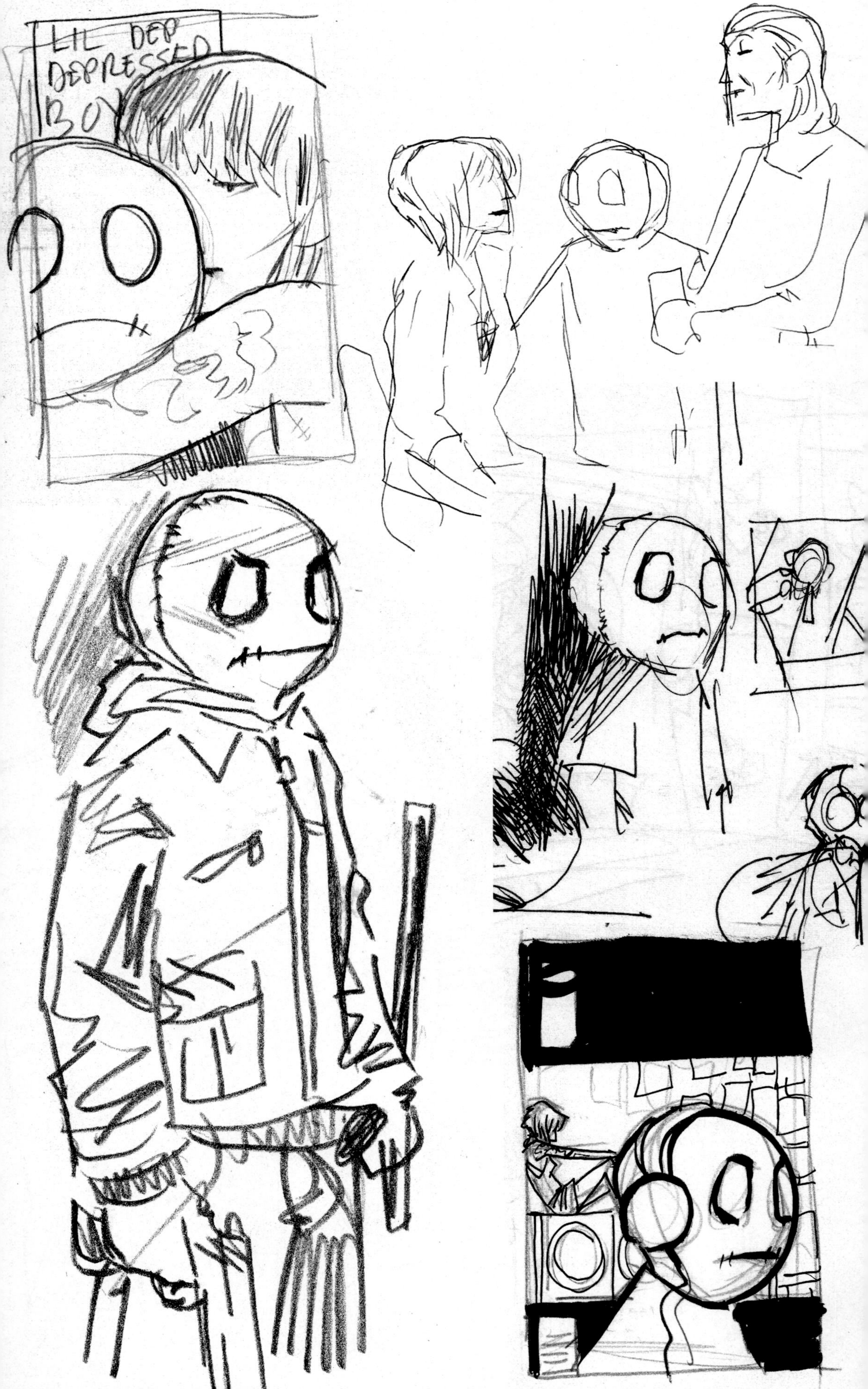
LIL DEP
DEPRESSED
BO

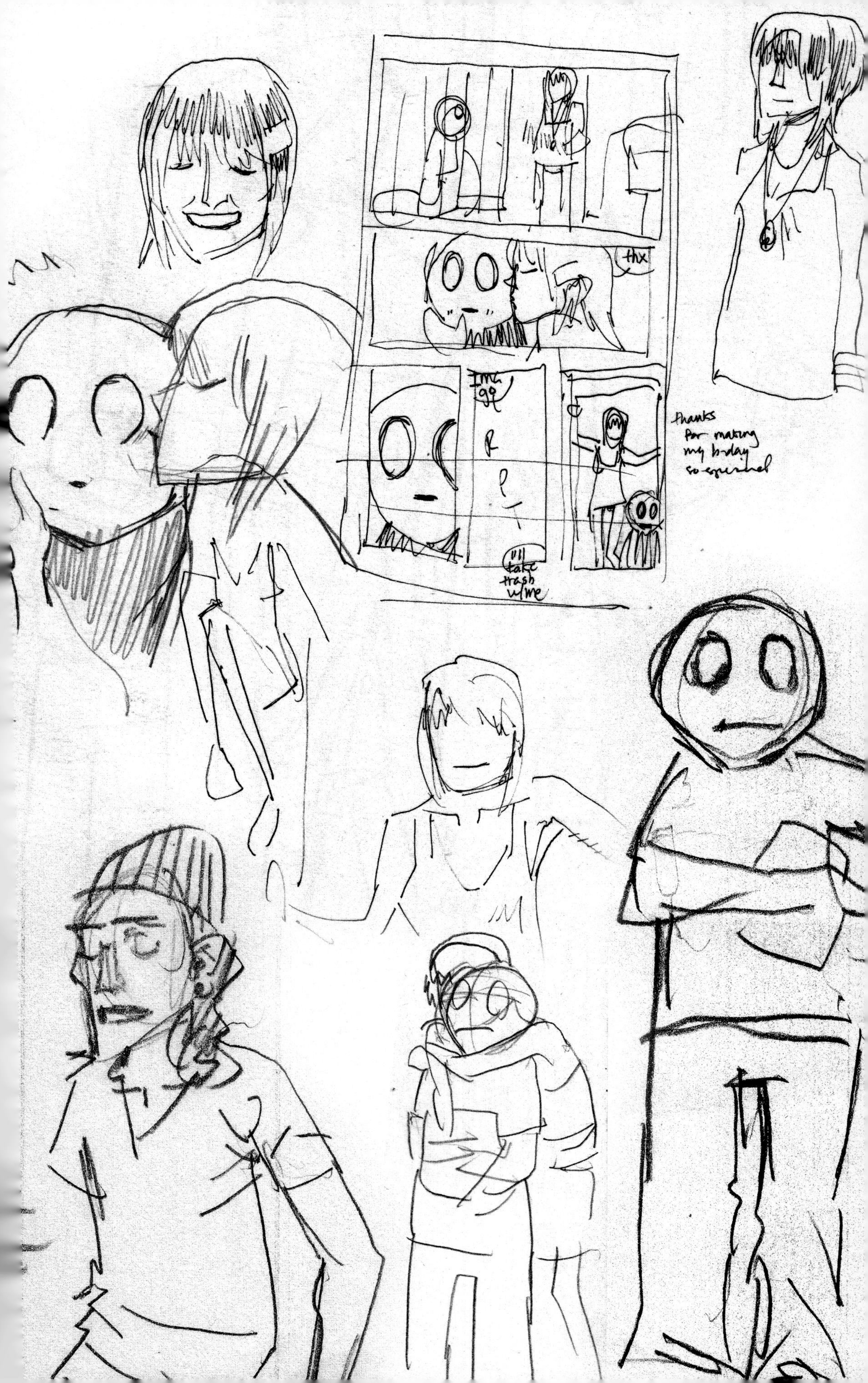
thx
Ima go
I'll take trash w/me
Thanks for making my b-day so especial

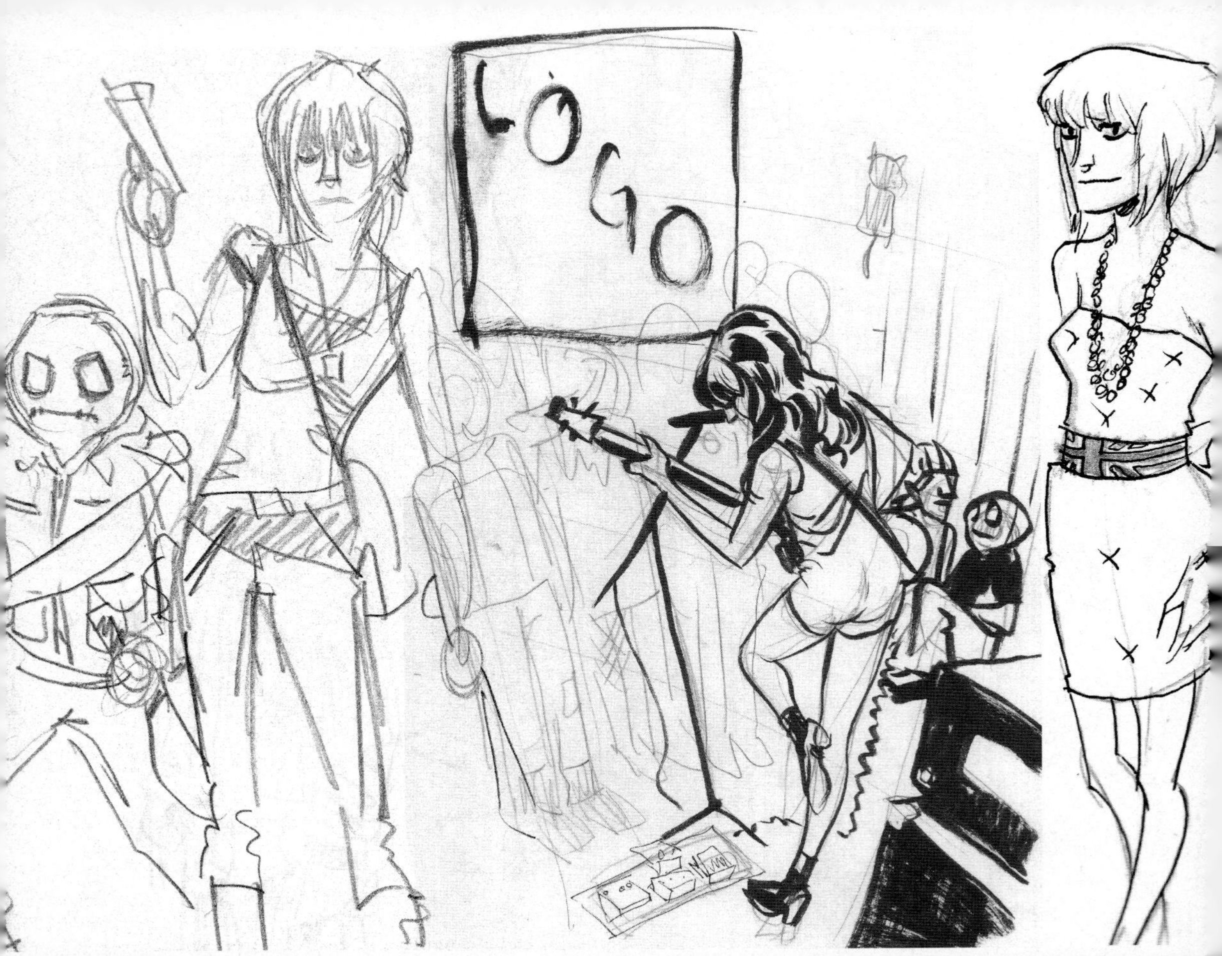
LOGO

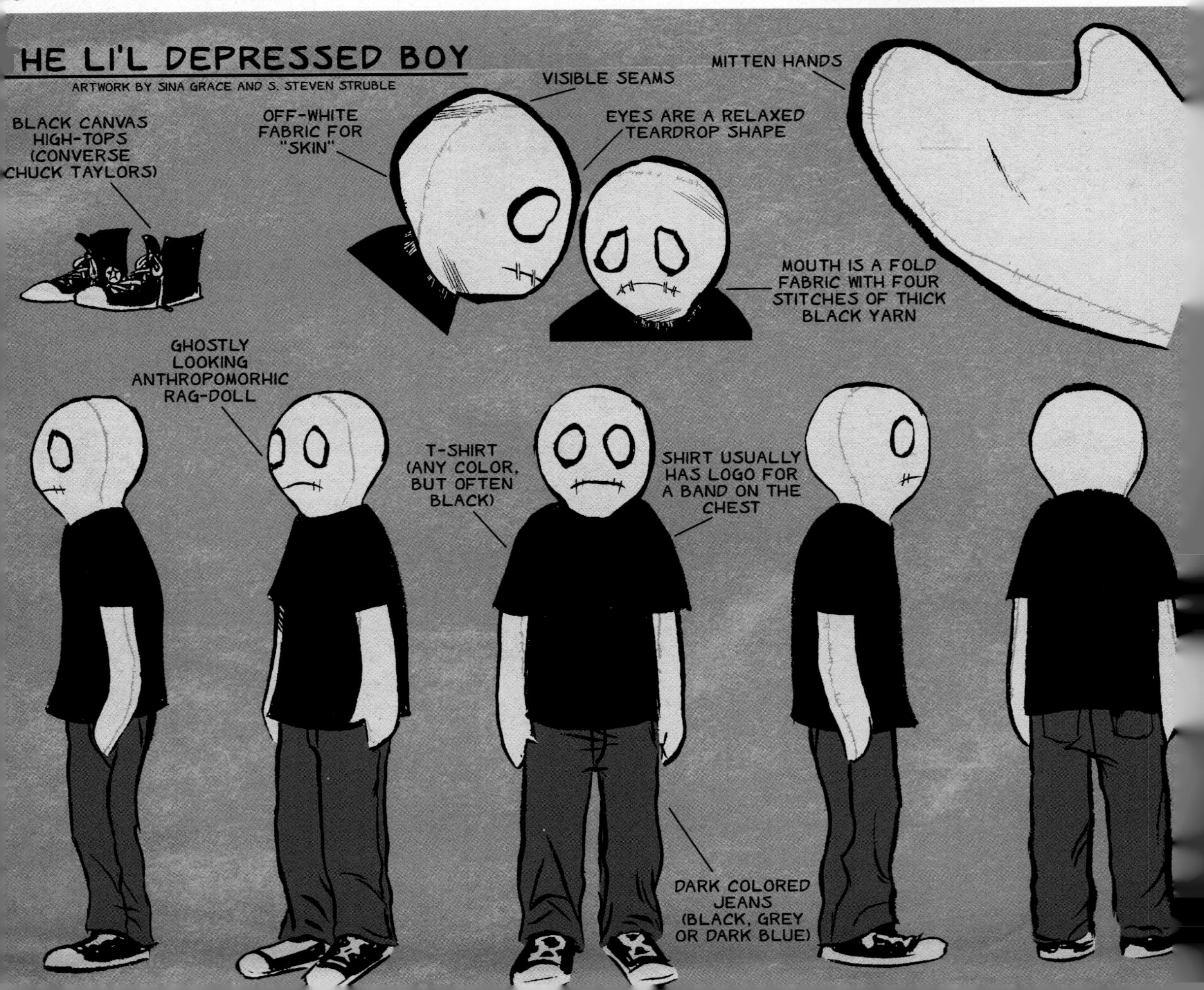
HE LI'L DEPRESSED BOY
ARTWORK BY SINA GRACE AND S. STEVEN STRUBLE
VISIBLE SEAMS
MITTEN HANDS
OFF-WHITE FABRIC FOR "SKIN"
EYES ARE A RELAXED TEARDROP SHAPE
BLACK CANVAS HIGH-TOPS (CONVERSE CHUCK TAYLORS)
MOUTH IS A FOLD FABRIC WITH FOUR STITCHES OF THICK BLACK YARN
GHOSTLY LOOKING ANTHROPOMORHIC RAG-DOLL
T-SHIRT (ANY COLOR, BUT OFTEN BLACK)
SHIRT USUALLY HAS LOGO FOR A BAND ON THE CHEST
DARK COLORED JEANS (BLACK, GREY OR DARK BLUE)

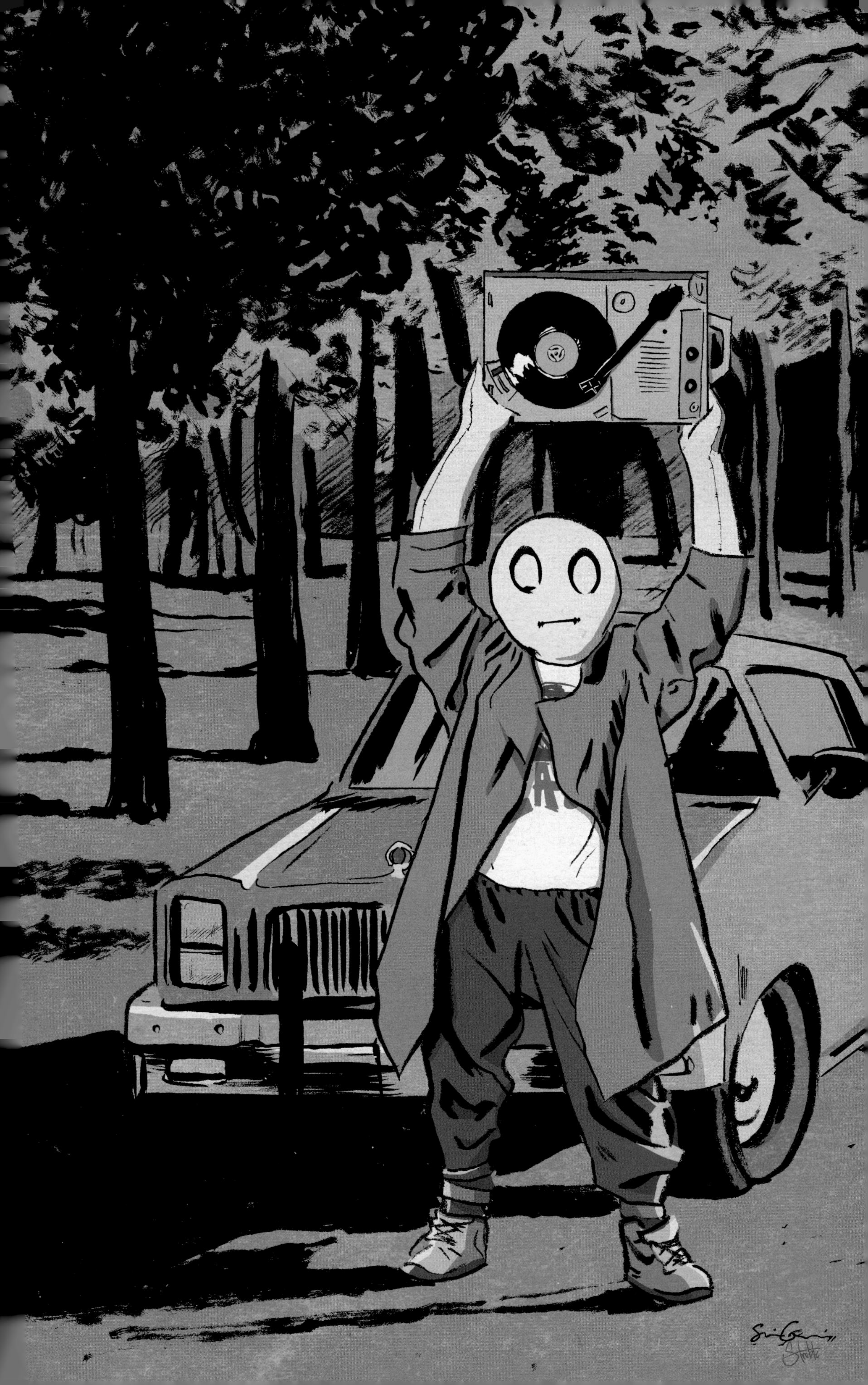

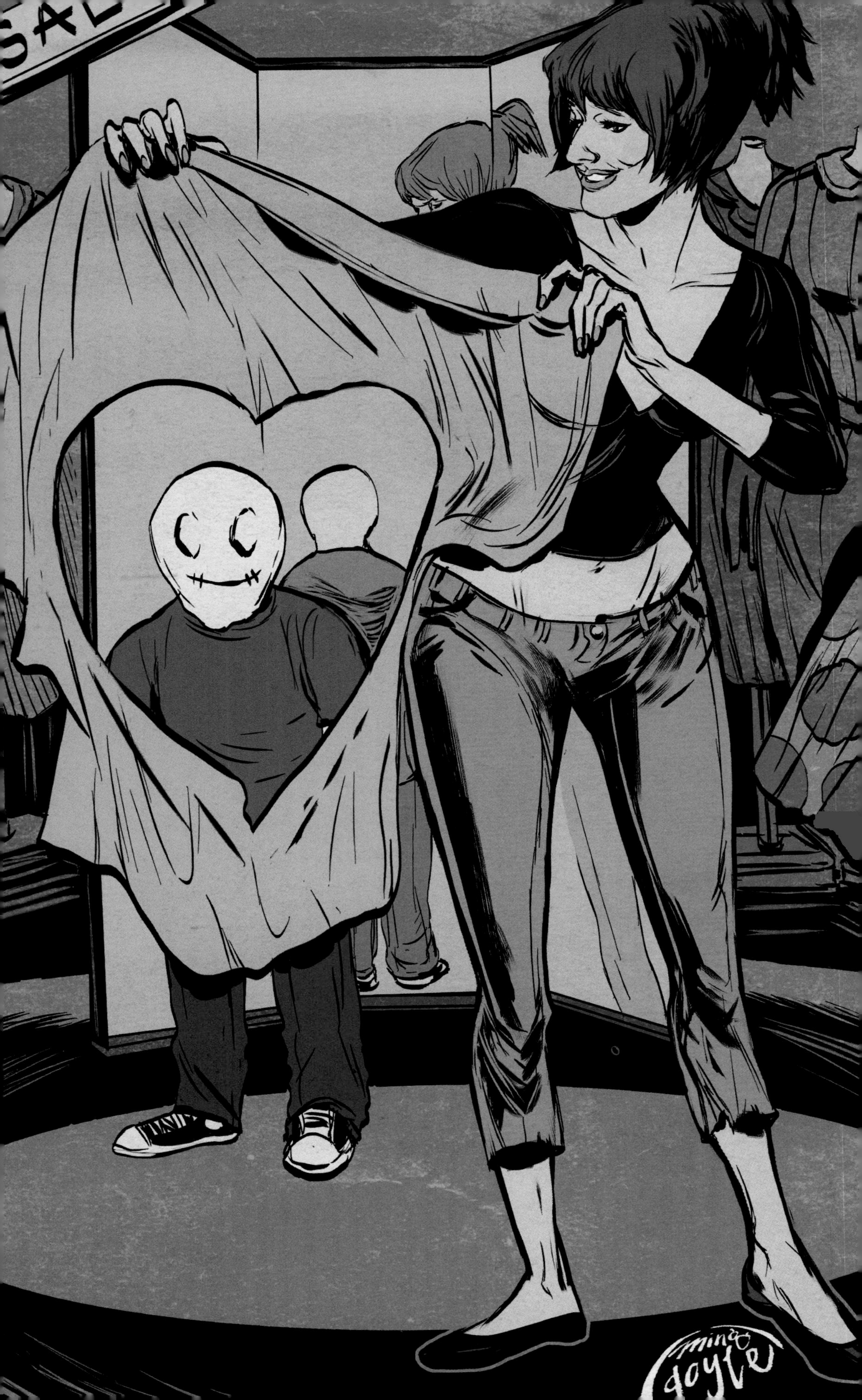
SAL
mina doyle

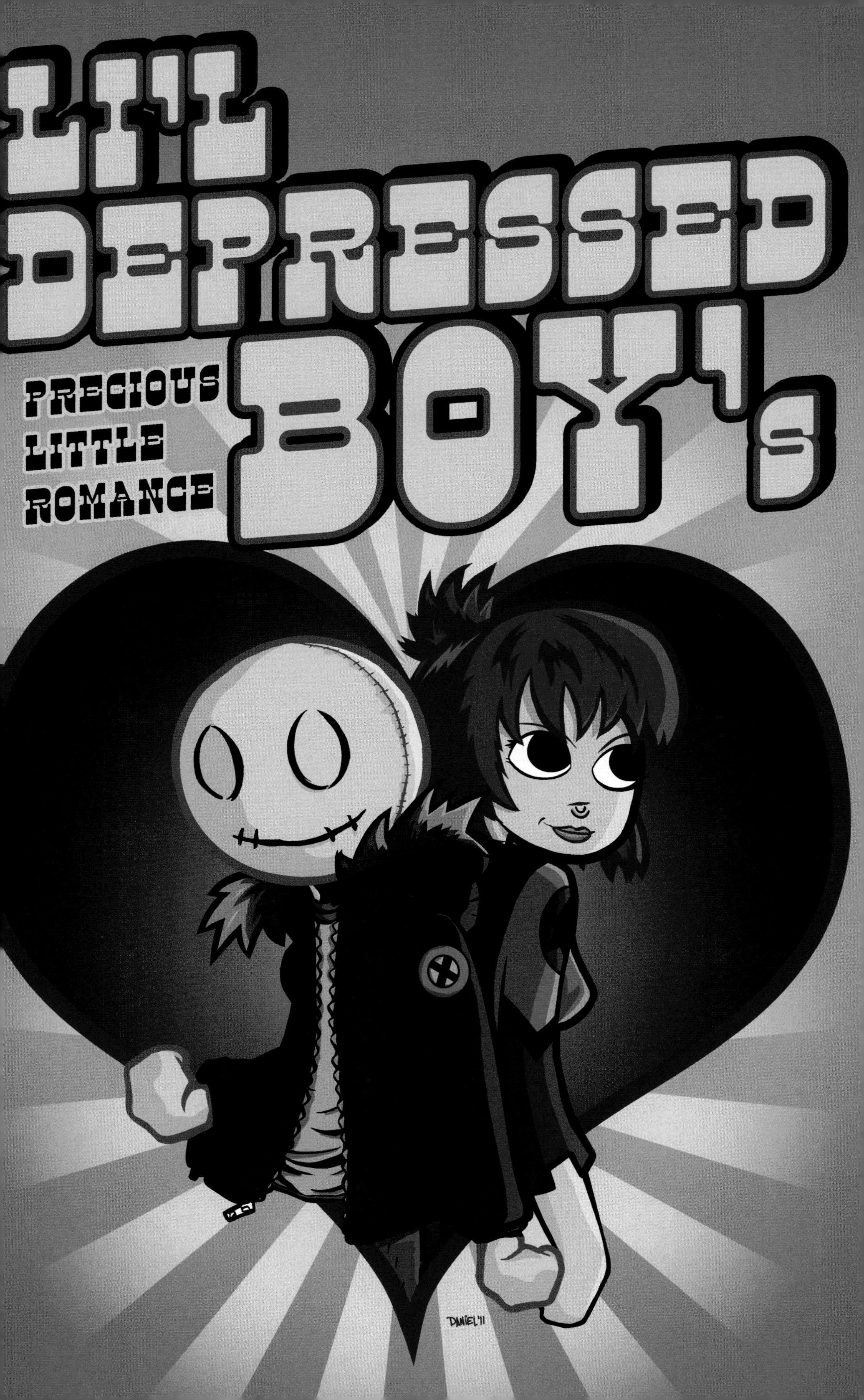
LI'L
DEPRESSED
BOY'S
PRECIOUS
LITTLE
ROMANCE
DANIEL'11

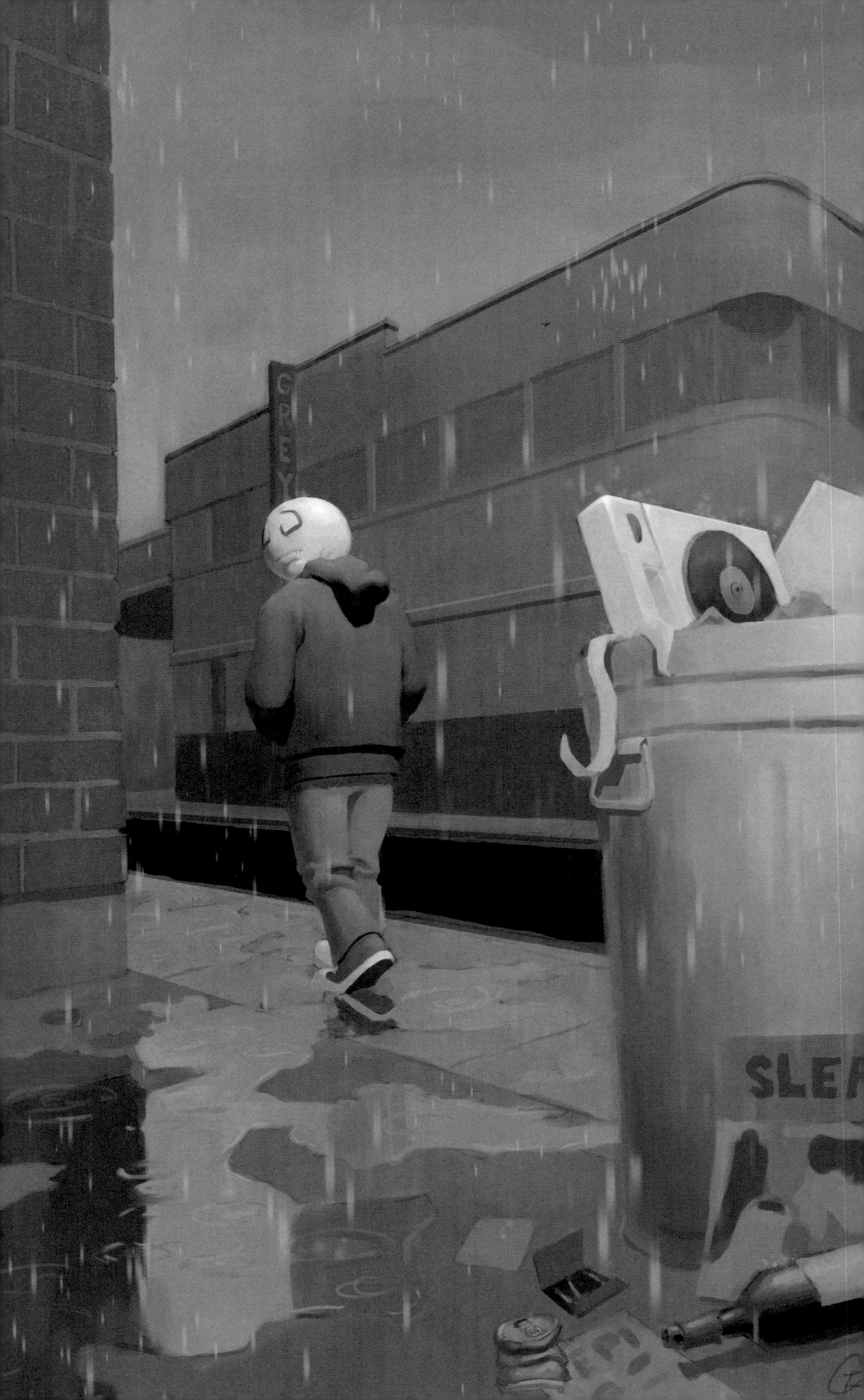
SLEA

Pinups by:
Ming Doyle -- http://mingdoyle.com
Tim Daniel -- http://hiddenrobot.com
Chris Fenoglio -- http://chrisfenoglio.com

Special thanks to: Ron & Lisa Chase, Chris Fenoglio, Jose Garibaldi, Lindsay Jane, Sam Kieth, Jim Mahfood, Jamie McKelvie, Roman Muradov, Justin Stewart, Kris Struble, Ed Tadem, Kanila Tripp, Zach Trover, Cory Walker, Rich Boucher, Jeff Bridges, Tyler Shainline, Evan DiLeo, Paul Daniels, Justin Heeren, Scott Arnold, Kat Cahill, James Parker, Jim Valentino, Betsy Gomez, Jocelyn Broadwell, Robert Kirkman, Drew Blood, Spencer Alcorn, Raul Rodarte, Eric Stephenson, Rob Guillory, Sarah DeLaine, Amber Benson, John Layman, Tvhead Jimmy, Leo Burke, Mikael Sebag, Travis Fox, Scott Morse, Jonathan Chan, Steve Rolston, Nicholas Brandt, Harris Miller, Jenna Hodges, our wonderful families, and you. This book in your hands wouldn't exist without the help of these amazing people.

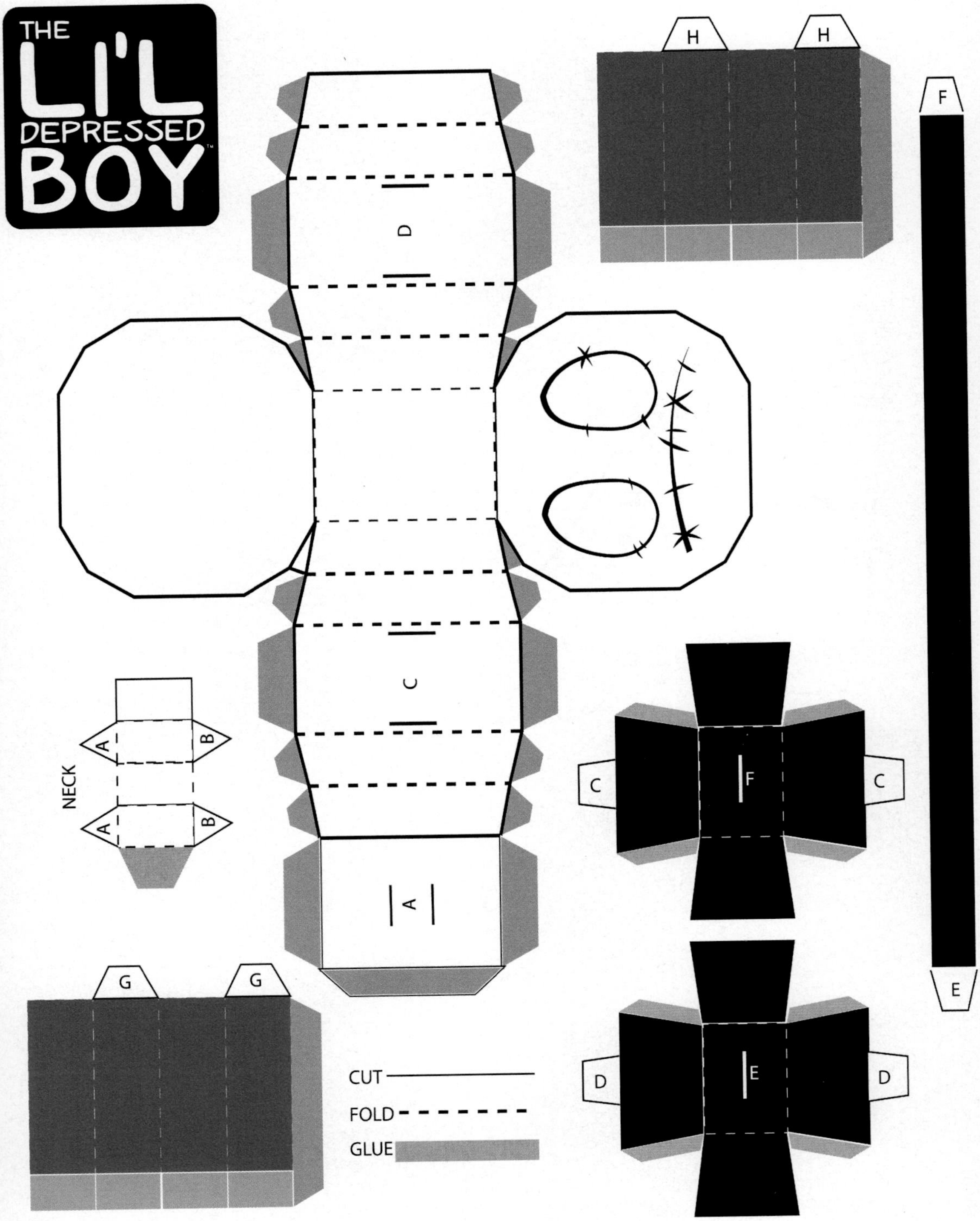
THE LI'L DEPRESSED BOY™
H
H
F
D
C
NECK
A
A
B
B
A
C
F
C
G
G
E
D
E
D
CUT
FOLD
GLUE

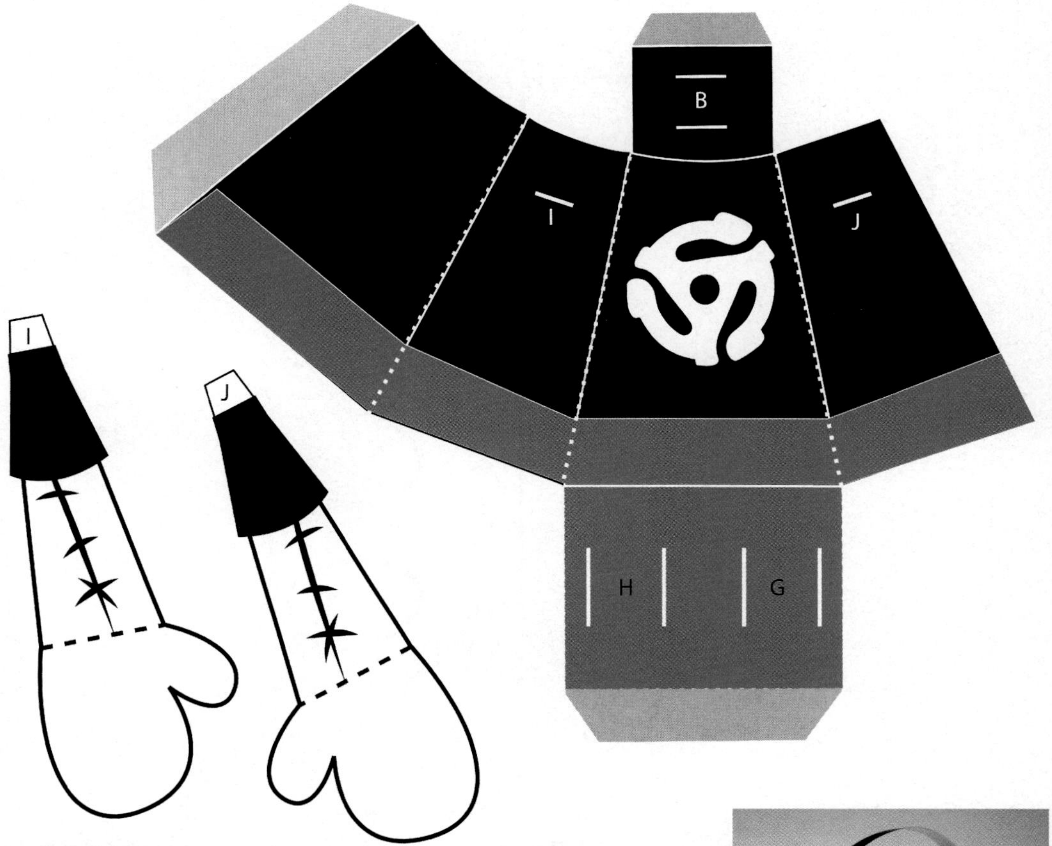
B
I
J
H
G
I
J

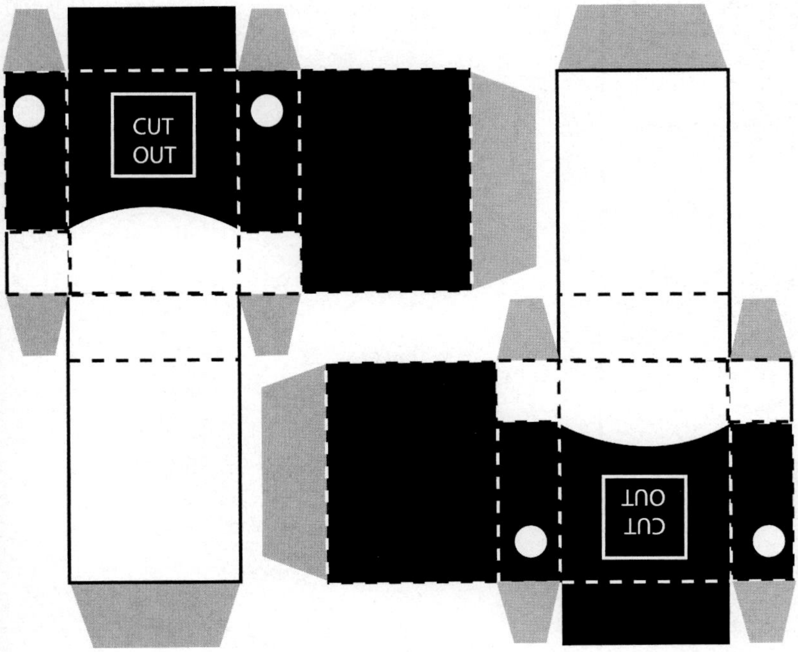
CUT
OUT
CUT
OUT

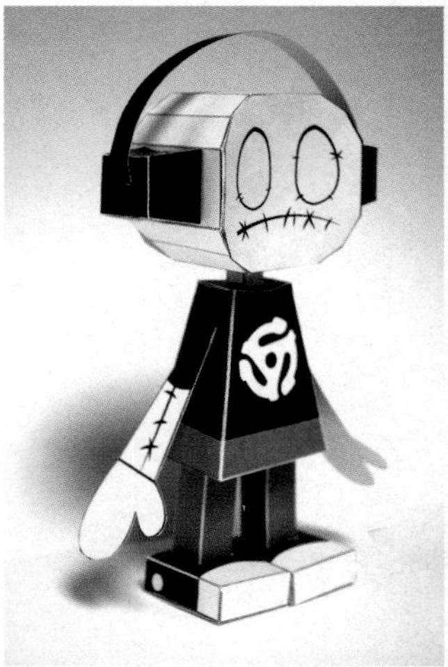

Paper LDB Designed by
Zachary Trover
www.too-hectic.com

S. Steven Struble moved to Amarillo, TX to write comic books. Surprisingly, this plan actually worked out!
In his spare time he also colors other people's comics and competes on the poetry slam circuit.

More at www.illiteraterainbow.com

S.STEVEN STRUBLE

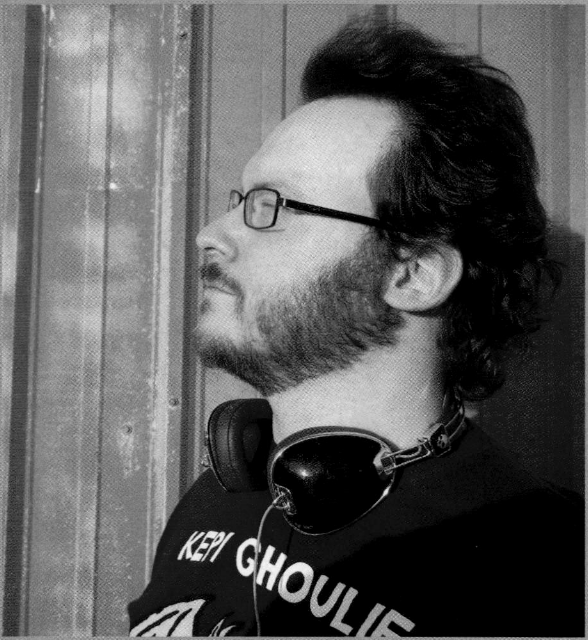
KEPI GHOULIE

PHOTO: JENNA HODGES

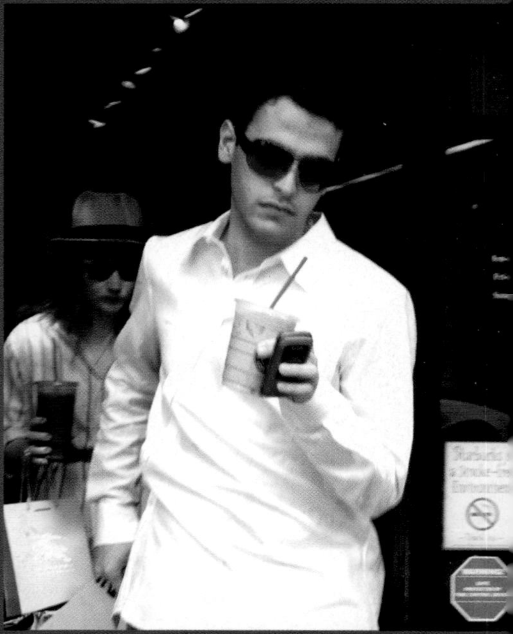

PHOTO: INDIA BROOKOVER

SINA GRACE

Sina Grace draws comic boo (The Li'l Depressed Boy), kic books (Among the Ghosts), ar big-people books (Cedric Hollov in Dial M for Magic) in coffee sho all around Los Angeles. When he not doing that, he's busy handli duties as Editorial Director f Robert Kirkman's Skybour imprint at Image Comics.

More at www.sinagrace.com